THE MAN

WHO INVENTED

ROCK-N-ROLL

VOLUME ONE

By Warren B. Burdine, Jr.

Bird in Flight Publications

For further information, contact the author at:
wburdine@pratt.edu

The Floating Gallery:
244 Madison Ave, #254, New York, NY 10016
877-822-2500   www.thefloatinggallery.com

Printed in Canada

Warren B. Burdine, Jr.
The Man Who Invented Rock-n-Roll

1. Author   2. Title   3. Fiction
Library of Congress Control Number 2002116462
ISBN 0-9726777-0-4

I am especially indebted to the following relatives, friends, mentors, and colleagues who played a direct role in the writing of *The Man Who Invented Rock-n-Roll:*

Warren B. Burdine, Sr. (of course)
(Cousin) Joseph Armstrong
Marie Brown
Carol Bugge
Arthur Flowers
George Guida
Joel Hochman
Dexter Jeffries
Kathleen Hopkins
Brian Keener
Larry Leichman
(Aunt) Mildred Netherland
Warren Parker
(Cousin) Aleece Netherland Stewart
Also, my late Uncle Thomas Lovely
And, my hundreds of heroes who made and played the music

Part One

"Cora Ann"

CHAPTER ONE

Sunday, April 10, 1955; 1:12 a.m.
The Full Moon Lounge. Knoxville, Tennessee.

"Ah, yeah! Rock them blues, yawl—rock them blues!"

"Ooo-weee, baby! I like it like that!"

Onstage, the Jimmy Jameson Quartet sent the beat skittering like a funky rubber ball across a hot blacktop highway of rhythm. It bounced about the tightly-packed room, causing heads to bob, fingers to pop, hips to sway, hands to slap thighs, and toes to tap the floor. The opening bars of the song, an original and one of the group's signature tunes, throbbed from the tiny bandstand.

"Yes, indeedy! Sat'day night, boogie-woogie blues: makes the rest-a the week *tol'rable!*" wailed a buxom brown woman in a tight turquoise dress.

"Honey, that brown-eyed handsome man couldn't git no finer if he spent the rest-a his life tryin!" shrieked one of her three female tablemates, referring to the vocalist.

"Girl, who you tellin?" another testified.

Training a well-practiced, all-encompassing leer onto those crammed into the club, the vocalist and guitarist, Louis Cannon, Jr., growled the opening lyrics: "You left me, pretty baby, of that I've noooo re-gretsss..."

The chicks went wild. On the bandstand, Lou Cannon masked his self-satisfaction behind the bluesman's standard deadpan facade. He shouted on: "I said you left me, sugar mama, of that I've no ree-grets..."

"Sang it, Lou! Make it plain!"

"...You took my car, my clothes, my cash—but why'd you take myyyyy cig-a-rettes?" Lou moaned.

"Hunny, give that man *back* them cigarettes!" a two-hundred-pound mama in a cinnamon-colored wig roared.

The band slithered into the second chorus. By now half the crowd was singing along.

"One day you said you loved me,
Then the next: 'Go take a hike!'
You promised that you loved me,
Then said: 'Go take a hike!'
The least you could-a done waaasss
Leave me my Lucky Strikes!
Leave me my Lucky Strikes!"

The quartet nestled into an instrumental break. Lou turned to his right and gave the audience his profile. As always, he pretended to blank out the patrons during the break, dimming his eyes to half-mast, seemingly in another world, yet studying the crowd closely. He searched for one in particular...and pushed back a pang of disappointment when he did not see that person.

As the crowed twitched to Jimmy Jameson's piano riffs, Lou glanced over his left shoulder and panned, left to right. The Full Moon Lounge was literally a barn or, more precisely, had been converted from a Knoxville Transit Company streetcar-repair barn on the corner of McCalla and Bell. To the left and perpendicular to the bandstand, a chest-high oaken plank roamed the length of the wall for standees to lean on and rest their drinks. Parallel to the bandstand, a long picture window abutted McCalla Avenue. The main entrance bisected the window. Burly crimson drapes staved off the rest of the world from the Full Moon.

The well-stocked bar dominated the length of the wall to the right of and perpendicular to the stage. Lou grinned as he watched the club's owner, Kelbert "Moon" Mullins, issue drinks, his face set in his trademark dour expression. He was a stocky brown man of medium height in early middle age. As always, his wife and a younger brother assisted him behind the bar. Moon squandered not one drop as he poured the drinks, placed them on trays, and dispatched them to a platoon of comely waitresses, costumed in tight-fitting, lime-green uniforms.

Lou hooked Moon's glance for a moment, head-pointed toward the lively crowd, and smiled. Moon replied with a neutral wag of his head. Lou then eyed the couples squeezed onto the dance floor, a thirty-foot-by-thirty-foot oasis of linoleum in the wooden floor. He marveled as the dancers flailed their arms, rolled their heads on rubbery necks, and whirled their pelvises without inhibition, locked into the music—his music.

He was still getting used to this brassy, jumping, smoke-filled scene. Except for a few tag-along trips to similar places while in the

Army, he had never stepped into a juke joint in earnest until he began to perform in them. The only lure they ever held for him was the music that blasted from inside as it had a life of its own. The pulsating pianos, snorting saxophones, and squalling guitars seemed to come from a mysterious, exciting, and forbidden universe.

Now, after five months with the Jimmy Jameson Quartet, the Full Moon and other clubs they played still held Lou in a near-magical grasp. The permanent smell of beer, hard liquor, tobacco smoke, perfumes and colognes from all spectrums of the price range, and the funk of honest, hard-working human sweat nourished him as he picked and shouted on the bandstand.

And the music—the music he was creating—was a ticket to...

To a place he could not identify, not even in his fantasies.

He continued his surveillance. Save for the standees on the wall to his left, and those on the dance floor, most of the revelers sat at the round wooden tables that dotted the huge room. Each table sported a red-and-white checked cloth, and a green wine bottle in whose neck a candle burned. A dozen fans descended from the twenty-foot ceiling. Their fat metal blades sliced languidly as they stirred the close air on the unseasonably warm early spring night.

Lou's gaze rested on a cluster of tables in the back half of the room, slightly to the left of the center. At least forty whites seemed right at home as they bounced and swayed to the beat. *It's a good thing the Jim Crow laws don't cut both ways*, Lou told himself. *You wouldn't find any—let alone forty—colored folks at a white roadhouse. No, sir.*

The presence of the white patrons reinforced one of the main goals for his compositions: *Make music everyone can dig. Not white music. Not Negro music. Notes, harmonies, melodies, lyrics—they don't come with a color attached. The barriers are in the listeners' heads. Got to break down those walls.*

Without appearing to do so, Lou avoided the gazes of three young women as they tried to ensnare his attention. Seated just a few feet away, they had been front and center at the last six Full Moon shows. He remembered them from high school, where they had never given him the time of day. Like many, they had surely considered him a square of a preacher's kid who wouldn't be much fun to run with.

He continued to soak in the crowd as the instrumental break ended and he resumed singing. He warbled the lyrics by rote while he did an approximate headcount. *Gotta be over three hundred here tonight—in a place the fire marshals limit to two-fifty. Moon must've slipped a few folks a few dead presidents.*

He took one last look for that certain person. *If they'd've been here tonight, I would've seen them.* He wailed as the waitresses scurried, serving drinks and platters of chitterlings, fried chicken, collard greens, potato salad, cole slaw, and macaroni-and-cheese from the kitchen run by Moon's mother. *Moon's making a pretty penny off us. We need to get a cut of not just the cover charge, but the bar and kitchen profits as well.* He would raise the issue with Jimmy, the band's founder—but not just yet. He had not been with the group long enough, and did not know the private, moody Jimmy well enough to make such a suggestion.

Still, it was common knowledge that before the Jameson Quartet began its run as the unofficial house band, the four weekend shows did well to attract one hundred patrons per set at the Full Moon. Most in that crowd were regulars, attracted by the club's congenial, working-class ambiance. Then word spread of the hot new blues band that was not really new and whose repertoire extended beyond the blues.

Lou nearly bobbled the closing lyrics as a form waltzing forward from the back of the room caught his eye. *Is that Alba? Coming this late? Or has she been here all the time?* Unlike his parents and two younger sisters, who had yet to see him perform in a blues club, his girlfriend Alba Evans had—once. And in Kingsport, nearly two hours away, where hardly anyone she knew would see her. They had been going steady for two years now, and though she claimed she had no misgivings about his boogie-woogie avocation…

Nah, that's Brenda Miles, not Alba, he determined, as he got as good a look as possible in the dark, smoky room. Brenda and Alba were the same age, and distantly related. Yet, Lou could not blame Alba for not coming to see him perform. She was uncomfortable in this setting and, unlike many of the Full Moon regulars, *did* have to be up early on Sunday morning, to teach Sunday school.

That's all right, baby, Lou told his girl in absentia. *I know you understand…*

The band put the finish on "Cigarette Blues." Lou nodded graciously to the applause. "Thank you! Now we want to slow things down a bit," he said, and gave his mates the cue for their next-to-last number. After a few bars of piercing guitar chords, Lou howled: "I don't miss ya, baby, when the sun is bright…"

Gotta mix these tunes just right, he thought. Since their last number was a mid-tempo "boogie-waltz," as Lou dubbed "Cigarette Blues," and the final song would be a roof-raiser, it was best to bridge them with a sultry ballad.

"No, I don't miss ya, baby, when the sun is bright..." Lou turned toward his bandmates, who formed a triangle behind him. At the apex was the drummer, Edgar "Blondie" Purcell, who was responsible for getting Lou into the Quartet, and had been Lou's best friend since either could remember. One look at Blondie provided the source of his nickname: he was a champagne-colored Negro with gray-green cat eyes and curly hair the color of wet sand. Blondie winked at Lou as he laid down the backbeat as cleanly and steadily as fat raindrops pelting on a tin roof.

Lou smiled at Charles "Deuce" Hurley, on stand-up bass. A former two-way tackle for the Tennessee A & I Tigers, he was six-feet-four and weighed a still-solid two-forty. The strings of Deuce's bass thrummed as they yielded to the delicate power of his thick fingers.

Lou glanced over his right shoulder toward the Quartet's founder and pianist, Jimmy Jameson. Locked deep within the music, Jimmy's oversized eyes fixed on a target only he saw. His blank expression never changed while he performed. Brown-skinned, plump, round-faced, at five-feet-seven inches tall, he was at least a half foot shorter than the other members.

Lou scanned the crowd as he sang. Suddenly, his heart made a stutter step and he almost flubbed the lyrics.

Well, I'll be! Swampcat made it here tonight. Finally!

Lou had telephoned Leroy "Swampcat" Newsome twice a week for the past month and mailed several reminders, imploring Swampcat to check out the Quartet. Swampcat was the owner of RICKY, a station in Nashville, and its most popular deejay. Transmitting with 25,000 watts, it boasted the most powerful signal of a Negro-owned station in the Southeast. On a clear night it fanned throughout Tennessee from the Smokey Mountains to the Mississippi River, the northern counties of Georgia, Alabama, and Mississippi, and much of southern Kentucky.

Lou had not invited Swampcat until he thought the band was ready to play before such a V.I.P. After four straight weeks of Swampcat not showing, Lou feared he never would.

Lou studied Swampcat, while Swampcat studied him in return. Seeing Swampcat for the first time, he looked much like Lou had pictured him, based largely on the whiskey-and-cigarettes baritone: early fifties, dark-brown-skinned, broad-featured, large-framed and well-fed, his hair done in a conservative process, and wearing a dark gray double-breasted suit that was equal parts businessman and hustler baron.

Certain he had caught Swampcat's eye, Lou gave him a big wink.

From the table he shared with his favorite cousin, Swampcat winked back.

"Oooo—his face lit up like a little boy's on Christmas morning when he saw you, Leroy, hunny!" Maynelle Byrams cried.

"Yeah," Swampcat replied, "whether he realizes it or not, it's his little-boy charm that helps him connect with his audience. He's havin the time of his life up there, like a kid ramblin wild at recess time. And the crowd digs how he busts his ass for 'em."

Maynelle slid closer and shouted: "And what do *you* think of these guys?"

"Not bad. Not bad at all," Swampcat answered after a moment's thought. "They're a bit raw, but they got—potential. I like the way they throw all types-a stuff together, yet somehow make it work."

"They are different—that you gotta give 'em credit for."

Swampcat motioned toward the crowd with a lazy sweep of his hand. "Main thing is the band's got the joint packed and jumpin. And get a load of all them white folks over there."

"Yeah, hunny. Each week, ten, twelve more show up. This keeps up, there'll be more-a them here than us Negroes," she said, laughing.

Swampcat continued to eye the white patrons. "Mercy! That many hoojies in a spade joint—that means the band's *gotta* be sayin somethin!"

"Don'tcha just know it, hunny!"

"Those original tunes—who wrote 'em?" Swampcat asked.

"That good-lookin boy on lead vocals and guitar."

"I figured that. The kid's got spunk. Been houndin me for a month. Me, I didn't think nobody *this* good could come outta Knoxville—or nobody I never heard of yet."

"Everybody's gotta start somewhere," Maynelle said. "Now ain't you glad *I* stayed on you for the past two weeks to come and see 'em?"

"Yeah—and I'd-a been madder'n a broke-tail dawg had you made me drive two hundred miles to see some stiffs. But they're definitely worth the trip." He returned his attention to the stage as Cannon pled his case into a microphone the size of a muscular man's forearm. A kiss, a tear, and a prayer made up equal parts of his petition.

...My heart feels like there's been a theft of you, baby/'cause my life's been so bereft of you, baby...

Swampcat continued to size up Cannon as a bettor would a thoroughbred before a race. "That Cannon's one fine-lookin boy—"

"He turned up the tem'prature in *this* joint a few degrees, I'm here to tell you... "

447794

"The voice is good enough—but he'd never make Billy Eckstine or Nat Cole phone in sick. He's got them nice black-Injun features—he's not too light, not too dark. A pretty middlin shade…"

"Yup. His skin looks just like a Hershey's Chocolate bar. Tall, too. He was a decent basketball player at Austin High," Maynelle added. "The high-bright drummer, too."

"Yeah, I saw 'em play a coupla times against Pearl High. The big dude on bass, too, a few years before them." He signaled a waitress for fresh drinks. "The other cats in the band are nice-lookin, too—but more importantly, they look good *together*." A nagging thought resurfaced. He stared hard at the lead singer. "That name and that face. Why they so familiar?"

She gave him a surprised look. "That's Reverend Cannon's boy."

He reeled through his mental file. "Isn't Rev Cannon one of the biggest preachers in town? Brighter Hope Baptist Church?"

"Brighter *Day*. Yup."

"Damn, sam! Does he know his boy sings boogie-woogie in juke joints?"

"'Course he does. In a town this size?"

"Don't the good rev have a problem with that?"

"Not as far as I know," Maynelle answered. "I doubt he's seen his boy perform at one-a these places, but he's never planted himself outside none, either, barrin Junior's way."

"Goodness! Most ministers would have a shit fit if their kids—"

"Hunny, Reverend Cannon ain't hardly no by-the-book type. Some say his services are like a Broadway musical, the way he mixes the sermon, songs by the choir, and his own solos."

"Is that a fact? Guess that's where this kid gets his showmanship," Swampcat replied, and refocused on the musicians. Though they had kept the crowd in a tizzy for nearly two hours, Swampcat did have some qualms about them—which he would discuss with them, if they wanted to hear them. *Yeah, the locals dig 'em, but will this—sound—play in black metropolises like Harlem or Southside Chicago, or with white folks, anywhere?*

A waterfall of crashing drums, guitars, bass and piano heralded the end of the blues dirge and brought Swampcat back to where he was. After the applause faded, the lead singer grinned and bowed politely.

"Thank you-all for coming out tonight."

"Hey, Lou!" a foghorn voice blared from way in the back. "Do that hillbilly goof!"

Lou shaded his eyes with his left hand, squinted, and searched for the speaker, greatly befuddled. "Repeat that please; I couldn't hear you!"

"Hillbilly goof! Hillbilly goof!" The chant began slowly, but steadily snowballed.

"*This* is the song I was tellin you about! It's *murder!*" Maynelle squealed.

"*This* I gotta see! A colored cat pullin off a Hank Williams country-ass song in a blues joint," Swampcat said, with skepticism and hope.

"Hillbilly goof! Hillbilly goof!" The demand spread like a flame on a tiled floor coated with kerosene.

Swampcat swiveled his head to take in the rising clamor. "Mercy!" he hissed. "And the white folks is callin the loudest!"

"HILLBILLY GOOF! HILLBILLY GOOF!"

Swampcat made an arching gesture to the room. "This—ritual. Cute."

"Ain't it, though? Ooo—look, hunny—he's winkin directly at you again!"

Swampcat acknowledged the handsome vocalist's wink with one of his own.

On stage, Lou smiled when he caught the radio kingpin's wink. *Man alive! He's actually* here—*and seems to be enjoying the show*! That notion gave him another shot of adrenaline.

"HILLBILLY GOOF! HILLBILLY GOOF!" By now all were on their feet, many pumping fists into the air, threatening to rip a hole in the ceiling with the sheer dint of their fervor. Lou plastered on a confused look, clutched the microphone for support, searched into his audience, and cupped his hand around his left ear. "Did you-all say something?"

"HILLBILLY GOOF! HILLBILLY GOOF!"

"Do you *really* want me to?" he sighed, breathlessly.

"Hell, yes!" the crowd roared back.

"But will you *respect* me in the morning?" Lou trilled, trying to keep a straight face, so he would not betray he was having more fun with this than they.

"This *is* the morning, Lou! Now quit diddlin us and sing the daggone song!" foghorned the same voice that had first demanded the tune. Laughter and applause greeted that.

"It's not gonna hurt—*that much*—is it?" Lou whimpered, as he furiously batted his eyes, with apprehension and visions of impending delight. The three hundred-plus assured him it would not.

"Promise?" he whispered hoarsely into the mike. From the corner of his eye, he saw Moon make a slicing motion across his neck and point to his watch. The two a.m. curfew approached. Lou winked at Moon, then returned to his crowd.

"If you say so," he exhaled with resignation. "I'm taking your word for it." He nodded to his bandmates. "Five, six, seven, and..."

The Jimmy Jameson Quartet exploded into "Cora Ann."

The tiny dancing area attracted people as if it were a flesh magnet. All else stood and shook and shimmied. Those who knew the lyrics sang along. Maynelle was up, too, swiveling her shapely, ample hips and waving her strong, fleshy arms to the boisterous backbeat. Swampcat, still seated, kept an eye out for wayward elbows. He felt like a tiny boat on a roiling ocean of country and boogie-woogie.

"Oh, Cora Ann!" the lead singer shouted, and his bandmates echoed him.

"Oh, Cora Ann!
Why you wanna go and marry that Smilin' Dan?
Didn't you know I wasn't playin'
When I vowed I'd never be strayin'
Now you done gone off wiiiiith
Some other man
Some other man!"

"Aw, yeah! That's *it*, hunny—that's it!" hollered a woman in a green silk dress.

Lou wailed on:

"Here I am, hidin in the lurch,
Layin' low down in my perch
Stationed half a block down from the First Avenue Baptist
   Church
So doggone mad I'm about to swoon
It's drivin me crazy as a loon:
Cora Ann an' Smilin' Dan are gonna git hitched at noon!

Nearly everyone sang the chorus with him, then he ripped into the second verse:

"Folks flockin' to the church all in a bevy
Cora Ann's climbin' out her daddy's Chevy
My heart's pound-pound-poundin' fast and heavy!
There's ol' Dan all sharp and smooth
Now they're playin' the 'Weddin' March' Groove
No doubt about it, brother—time to make my move!"

"Make that move, baby!" a woman shouted as Lou—and most of the audience—shouted out the chorus again.

"A second 'fore they took that final vow
I told myself: 'It's never or now'
I jumped on Dan and combinated—left, right, left, right,
    pow-pow-pow-pow!"

"That's right, baby—fight for your girl!" a young white woman jumped up and shouted.
"Whup his ass like you Sugah Ray, baby!"

"Nobody knowed what hurricane hit
Dan and his folks was pitchin' a fit
But by then me and Cora had hit the grit!
While everyone was reelin' from the shock
Me and Cora got hitched in Little Rock
Where we been rockin' and rollin' all 'round the clock!"

"That's right—you won her, now *rock* her!" howled the hefty woman in the turquoise dress. The musicians reprised the final chorus as if their lives depended on their energy level.

"Was I lyin when I told you how good this tune was?" Maynelle shouted. Swampcat replied with a gesture toward the turmoil that surrounded them, then flashed a gold-toothed smile and pointed a thumbs-up at the vocalist.

On the bandstand, Lou howled internally. The single, simple vote of confidence from Swampcat meant more than the crazed approval of the crowd. Lou nodded toward the dressing room in the back. Swampcat tipped his highball glass in acknowledgement.

As always, the crowd demanded encores of "Cora Ann." After the second, it was time to call it a night; both the audience and band were totally spent. Lou graciously thanked the crowd on behalf of the Quartet and the management, bade all a safe journey to their next destination, and reminded them the band would return next weekend, same time, same station. He was only half-joking when he suggested that everyone go to church on Sunday. Foghorn Voice re-reminded Lou it was already Sunday.

Moon put a capper on the carnival. "Last call for alcohol!" he hollered. "Yawl ain't gotta go home—but you sure gotta pull a Houdini from here! See ya next week!"

The patrons filed out. Some would head for the city's one reputable Negro after-hours joint; others, as Lou heeded, would try to get some sleep in order to make a morning service.

Lou again caught Swampcat's eye. He had not budged from his table. Lou signaled "twenty minutes" by flashing that many fingers. Swampcat replayed Moon's gesture by giving his watch a hard look and tap, then cut his eyes in the direction of Highway 40 back to Nashville. Lou gave him the "okay" sign, then followed his bandmates into the dressing room.

The room was but a twenty-foot-by-twenty-foot wood-slatted compartment that Moon had hammered together. Five clothes trees complemented a row of coat hooks nailed into the wall. The furniture was comprised of a dresser drawer, two short couches, a coffee table, and two armchairs Moon had intercepted between friends' homes and the junkyard. Lou and Blondie collapsed onto a couch, Deuce sprawled his massive frame in the other, and Jimmy commandeered a chair. They had burned adrenaline for the better part of five hours, and now fatigue descended on them like a clunky curtain.

A waitress had set out their favorite drinks just minutes ago. Jimmy swigged from a double Cutty Sark on the rocks. Deuce sipped from a water glass half full of Wild Turkey, straight. Blondie swilled down the first Budweiser with shameless gusto, then took his time with the second of three placed for him on the coffee table. Lou chugged on an Upper Ten soda. Allowing themselves a collective peaceful moment, they lit cigarettes and peeled off their flame-green, black-bordered, imitation silk jackets.

As usual, Jimmy gave them a few minutes to wind down before he critiqued their performance—in total, and individually. He took mental notes throughout, and never missed a sour chord or ill-timed entrance. After the evaluation, Jimmy opened the floor to comments. They knew they had less than a half hour; by two-thirty, Moon would have the place padlocked.

As usual, it was Blondie who cracked the silence. "Gents, we put the wood to it tonight!" he crowed, his cat eyes dancing with still-unburned energy.

As usual, Jimmy responded in a "yes...but..." manner. "That we did, but we still got some kinks to iron out." He paused to find the correct note on which to begin the discussion.

A trio of hard thwacks on the door startled them. Moon's voice followed. "Hey, fellas—yawl's got a visitor. A very im-por-tant visitor."

The musicians batted around looks. Only Lou's was not puzzled.

"Can it wait? We got things to discuss," Jimmy said, not bothering to hide his irritation.

"Boys, you *wanna* meet this cat," Moon persisted from the other side of the wall. Before anyone could protest, the door swung open. Moon and the guest strolled in. The chunky, well-dressed man beamed at Lou, then smiled generally, his expression an outstretched hand to all.

"Hey, dudes. Yawl ain't half bad," he drawled.

Moon gestured to the stranger. "Boys, meet—"

"Swampcat Newsome!" Deuce and Blondie howled in unison. As often happened with radio personalities, people recognized the voice before they placed the face.

"I'm afraid that's me," Swampcat said with a modest smile.

"I listen to your show—religiously!" Blondie gushed.

"You the man! You the *main* man!" Deuce rumbled.

Lou had yet to say anything.

Jimmy eyed the visitor with equal parts wariness, wonder, and appreciation for his presence. He half-smiled. "So...what brings you to our little neck of the woods?"

If Swampcat caught the glimmer of challenge in the tone, he did not respond to it. He grinned coolly at the bandleader, and seemed to relish the anticipation the others had for his answer. He reached into his vest pocket, pulled out a large cigar, slowly unwrapped it, and licked it languidly. By the time he eased it into his mouth, Blondie and Lou had flaming lighters at the ready. He accepted a light from both, drew hard upon the cigar, and finally spoke:

"You cats are what brought me here."

Blondie, Deuce, and Lou's faces slackened with relief and joy; even Jimmy let a light grin slip. The four introduced themselves, and punctuated their names with firm handshakes.

"How'd you hear about us?" Blondie asked.

Swampcat's gaze slid toward Lou, but before he could answer, the vocalist squeezed his eyelids, hard: *No.*

"Word travels," Swampcat said vaguely. "You'd be surprised how tiny the world of R & B is. Everyone knows who's doing what, be it good, bad, or mediocre."

"Which one are we?" Jimmy asked, his challenging tone more pronounced.

Swampcat hesitated before he answered. "Me—I think you studs are...better than just good. You're hip to what *your audience* thinks about you." He paused to see if they had caught the emphasized words. They had, so he continued: "*I* think you're as good as or better than seventy, maybe eighty percent of the artists on the R & B charts." He paused. "But...it's hard to gauge how well any fish can swim out of familiar waters."

Four faces clouded. Lou spoke carefully, bracing himself. "Just what is it you're telling us, Mister Swampcat?"

"I'm saying, if you boys have already discussed auditionin for a record company, by all means give it a go."

"You think we're *that* good?" Blondie blurted.

"Whoa! Slow down, son. Anyone can *audition*," Swampcat backpedaled. "But, yeah—you guys got a sound that's...different. I'll say this much: you boys're too good *not* to try to get your stuff on wax. Just lissen to all the mediocre mess on the radio. What've you got to lose, 'cept a few hours and some gas money? You don't wanna be sittin on your livin room couch when you're seventy, wishin you gave it a shot back in '55."

Jimmy eyed Lou, then Swampcat. "You *really* think we're good enough to—?"

"I don't know you cats from Adam, ain't got no reason to try to kiss your asses," Swampcat replied. "This is a recording: *I* think you cats can make a splash...but..."

"Oh, Lord," Blondie moaned, "let's hear it..."

"Coupla problems you might face. Knoxville is stuck in the middle-a nowhere—"

"We're just four hours from Nashville, the country-music capital—"

"Will you *please* let Mister Swampcat finish, Blondie?" Lou squalled.

"Sorry. Go 'head, Mister Newsome."

"Yeah, the *country*-music capital, but a hotshot R & B band cuts little, if no, ice there. You'll have to get record company folks in the big cities—New York, New Orleans, Chicago—interested, *and* you'll have to do one helluva persuasive job just to get an audition."

"Why's that?" Deuce asked.

"The big wheels in the top recordin outfits just don't believe there's any worthwhile talent in a li'l off-track burg like Knoxville."

"Where's it written you gotta be from New York or one-a them places to have talent?" Blondie fumed.

"It ain't right, but that's the way those cats think," Swampcat replied. "If you want a shot at a record deal, yawl's just gonna hafta work around that fact."

"What's the other problem you foresee?" Lou asked.

"Don't take this the wrong way. Much of your local popularity lies in a—gimmick. Yeah, Lou's other original tunes are cute, clever, and catchy, but the one that's gonna make or break yawl is the hillbilly goof."

"Folks love it here, so why wouldn't they dig it elsewhere—?"

"Blondie! Let. Mister. Swampcat. *Finish*!"

"Sorry!"

"In this town and other burgs like it, where colored and country cultures kinda rub elbows naturally, that sound'll work. But in the more—sophisticated—big cities..." The musicians frowned, so Swampcat amended: "Then again, it could be the novelty that gets the song over, big-time. Which brings us back to Square One. Only one way to find out..."

"Is to grit our teeth and take our shot," Lou said, then took two short, careful steps toward Swampcat. "Can you make some calls, alert some record folks about us?" He pretended not to notice Jimmy's peeved look.

"Whoa, again! Let's get somethin straight, *like right now*! My dealings with the record folks is about playin their product. I *don't* scout talent for them." He paused, pulled deeply on his cigar, and slowly let out the smoke. "Yawl make me out to have more clout than I truly got."

"But you *must* know every wheel in R & B—"

"You're not *hearin* me," Swampcat cut off Blondie. "What I do is 'break' regional hits in this area. Only a few hotshots in Chicago, L.A., or New York can do what yawl *think* I can."

"Still, can't you call—somebody—tell 'em you've heard us, think we're—"

"Two-part answer on that, Lou. One: I'm just too doggone busy. Runnin a twenty-four hour station is a twenty-seven-hour-a-day job, nine days a week. Two: You dudes are gonna hafta contact them folks your ownselves. Make 'em know you're hell-bent for success." He paused to make eye contact with all. "That is, if *all* you studs are as gung-ho about all this as some seem to be." He paused again. "*Everybody's* gotta go balls to the wall."

Lou squelched an impulse to steal a glance at Jimmy. And Deuce.

An ironic grin suddenly split Swampcat's broad, dark face. "Uh-oh. Looks like the idea of recordin is *news* to some-a you cats." Grimaces confirmed that. "I know. The mere thought of *auditionin* is like stepping off a cliff. I understand that. Here's my advice: discuss among yourselves if you wanna take the time and energy—and suffer the disappointment—of shoppin your product around. But if you *do* decide to have at it..." He paused, almost coquettishly. The four leaned closer, wide-eyed.

"*You* contact the small, independent labels that produce R & B. Forget about the majors, at least for now. I assume that between you four, yawl's got most-a the latest sides…"

"That we do, sir," Lou replied.

Swampcat told them what to do: find out each label's home city, call information and get the firm's general number—or, if possible, a direct line to the owner. Call the record people early and often. Sound like you're used to getting your way. Don't let them put you on hold, or turn you down over the phone—*talk* to them. "Make a list of *exactly* who you spoke to," Swampcat advised. "I'll give 'em a follow-up call…for whatever it's worth. *That's* the best I can do."

Silence, then Jimmy spoke: "Lotta legwork. And a lotta getting shit on by fat cats who naturally assume anyone from *Knoxville* is a no-talent hick," he said, softly but acidly.

"Can't take that attitude, my friend," Swampcat flatly declared.

"No, *we* can't," Blondie echoed, archly.

Swampcat spoke, slowly. "There's three labels where I got their ear: Jay-Vee in Chicago; Monarch in Cincy; and Unique, out of New Orleans. Of course you cats've heard of 'em."

"Sure," Lou chimed in. "Little Robert and Louisiana Fats are on Unique; Moanin' Lisa and Little Johnny Wills on Monarch—"

"Very good." Swampcat gave them specific names to ask for.

Moon knocked and entered in the same motion. "Sorry to rush yawl, but…"

"We understand," Swampcat said. "Just lemme give the boys one last bit of advice…"

Moon smiled, pointed to his watch, and stepped out.

"However far you cats try to go in this business, you're gonna meet some-a the slimiest snakes that ever crawled from under a rock. Even the nicest, most honest cats are gonna try to take you for a ride a time or two."

"We know," said Deuce.

"Some-a them cats would hand their own mama a rope to hang herself with if it meant an extra dollar in their pocket," Swampcat continued.

Jimmy looked at Deuce, then said: "You ain't tellin us nothin we don't already know."

Lou caught Blondie's eye, and they angled baffled looks at the senior members.

"Just so you'll know," Swampcat said. "Look—if I seem to be leadin you on, and puttin you off at the same time…well, that's the crazy nature of this business…"

"We understand," Lou replied. Outside the room, Moon loudly cleared his throat. Lou extended his hand to Swampcat. "We cherish your advice. Thanks for everything."

Swampcat squeezed the hand. "Just tryin to be of whatever help I can." He shook the other hands, then turned for the door. "Be good, be aggressive, but most of all—be careful. Good night and God go with you."

After Swampcat left, Moon thrust an envelope into Jimmy's hands. "I hate to seem like I'm kickin you guys out, but—"

"Yeah, yeah, Moon—"

"—I got two curfew violations already. Them paddy boys'll be on me like grease on fatback if they catch me a third—"

"Yeah, yeah," Jimmy repeated. In five minutes they were in their street clothes and out the door.

As they stepped outside, a car horn pealed three times. Blondie sighted his '53 Ford convertible and waved. "Hang in there, girls!" he shouted.

"C'mon, Edgar—it's late enough as it is!" a female voice groused from behind a half-raised window.

"Calm down, Sugarpie. No need to rush!" Blondie called. He grinned at the looks from his bandmates. "Women! Boy, I tell you..."

Jimmy counted out each man's pay. "Since we didn't get around to our usual after-show chat, we'll discuss that—and other matters—Tuesday. My garage, seven p.m. Light rehearsal, as always." His eyes narrowed as they connected with Lou's. "And in case anyone has forgotten, this is *still* my group; I still call the shots—"

"I never said differently!" Lou protested.

"What makes you think it was Lou who contacted Mister Swampcat?" Blondie asked. "He might've come on his own, don'tcha know! And if Lou *did* invite him, it was for the band's benefit—"

"*I'll* decide what's for our benefit!" Jimmy shot back. "If and when I think we're ready for a major move, I'll make the calls and—"

"Lord have mercy, Jimmy!" Lou wailed. "If I'd've known you'd react like this, I'd've never invited Mister Swampcat!"

"Lighten up, Jimmy," Deuce cut in. "He didn't think he was steppin on your authority."

The horn on Blondie's Ford brayed three more times.

"Hold it just a damn minute!" Jimmy barked, causing the others to recoil. He turned back to Lou and sized up the much taller man for a long count. "You're how old, Lou? Twenty-three?" Lou nodded. "And a *young* twenty-three, at that." Lou grimaced slightly. "And I'm not just sayin that 'cause you're a preacher's kid," Jimmy added. "But you—and Blondie, to a certain extent—are quite...naive."

The junior members started to protest, but Jimmy beat them to the punch. "You boys grew up a bit easier than a lot of us colored folks—"

"Oh, yeah," Blondie parried, "we always gotta be careful not to choke on these-here silver spoons in our mouths."

"You know what I mean. Yawl never had to scuffle like me and Deuce. And we *already* been on that road you're thinkin about travelin," Jimmy said softly.

Lou and Blondie stared quizzically at Jimmy and Deuce.

"So if we don't quite share your desire to go flyin off on some R & B treasure hunt, you'll have to forgive us," Deuce said.

Lou dug his heels into the parking lot's gravel. "So what happened to you guys?"

"It's a long story," Deuce sighed.

"No, it's not, really—but too long to be recountin tonight," Jimmy amended, and punctuated it with a yawn. "We'll bend your ears about it later. Tuesday night."

"Then what do I do about all those calls Mister Swampcat advised us to—?"

"We'll discuss that Tuesday," Jimmy said in a case-closed tone, then climbed into his '49 Cadillac Seville and started the engine.

Lou and Blondie looked at Deuce, who grinned vaguely and slid into his royal-blue '54 Buick Electra 225. Soon his engine revved in perfect harmony with Jimmy's, then they rolled out of the lot.

"Man," Blondie began when they were gone, "later for those fossils. Let's split, find ourselves some truly gone cats who're horny for a hit record and—"

"Relax. Let's hear what they have to say on Tuesday, and take it from there."

"I'm tellin ya, Lou—let's drop these Methuselah fogies and—"

"Blondie, what we've got is a *sound*. The four of us. We're like— the right chemicals compounded together to form the right..." He fumbled for the correct word until he clutched it, "...combustibility."

"Yeah, well, I'm sure you remember how I was a lost ball in chemistry class—"

"Let's just play it by ear, Blondie."

Three more protests bleated from Blondie's car horn. "C'mon, Lou—got some chicks I want you to meet."

In the overspill of a streetlamp, Lou recognized the women in Blondie's car—the girls from Austin High who now sat up close at the Full Moon shows. "It's late, and—"

Blondie hooked his right arm under Lou's left and began to walk him to the car. "They been houndin me to introduce you to them since—"

"*Introduce?* We went to grade, junior high, and high school with them, remember? They barely said 'boo' to me in all those years. *Now* they want to meet me?"

"You're a *star* now, boy! You know how women are—"

"*Some* women, Blondie. Some."

"Aw, Lou, don't be such a drag. I promised those chicks you'd slide on over with us to Red Hogan's after-hours joint and then—"

"Excuse me, but some of us have to get up early. Church? Remember? Sermons and singing and Jesus saving souls and—"

"Blah, blah, blah. Spare this hell-bound sinner the lecture, Lou."

"Edgar! Are we gonna sit here all night, or what?" a soprano squeal rang from the car.

"Keep the mustard warm, honey! I'm workin on it!" Blondie hollered back.

"Alba Evans. Does that name ring a bell, Blondie? My...girl-friend..."

"Lou, Lou, Lou. What she don't know won't hurt her—"

"BLONDIE!"

"Just tryin to look out for you, brother."

"That kind of looking out for I don't need."

Blondie shrugged. "Have it your way. But if we ever get this R & B thing going, we'll see how long you can keep up this 'Saint Louis' act in the face of all the cooz that'll get thrown your way."

Lou took a step toward his car. "Thank you. And good night."

"Okay, man. The girls're gonna be disappointed, but the Blond One will do his best to take up your slack. More wool for me, brother."

Lou climbed into his car. "Wear some protection, fool," he advised. Blondie rolled his eyes theatrically. Lou switched on the engine of his '51 Delta 88. As he waited for it to warm up, he heard the conversation in Blondie's car, just five yards away.

"What's wrong with your boy? He funny or somethin?"

"Nah. He's in looooove, is what he is," Blondie replied.

"Oh, yeah," a second female voice cut in. "I know his girlfriend. Kinda cute, if them church-girl, bookworm types is your speed."

"Like *attracts*, hunny" a third female voice chimed in. "Guess it's no big loss."

"Make the most of the night with the one you're with," Blondie said. "Let's roll."

"Your boy don't know what he missin! And I know *she* ain't comin up off-a nothin!"

The next sound Lou heard was Blondie's screeching tires as the Ford shot past his Olds, purposely missing it by inches. Lou goosed the gas pedal and eased out of the lot. Now that he was alone, he realized how tired he *really* was. He looked at his watch: it was a quarter to three. He could catch about five hours of sleep before church. He smiled as he thought of how much easier it was to perform before a packed juke-joint crowd at one a.m. on a Sunday morning, than face a Sunday school class of a dozen ten-year-olds eight hours later.

Twenty minutes later, he was home and in bed. As always, he was so keyed up from the performance that it was nearly an hour before he fell asleep.

CHAPTER TWO

Sunday, April 10, 1955; 10:33 a.m.
Brighter Day Baptist Church. Knoxville.

"But now I know my soul is blessed
  Because I've finally passed the test
  The test of faith my Beloved Lord
  Has given me…"

"Aw, yeah, sang that gospel, Sonny-Boy, sang that gospel!"
"Make us feel it, Junior! Make us feel your soul!"
The church band climbed to a crescendo ending as Lou held the last notes. It was the first time he had tried out this composition, and was glad it was over. He was never confident about his creations until he got feedback from an audience, be it in a blues club or church. He stole a glance and a wink at his girlfriend, Alba, in the women's choir. She flashed a deep-dimpled smile and wrinkled her short, pert nose at him.

The Reverend Louis Cannon, Sr., rose from his high-backed chair at the right of the pulpit and swiveled toward his son. The senior edition looked as if someone had added an inch, thirty pounds, and a quarter century onto the junior model. Both had the same chocolate-candy complexion, with copper undertones. The main difference was in their hair length and texture: Lou's curling waves were close-cropped and plastered down with Duke pomade; the reverend's hair fell in large black ringlets to his broad shoulders. He was not shy about flailing his thick mane, Cab Calloway-style, at strategic moments.

The reverend peered out at the gathering. It had not escaped his notice that the six hundred-seat church, which had been filling from eighty to ninety percent of capacity since the end of World War II, was overflowing since Junior had gained local popularity as a blues-man. Most of the newcomers were young and female.

In the front pew on his right sat his wife, Florence, and his widowed mother, Beatrice, known to all as Mother Cannon. Flanking them were Lou's sisters: twenty-one-year-old Ruth, and Sarah, one year Ruth's junior. Three spaces beside them were prominently empty: those that Florence's late parents and Reverend Cannon's long-deceased father once occupied. In the front pew to the reverend's left sat Sam and Hurlene Evans, Alba's parents. Scattered throughout were at least three dozen members of the extended Cannon family.

The reverend breathed deeply of the church's smells. Early April: the first flowers of the spring, the sweet natural mustiness of the church itself, and the scents from too many sisters who had doused on too much perfume made for a delightful mix of fragrances.

Cardboard fans advertising Baird's Funeral Home fluttered before black, brown, tan, and ivory faces; it was unseasonably warm. Reverend Cannon made a mental note to commend his wife for ordering the smart new burgundy curtains. To his left was the women's choir; to his right, the men's; on the back wall was the requisite painting of Jesus Christ.

This portrait of The King of Kings, however, was different. Jesus was a walnut-colored man with a waterfall of coarse black woolly hair. Depending upon the viewer's angle, He resembled Joe Louis or Frederick Douglass.

The reverend returned his gaze on Lou, then gestured toward him. "Yes, Lord! The song you just heard was by my son, another original composition, written in the service of Jesus!"

"Go 'head on, Junior!" cheered an elderly sister.

"Glory to Gawd on high!"

"Louis, Jr.! My soul!" shrieked a sister close to Lou's age. Many chuckled; she obviously admired more than Lou's gospel singing. As he sensed all eyes upon him, he grinned sheepishly, then glanced toward Alba. She glared at the woman, then cut her eyes toward Lou. He gave her a wan smile.

The reverend pointed his eyes Heavenward, released a long sigh, gripped the podium tightly, lowered his head, and frowned. Many recognized this shift, and braced. "Y'know, brothers and sisters," he said as he gestured toward the combo, "there're those who have the nerve to be *upset* because I have a five-piece band playing the Lord's music." He hunched over the podium and shot out a disbelieving look. "Some peeee-ple got nothing better to do than worry about who or what Reverend Cannon's got sending out the gospel of the Lord!"

Only a handful murmured in agreement. The reverend hunched over farther and shook his head. "Yawl don't hear me."

"What do *they* know, Rev?" shouted Sister Mary Purcell, Blondie's mother.

"They need to find somethin better to do with they time!" added Mother Cannon. Others muttered similar sentiments.

Now that he had a passable response, the reverend continued: "They say you don't need a piano, drummer, a clarinet, and two gee-tars to sing the songs of the Lord! Some say I gots me a 'rhythm-and-blues' band in my chu'ch!" Despite two degrees from Howard University, the reverend often lapsed into incorrect grammar, as did most Southern Negro ministers. Yet, each conscious error forced a cringe from his wife, an English teacher at Vine Junior High School.

"It's *your* church, Rev! You can have *ennythang* you want in it! Praise Gawd!"

"People, I'm here to tell you, it doesn't matter *who* or *what* is playing The Lord's music—as long as it *is* The Lord's music! Now whatcha got to say to that?"

Six hundred voices rose in a cacophony of agreement, with vary-ing degrees of sincerity.

"I looked; my wife searched; so did all three of my children; five of our deacons went over the Bible, front to back, top to bottom, and *nowhere* does it say that Reverend Louis Cannon, Sr., of the Brighter Day Baptist Church, 550 Patton Street, Knoxville, Tennessee, could *not* have a five-piece band play the Lord's music on the Lord's Day! Praise Him on high!"

"Glory to Gawd!"

"Preach, Rev, preach!"

"And one other thing along those lines." The Reverend leaned back, rolled his head slowly, then hunched over the podium again. "Those same busy-bodies want to make something over my son spending some of his well-earned spare time performing with a—" he paused, swirled the words on his tongue, and spat them out: "—blu-uuuues band!" He surveyed the congregation to see who flinched.

"I don't like to take up chu'ch time on issues of a *personal* nature, but the back-biters are working my last nerve with their uninformed talk! Was Junior here at nine sharp to teach his Sunday school class as always? Yes he was! Was he here at ten sharp to lead us in the first prayer? Yes he was! Does he stand before you now, in the songful serv-ice of Our Lord? Yes he does! Then I guess the blues and the gospel can coexist, at least where Junior is concerned. Am I right or wrong?"

"You right, Rev! Lawrd Gawd A'mighty!"

"Maybe someday his name will be in lights, Rev!"

Lou watched as the parishioners bounced looks from the rev-erend to him. He was surprised—and grateful—for his father's unso-licited defense of him, but he displayed no emotion.

"But wait a minute!" The reverend continued. "Some of you might argue that the blues is *still* the Devil's music!" He glared at Deacon Smiley, then Mrs. Smiley in the choir. He knew they had complained the loudest. "These busy-bodies keep insisting you can't do the Devil's work on Saturday night, and The Lord's work the next morning! Well, children, I'd say that was The Lord's call. If and when He feels Junior's sinning with his boogie-woogie, then He'll give us some kind of sign."

"You right, Rev! Ain't *nobody* heard The Lawd Himself say the blues was the Devil's music!" Blondie's mother shouted, to raucous agreement.

"The blues is *the black man's music!*" The words rang like a shotgun blast. Many recoiled. "It was the blues that got our ancestors through those scorching summer days on the plantations. It was singing the blues during their precious few leisure hours that kept them from going insane. The blues may not all be pretty, the blues may not all be clean, the blues may not be sweet, but it washed the dirt and lifted the spirit of many a Negro! The blues are the *flipside* of the songs we sing here in service to Our Lord! They serve the same purpose! And you don't need to listen too awful close to realize how *similar* they sometimes sound! Now say hallelujah!"

"HALLELUJAH!"

"Make it plain, Rev, make it plain!"

"Preach the good sermon! Lord ha' mercy!"

"You hate the blues, you hate your heritage, you hate yourself! If you believe the blues, the *black man's music*, is the Devil's music, then you see yourself as of the Devil, and not of the Lord God Almighty!" roared the reverend. The congregation thundered its approval. Satisfied he had hammered home his point, Reverend Cannon was ready to press onward. With a nod of his head, he cued the band and choirs to begin the next song. He resumed his place in his magnificent chair.

Lou felt his eyes moistening. He beamed broadly at his father. Though the reverend did not move a facial muscle, he leaned his head slightly toward Lou, smiled in return with his eyes, then continued gazing at the flock before him.

The rest of the service passed smoothly. When it was over, Lou joined his parents, grandmother, and sisters in the ritual greeting of the worshippers as they filed out. The Cannons shook everyone's hand firmly and thanked all for attending. When Alba left with her parents, Lou clutched her wrist and whispered, "Love you."

She wrinkled her nose, and when she thought no one saw her, stuck out her tongue. She tapped her watch and mouthed the word "dinner." He tapped his in return and winked.

As she walked off, his eyes followed her rolling backside until he felt a sharp elbow in his ribs. He turned to see Sarah grinning, rubbing her left forefinger with her right one, and shaking her head.

It's a good thing you're too dark to blush, bud, he teased himself, then returned to thanking the worshippers.

* * * * *

At 3:57 sharp Lou pulled in front of the Evans' neat, red-brick, two-story house on Surrey Drive. He parked in the driveway, behind the family's station wagon, and crossed to the porch. The outer storm door was slightly ajar; the inside door wide open. He peered into the short vestibule and saw Sam Evans in the adjacent living room, anchored in his favorite chair, staring at the television. *He knows I'm out here.* He felt something brush against his left calf. It was Ajax, the ancient, barrel-bodied blue tick hound. Lou bent to pat Ajax, which caused the dog to yelp in joy. *He* must *have heard that,* Lou thought as he again peered in. Sam Evans had yet to blink.

Still, Lou knew better than to march into Sam Evans' domain through an unlocked door, even if he was expected, until someone granted him entry. As he stared at Sam in the living room, Lou pressed the doorbell button. It came as no surprise that Sam gave no indication of hearing it. He pushed the button again.

"Alba! Get the door!" Hurlene shouted from far back in the house. Seconds later, Alba swept into the hallway, clad in a white apron with red polka dots over the blue cotton jumper she had changed into. She opened the already unlocked door.

"Hey, honey! Four on the dot," she gushed as she put her cheek up for him to kiss, but not until she glanced into the next room at her father.

"Hey, Doll Face," he said as he bussed her lightly, quickly.

"That you, Louis, honey?" Hurlene called from the kitchen.

"Yes, ma'am!"

"Just make yourself to home! Dinner'll be ready in about ten minutes!"

"Yes, ma'am! Will do!" he said. Alba squeezed his hand and steered him toward the living room. Without having to be reminded, he removed his shoes and placed them in a hallway corner. Sam Evans had paid far too much for the deep, soft, gold carpet on the living and dining room floors for anyone to track anything onto it. Lou entered the living room, and without catching Sam Evans' eye, addressed him. "Mister Sam, sir," he said, tonelessly.

Sam Evans tendered an abrupt nod of his head. "Louis."

Sam Evans was a bespectacled, pecan-colored man on the shorter end of medium height. Lou knew he was two years younger than the reverend, which put Sam at forty-six. Sam's close-cropped, reddish-brown hair was graying and thinning. His compact, muscular build suggested he might have been a decent track-and-field athlete or baseball player in his youth.

Lou eased onto the navy-brown sofa, neither too close nor too far from Sam. He turned to the Motorola television that held Sam riveted. Lou recognized the voice of Edgar R. Murphy, the host of *Face America.* "Anyone interesting on this week?" Lou asked.

"Mmm-hmmm."

Lou took that as a "yes." Seconds later, the smoky, well-modulated voice of someone from the Deep South rumbled from the set. "Isn't that Senator Theophilis Briscoe?" he asked.

"Yep. The patron saint of segregationists."

"Good. That Edgar R. Murphy doesn't mess around. He'll throw some hardball questions at him, the kind everyone else is afraid to ask," Lou said. Sam nodded slightly. "Have I missed much?" Lou continued.

"Just began."

The camera moved in closely on Senator Briscoe. His face was broad and capped by a high forehead from which a mane of hair was brushed back, unusually thick for a man in late middle age. Below the forehead sat a pair of small, drill-like eyes: darting, probing, ever in control. Lou thought the bulbous nose resembled Babe Ruth's. Yet, despite the beady eyes and bourbon-lover's snout, only a sliver of a mouth—which appeared even thinner in contrast to the fleshy jowls—prevented Briscoe from being quite handsome, in Lou's estimation.

Another camera angle revealed Briscoe seated deeply in his chair, his hands folded across his fleshy midsection, relaxed, like a supremely confident prizefighter awaiting the opening bell. Murphy began in his trademark no-nonsense staccato. "Senator, your separatist views are well known. Can you explain why you are so adamant that the races be kept apart?"

"Let me begin by saying that two of the greatest Negro leaders—Booker T. Washington and Marcus Garvey—held similar separatist views. Garvey's plan in the 1920's was the same as Lincoln's in the 1860's: all American Negroes should return to Africa…"

"*Return* to Africa?" Sam snarled. "I've never even been there! I'm from Tennessee!"

"...While the esteemed Doctor Washington, in his famous 1895 Atlanta speech, pressed for, in lieu of 'social equality,' separate-but-equal facilities in terms of education and basic creature comforts."

"'Separate but *equal*?'" Sam gasped. "Just *you* ride in a rickety Jim Crow railroad car, or use a filthy 'colored only' toilet!"

"And frankly," Briscoe continued calmly, "I don't see why so many Negro leaders demand that their people be allowed to eat next to whites in restaurants, drink from the same fountains, sleep in the same hotels, use the same rest rooms. What would that prove, beyond some abstract, 'symbolic' victory? Only a Negro who despises his own people and himself would trespass where he is unwelcome, in the name of—equality? The races are *already* equal in the South, but separately so."

"Lord," Lou moaned, "can *he* actually believe that?"

"Maybe not that—fully," Sam speculated. "He's a politician, remember. Those actors spout whatever they think will get them more votes."

Briscoe further defended his views, culling more quotes from prominent Negroes, past and present. Murphy listened patiently, reminding Lou of a rattlesnake waiting for the best moment to uncoil, then he finally pounced. "Senator, you are on the record as saying a major reason you resist integration is because you feel Negroes are mentally and morally inferior. Can you elaborate on that?"

Briscoe grimaced. "Let's get one thing straight. I hold no *personal* dislike toward anyone because of his race. Some of the finest people I know are Negroes. Ministers, educators—"

"I understand that, Senator—"

"Please do not interrupt me again, sir," Briscoe said coldly. "I know Negroes who are as smart—or smarter—than the average white person. That said, the *average* person of Western European descent is much smarter than the average Negro and people from other tropical climates. History bears me out. *All* the great scientific inventions are the works of Nordic scientists. And though the music and dances the black and brown races give us are at times a sweet diversion, drumming, dancing, and singing do *not* a forthcoming civilization make."

"At the risk of offending you, Senator, some of your remarks sound alarmingly close to Adolph Hitler's belief in the so-called Master Race."

"Yeah—that's right—go get 'im!" Lou cried.

"I cannot disagree with Hitler that the Nordic race is superior—in terms of intellect and culture. However, I *cannot* agree that the races he deems inferior should be eradicated," Briscoe replied.

"So, Senator—can you provide us with—scientific—proof of this gap in intelligence?" Murphy asked, doing little to disguise a sardonic tone.

Briscoe fielded the question like Jackie Robinson handling a lazy ground ball. "The changing seasons," he said, simply.

"Sir?" Briscoe's nonchalance caught Murphy off guard.

"In the tropics, with year-round warm weather, the vegetation is right there for people. Just pluck it and eat it. Temperature's the same, day in, month out, so there's no need to make adjustments for the change in seasons. However, the Europeans had to learn when to plant crops, how to nurture them, when to harvest them, how to hunt animals in adverse weather, how to make clothes and build shelters to protect them from the cold. Planning. Discipline. Two things tropical races—to this day—are notoriously lacking. In short, the Europeans were forced to become *critical thinkers.*"

"I'm sorry, Senator, but we must pause for a commercial," Murphy said, reluctantly.

A minute later, the interview continued. Briscoe explained his views on the perils of integration: "The Negro will suffer the most. Schoolteachers, businessmen, lawyers, doctors—many will be shunted aside when their people can patronize their white counterparts."

"He's got something there," Sam concurred. "Good thing I own a barbershop. White folks won't be cutting too many Negroes' heads, no, buddy."

"Soup's on!" Hurlene announced as she stood in the wide archway that divided the living and dining rooms. "Come and get it."

Lou was slow to rise. "I'd hate to miss the rest of this..."

"Me, too, but..." Sam nodded toward the dining room. He rose and crossed to the set.

Before Sam touched the knob, Lou called out, "Mister Sam, can we position the set so we can see the rest of—"

"Sunday dinners at my house are for eating Sunday dinner, not for watching television. You know that, Louis."

"Yes, sir, but the discussion was so enlightening—"

"Louis. If you want to stay in here and watch television while your hosts partake of dinner on the Lord's Day, you are more than welcome to do so."

Lou swallowed before he spoke. "I apologize if the suggestion offended you in any way," he said, allowing a trace of irritation to filter through.

Sam grunted and clicked off the television. As Lou crossed into the dining room, Alba and Hurlene slipped him rolling-eyed smirks. He smiled back tightly.

Sam sat at one end of the oblong mahogany table, Hurlene on the other. Lou and Alba sat side by side. Lou noticed how, instead of a tablecloth, place mats lay beneath plates, serving bowls, platters, and saucers. Sam Evans did not want his expensive, glistening table to be obscured by a mere cloth. Like many objects in the house, Lou judged, the table was there as much to impress visitors as to be functional.

Lou hungrily surveyed the layout of the meal. A macaroni-and-cheese casserole, a huge bowl of mustard greens, a platter of smoke-cured country ham slices drenched in red-eye gravy, a plate of fluffy buttermilk biscuits, and a serving basin of candied yams reminded Lou of why he seldom missed a Sunday dinner here in the last six months.

"Louis," Alba chirped, "can you say 'grace' for us? I love the way you say it."

"Me, too," Hurlene chimed in. "Go 'head, honey, say it."

Lou glanced at Sam, whose flinty eyes did not seem receptive to that. "No, let Mister Sam do it. He keeps it short and sweet." Alba gave him a light kick under the table.

Sam bowed his head, closed his eyes, and folded his hands. The others did likewise. "Thank you, Lord, for this bountiful blessing."

"I lift mine eyes unto the hills, from whence cometh my help; my help cometh from the Lord, the maker of Heaven and Earth," Hurlene recited.

Next was Alba. "Yea, though I walk through the valley of death, I shall fear no evil, for Thou art with me."

"Go ye forth and preach my gospel," Lou contributed.

"Jesus wept," said Sam as he completed the circle. "Let's eat."

They did. A brief silence, then Hurlene spoke. "That was some powerful preaching your dad did, Louis. I'm sure it put to rest a lot of folks' doubts about you playing the blues."

Sam made a sound halfway between a hacking cough and a grunt. He mumbled an "excuse me." Nobody responded.

"Yep. My daddy's very broad-minded," Lou said with the straightest of faces. Beneath the table, Alba ground her heel into his ankle.

"Music isn't sinful, only people are," Hurlene added.

They passed most of the meal in silence. After a dessert of cherry cobbler, vanilla ice cream, and coffee, Sam uttered his first complete statement since blessing the meal. "Louis...I need to see you, in my den..."

Lou and Alba traded a glance because of Sam's tone. "Of course, sir," Lou responded, and followed Sam into the den. Lou thought the small room was unremarkable, save for three paintings on the wall: Sam had commissioned an artist to craft portraits of his parents, and both sets of grandparents, from photographs. Sam's strong resemblance to all six ancestors never ceased to amaze Lou.

Sam pulled out a decanter of brandy from the liquor cabinet. He poured two fingers into a snifter. "Since you don't drink, Louis..."

Lou's response was a watery smile.

Weighing his words carefully, Sam began. "Obviously, your father sees no conflictions with your boogie-woogie...sideline..."

Lou noted how Sam emphasized the last word, by letting it dangle.

"Thus, neither do I," Sam continued, "from a *moral* standpoint, anyway..."

Lou had a good idea of what was next. Still, he feigned naiveté. "...Sir...?"

"I assume you...love that music...and I also assume it is and will only be just a hobby...am I correct?"

"I don't quite follow you, sir," Lou lied.

"You and my daughter...though you have yet to officially announce anything, it's understood that you'll..." Again, Sam let his words swing in a breeze of silence.

"Yes, sir, it is."

Sam took a long, precise swig of brandy. "And when that happens, I'm sure you'll be ready to provide for her to the best of your ability..."

Lou waited before he replied. "Of course, sir..."

"Louis...I heard your cousin Tommy's construction company is doing so well, he's thinking about creating a chief assistant's post..."

"Uh...so he's been saying," Lou mumbled.

"As well-paying a job that a young colored man here could want, I'm sure it will be," Sam said as he packed some Red Man tobacco into his pipe.

"Tommy's no skinflint on payday," Lou said, evasively.

Sam lit his pipe, but did not look at Lou. "I heard he's offered the job to you first..."

Man alive—news travels fast in this one-horse town! Lou doubted that Tommy had told Sam, but a few others knew. "Yes, sir, he has," Lou said, neutrally.

"Well, Louis...given that your—marital status—could be changing in the foreseeable future, one wonders why you didn't jump at such an opportunity."

"I haven't told him I *wouldn't* take it," Lou said, and quickly regretted his defensive tone.

"You haven't agreed, either." Sam took another sip of brandy. "I hope this doesn't mean you'll be capriciously chasing R & B dreams, when such a fine job lies before you."

No use trying to explain anything to someone whose mind is already set, Lou mused sourly. He affected a look that was at once puzzled and innocent. "Sir—have I *ever* given you an indication I would just..." He aimlessly wagged his hand.

Sam gave him a probing look. "No, you haven't. But know this: the life of a professional musician—and never mind the flashy front many of them put up—is mostly for losers too childish, lazy, and stupid to assume workaday adult responsibilities."

Lou settled back in his chair. He had spent enough time in Sam's barbershop to know that a lecture was imminent. Sam continued: "And everything I say goes double for Negro musicians who play that barrelhouse blues, or boogie-woogie, or R & B, or whatever folks are calling it this week. That life is sotted with drug and alcohol addiction, all stripes of sexual deviancy, and the resultant diseases. To make a living on the road, yet maintain a responsible, Christian relationship with a wife and children is practically impossible."

Sam paused to gauge Lou's reaction. The young man's expression, however, remained that of an apt pupil soaking wisdom from a mentor. Sam forged onward. "And we won't mention how these musicians get constantly short-changed by club owners, the record companies, and their own managers." Lou listened silently; Sam paused to wipe his eyeglasses, which reminded Lou of two half-dollars on a wire.

"I know all this, Louis, because in my barbershop I've heard the grumblings of many an itinerant musician. Their stories are roughly the same, and always sad."

Lou shook his head in feigned accord and concern. "That's terrible. Pitiful."

Sam studied Lou some more and resumed. "Even the few 'successful' ones enjoy only temporary triumphs. Look at all the articles in the Negro press about this 'star' who filed for bankruptcy, or that one who is now a destitute street bum."

Lou again shook his head. "Sad. Sad."

Sam peered over the rims of his spectacles into Lou's eyes. "But of course *you'll* never have to worry about that, because you're too smart to even consider such a life—"

Lou looked puzzled. "Did you say all this because you think I would—?"

"A future father-in-law can *never* be too careful. No man who loves his daughter would hand her over to *any* man who is still unclear about his future."

"Sir?" Lou reprised his baffled look.

Sam smiled coldly. *Don't play dumb with me. You know exactly what I mean.*

Lou smiled coldly. "I hope you don't think I *won't* be able to provide for Alba..."

Sam leaned on a bookcase, puffed his pipe, and stared at Lou.

"I assure you when we get married, I will provide for her in line with *her* standards...and if she thought I could not, I'm sure she'd have the sense and self-respect to call it off."

Sam's eyes narrowed. "Everything remains to be seen." He crossed to the liquor cabinet and poured more brandy. With his back to Lou, he said, "Enjoy the rest of your day..."

Lou hoped Sam could feel the eyes on his back. "Indeed, sir," he muttered, and drifted out of the den and back to the dining room, where Alba was running a cloth along the table. She tried to smile. "What did you-all discuss?" she asked, too casually.

"I'll tell you as we're riding." She frowned. "Nothing to get upset about," he added. "About ready?"

She tried again to smile. "In a jiffy." She vanished into the kitchen and returned moments later with Lou's Austin High basketball letter sweater wrapped around her waist. "Let's motorvate," she said.

Minutes later, Lou was wheeling along Boyd's Bridge Pike, headed for Armstrong's Lookout. The Lookout, ten miles past the city limits in Strawberry Plains, featured one of the most breathtaking views of East Tennessee. It was on land owned by the descendants of Oscar Armstrong, a colored man who had amassed some of the area's best farming land during the Reconstruction. Alba and Lou's last few Sunday rides had been to the Lookout. Until warmer weather set in, they would have it mostly to themselves.

As Lou drove, Alba nestled closer. "Okay, Lou. What were you two talking about?"

"Nothing of any great importance." He fingertipped her short, dark-auburn curls, glistening with and softened by hair oil. "Got you a new hairstyle."

"Yep. You like?" she said as she patted her short, immaculate page-boy cut.

"It's cute, though you couldn't get any cuter if you—"

"Back to the original question," she interrupted. "It was *something*. What was it?"

"We'll talk about it later," Lou said, with finality. "For now, let's enjoy the day."

"Alright, Lou—but we *will* talk about it!"

Lou pushed the Delta 88 closer to Strawberry Plains. He scanned the radio dial, though no Knoxville stations would be playing R & B or country songs—not on Sunday.

"Louis...do we have to listen to that music on the Lord's Day?" Alba pouted.

"Music? What music? I haven't found any yet."

"But you will, when we get to the Lookout. Sometimes I think *that's* why you go there, because that's the only way you can get stations from New York and Chicago and those big cities." Lou's smile was a giveaway. She pinched him on his shoulder. "See? I'm right!"

Lou continued to scan the dial; he could pick up only wisps of gospel or news shows. They rode in silence until they arrived at Armstrong's Lookout. Thankfully, nobody was there. They parked facing a sumptuous view of the pink-laced sun setting into the hills behind West Knoxville. Alba cuddled next to him; he savored the fragrances of Dixie Peach pomade, Cameo soap, and a light perfume he could not identify. He glanced at his watch. It was six on the dot—meaning it was seven up in New York City.

She could squawk all she wanted; he *had* to turn on that station.

He slithered his arm around her and turned the knob, careful to ease up the volume. He cranked it too high; a trumpeting flourish blared and startled Alba.

"Looouuu-iiiiis," she groaned.

"Cool it! This guy is the utmost!"

A voice with a bullet-proof Cockney accent boomed: "And now ladies and laddies, you are about to be entertained by a bloke 'ose 'ad 'is praw-cess insured by Lloyd's of London for 'alf a million bucks! WPLC is proud to present the 'ippest Man in the World, The Velvet Voice 'ose the Ladies' Choice, Mister Rhythm-and-Blues 'imself: Cooootie the Cuuuutie!"

Alba stared at Lou as he stared at the radio, like a child ogling his gifts on Christmas morning. "'Cootie the Cutie,' Lou? A grown man calls himself—'Cootie the Cutie?'"

"Girl, hush! I *love* this guy!"

A voice deep as a country well and dripping with honey-coated Southern comfort oozed from the dashboard radio. "Oo-papa-dootie, this is Cootie the Cutie, and I'm here with the rooty-tooty, set to do my duty, your rocky, stocky, cocky disk jockey! I'm the seventh son of the seventh son of that quadroon from the dark side of the moon. I have crossed the burning desert sands on my knees and hands to be with you, then made tracks from the stacks with five hours worth of *wicked* wax! It's a bet, Chet, that every side I ride is an ear-bender, a mind-mender, a top-ender and a solid sender!"

"Oh, my!" Alba gushed with amazed pleasure.

"Yes, dudes and dollies, we're kicking things off at seven bells for all the hipsters and swells, for all the cats and kitties on the farms and in the cities! We're gonna be steady buzzin, cousin, 'til the hour of the Dozen, then we'll turn things over to Captain Midnight, the wee-hour rover. 'Til then, Glenn, I'm gonna scatter some chatter designed to shatter your gray matter—LOOK OUT!!—let's get rockin with the latest platter by Mister Claude McPatter!"

"Is this guy even speaking *English*?" Alba asked.

"New York rhythm-and-blues hipster-ese," Lou answered authoritatively.

"Sounds halfway colored."

"He is."

"What? They let a colored guy on *that* far-reaching a station?"

"Most powerful Negro jockey there is. Young cat, not much older than me. He pushes your record—boom! Top Ten for sure. He's on the cover of this month's *Ebony*-book."

Alba thought for a moment. "Oh, yeah—light-skinned guy, wears a twenty-ton conk! Haaaand-soooome!"

"Heeeey! Careful, gurlie!" Lou bawled in feigned jealousy.

Within seconds they were lost in the song, as Claude McPatter & the Wanderers raved silkily about "The Honey With the Money." Lou sang along, mimicking McPatter's unique tenor; he'd read in a recent *Jet* article that McPatter's father was a Baptist minister. Lou grinned as Alba bobbed her head to the sprightly beat.

"Nice tune," she blushed when she caught Lou staring at her.

"Rhythm-and-blues—best stuff ever made," Lou declared.

The song ended and the Voice on the Radio resumed, holding court along the Eastern Seaboard. "Oo-papa-dower, we're gonna be lashing out with 50,00 watts of power 'til the mid-night hour, puttin down the latest sounds to Paul up in Montreal all the way South to Sammy in Miami, and to all points in between, Gene!"

"I'm starting to like this guy," Alba admitted.

"You've heard him before; you just never *listened*."

Cootie the Cutie continued to caterwaul: "Look out, Planet Earth, it's me, that wild, bad, wicked boy your mama *always* warned you about! So keep your ear near, dear—you're sure to love what you hear! Oo-papa-dullet, this next side is number-three with a bullet; they got their fingers on the trigger and're *dying* to pull it! Here's some baaaaad motor-scooters, Hal Dillard & the Moonlighters, creatin some itchin in the kitchen with 'Bunny's Got a Bun in the Oven!'"

"Lou! Is *this* the smutty hit record everyone's talking about?" Alba demanded.

"If it were *that* 'smutty,' he wouldn't be able to play it—"

"If it *is* a naughty song, I *refuse* to listen to it!" Alba charged past Lou's reply. "Turn off the radio, or change the station!"

Lou laughed. "Girl, you need to get over yourself. Get hip! Dig that crazy beat!" No sooner than he said it, the pulsating bass line and pounding percussion had her hooked. Lou smiled as she patted time on the dashboard.

"You like, hunh?" he asked.

"It is rather catchy. And cute—though, if you read between the lines, it *is* naughty."

"Then don't read between the lines. Just have fun with it."

When the song ended, Alba squeezed his hand. "Let's get out and stretch our legs," she whispered. They climbed out and walked less than a dozen paces before they embraced. He dipped his knees to make up for their nine-inch height difference. He covered her full, bow-shaped lips with his own, and they began a vigorous swordfight of tongues. Instantly he felt himself responding, and pressed his loins firmly, shamelessly against hers.

Alba came up for air. She tilted her head back to take in his eyes, then cast hers downward. "*Somebody* finds Alba quite...compelling," she said with a smirk.

Lou pressed harder. She did not back away. "You think?" he said, then snaked his tongue into her mouth. He withdrew it when she clamped her teeth on it. "Ouch!"

"Bad boy! I knoooow what you'd *like* to do," she clucked joyfully.

"You do, hunh?"

"We'll have plenty of time for that when we're..." She allowed her sentence to dangle.

He pressed even harder. "I *know*, baby—you tell me every—"

"Louis, we're good Christians, and good Christians, no matter how much they love each other, and how—excited—they get—!"

He shut her up with a kiss. His hands fondled the small of her back, then he eased them southward...

"Lou, honey, be niiiice," she purred.

"This *is* nice," he whispered as his long fingers lightly spanned her backside.

"Looouuu...you know the rule...you can pat the outer cheeks, but there will be *no* diddling in the...canyon..."

"And it's a *grand* canyon, don'tcha know, don'tcha know," Lou said, imitating 'The Kingfish' of *Amos 'n' Andy*.

She hit him on his shoulders. "You! A preacher's son! And on a Sunday!"

He grabbed her wrists, then noticed how close they were to a ledge. "Whoa! You'll get us killed before we even get to—"

She cut him off with a laugh. "And when we—do—you'll know how it feels to be on the business end of a dam that's burst..."

"Promises, promises." They fell into a more chaste embrace. Silence, then Alba spoke.

"Okay, Lou. What was that mysterious man-to-man talk you had with my father about?"

He recounted the conversation, and why he did not try to contradict Sam. As he spoke, he sensed her thoughts darkening. "Like I don't have any say-so in my own future?" she huffed after he finished.

"That's what I told him...in so many words. But I'm sure he got the message."

A sweet-sad look overtook her face. "Lou, honey, don't ever doubt my devotion—"

"I don't and won't, baby—"

"I'm with you, regardless. I know you'll be successful at whatever you do. And if ever you think I'm standing between you and your dreams—"

Lou clasped her shoulders. "I'd never think that, baby."

"But sometimes when we're together—we're *not* together. Sometimes you go deep within yourself, shut me and everyone else off—"

"That's just the way I am. Everyone who really *knows* me has to realize—and accept—that." He did not want to say it, but he *had* to add: "I'm an—artist."

"I know that, honey. I assume you're probably composing something, and..."

Lou squeezed her tightly. She responded half-heartedly, then disengaged. "I only want the best for you, Lou, whether I'm to share it with you or not—"

"You are, honey. Don't *ever* think you're not." He saw a tear pool in each eye. He let the twin drops escape, then kissed them before they got too far. "We're in this together. Corny as this may sound, but everything I do will be for *us*."

Alba laughed and cried at the same time. "Be corny as you want." She held him tightly. "I love you," she whispered, "and I knew you'd say what you just did. But I wanted to—*had* to hear it from you..."

"Honey, you're the swankiest."

She gazed up at him, and her face brightened. "But I *do* have a bone I've been wanting to pick with you for some time, mister."

Lou gave her a slightly wary look. "Let 'er rip."

"Those—floozies!"

He was genuinely baffled. "Floozies? What floozies?"

"You know who I'm talking about! Those gals from the Full Moon and other glad-pads who're suddenly showing up in church—"

"Oh, please! You're worried about *them*? Those silly jitter-dolls won't look at a man who's not in the spotlight or behind the wheel of a fancy car. They never give me a second look when I'm hauling stuff for Tommy. Girl, you need to quit!"

"Still, Lou—just the idea that they *think* they can—"

"Maybe if you showed up to see me perform more often, you know...protect your interest..." he said with a sly smile.

She punched his arm. "You *know* how out of place I felt when I *did* go to see you, up in Kingsport!" she said, the memory angering and amusing her at once.

Lou had to hoot. "You, your cousin Joyce, and Sandra Jones couldn't've stuck out more in that club than the Harlem Globetrotters dancing butt-naked at a Ku Klux Klan rally—"

"LOOOUUU!"

"You-all looked like you'd've felt *safer* at a Klan pow-wow!"

"I mean really, Lou! We were afraid a razor battle or gunplay would erupt any moment. Those people there were not at all—refined!"

Lou guffawed. "Don't worry. Jimmy would never book us into places *that* wild."

She nestled closer to him. "One good thing came of it, though. I got to see how crazy folks go over your music, that you *can* be a big-time musician if you want to be."

He nestled closer to her. "I'll bet you say that to all your preacher's-kid boyfriends who moonlight with a boogie-woogie band—"

"And when you *are* a big-time musician—"

"*If*, Alba—if!"

"*When*," she insisted, "and you're out on the road, lonely...feel-ing—you know—and all kinds of chickies are throwing themselves at you—"

Lou stopped her with a stern, wounded look. "You think I'd—?"

Alba looked away. "No, but I *had* to ask..."

"No, you didn't," Lou growled. Silence. "If you're worried about—that—"

"Lou, I'm *sorry* I brought it up. Okay?" Her face and voice light-ened. "I mean, after all, you are *quite* a handsome fella. I know *I've* been throwing myself at you almost all my life."

Lou smiled. "And now I've caught you."

"Took you long enough."

Lou kissed her on her nose. "And there won't be any free rides on my bandwagon—if I have one. I'm gonna put you to work, girl."

"Doing what?"

"Figures."

Alba blinked three times, hard. "Excuse me?"

"Figures. Budget. You're a whiz at math, right?"

Alba paused to ponder. "Uh...I *am* fairly good with numbers..."

"So you'll manage my money, and like your mom does for your dad, you'll make our every dollar spend like two." Lou laughed inter-nally. Sam Evans' shop surely enjoyed a decent profit, but from the way Hurlene stretched Sam's earnings, one would think he was one of the richest Negroes in Knoxville, which was far from the truth.

He saw doubt cloud her face. "How's that sound, Doll-face?"

"You may be giving me more credit in that area than I deserve."

"You'll be up to it." He paused. "One other thing. Let's put a lid on this 'when-Lou-hits-it-big' jazz. That could jinx it."

"Whatever you say, Louis," she said, flashing her deep-dimpled smile. "Honey, isn't it time we headed home?" she asked, nodding toward the last of the fire-fingered sunset. They were so engrossed in their conversation they barely noticed it. Soon they were on their return voyage down Boyd's Bridge Pike.

As they approached the city limits, Lou equated the sentry line of roadside telephone poles with the many obstacles he faced in his near future. He pondered the barriers he—and the band—would soon have to overcome, and tried not to let them daunt him. Yet, despite the bar-riers and pitfalls that faced *anyone* who braved that uncertain world, Lou *could* envision himself as an R & B star. The band's still-grow-ing local popularity was the best indication. *I know I'm somewhat naïve, but what drive 'em wild here can send 'em just as well in the bigger cities...*

He saw no difference in how he raised spirits in a juke joint on Saturday night and the way his father did in church on Sunday morning. Both had been given a talent to move people, make them feel better—if only fleetingly. Both relied on the combined power of words, images, and music. *Maybe you were—chosen—to reach people in that way.* There! That voice had said it again, something he did not want to think about, at least not consciously. That voice could be from a positive force, urging him to take the big step.

Or, it could be from an opposite force, leading him up a blind alley, filling his head with delusions of grandeur. *So you make some folks in this nothing of a hill-country town happy on weekends. That's gonna put you up there with Ellington and Armstrong and the other true greats? Wake up, Cannon! Act like you've got some sense and take that job Tommy's offering!*

"Lou." Alba pulled him back to his here and now. "You have the strangest smile on your face, like you're stone confident and worried to death—and over the same thing," she said.

Lou grinned and patted her hand. "You're right. I am."

Alba shook her head lightly.

A sudden thought struck him, and he bore down on the gas pedal. "Mind if we stop by my house before I take you home?"

"That's fine by me. But why?"

"Just remembered. Louisiana Fats is on *The Ned Mulligan Show.* If we get a move on…"

"Louis, Louis, Louis. Whatever am I going to do with you?"

Lou squeezed her kneecap. "Everything, Sweetie Peach."

CHAPTER THREE

"*Of course* it crossed our minds to record some of our songs!" Jimmy said as he looked at Lou and Blondie in disbelief.

Deuce nodded and said, "With the way folks go ape over some of our stuff, why not?"

The band was in Jimmy's garage for the Tuesday tune-up. On the side nearest the entrance to the kitchen, Jimmy leaned against a wall from which an armada of tools hung. Seated next to him on a lidded oil drum was Deuce. Opposite them, Lou and Blondie leaned against a 1940 Packard sedan Jimmy was trying to restore.

"So why don't we?" Lou squalled. "What's with all this—resistance?"

"First off, I don't appreciate you invitin Swampcat Newsome— or *anyone* you think can run interference for us—without consultin me and Deuce first," Jimmy replied.

"I wanted it to be a pleasant surprise—"

"It was a surprise all right, but not totally pleasant!" Deuce shot back.

"Daaaag! He's already apologized!" Blondie cut in. "How many times does he hafta say he's sorry?"

Jimmy exhaled through his nostrils, as if summoning saint-like patience. "The goal of recording would be to score a hit, right or wrong?"

"Of course," Lou answered flatly.

"So let's jump straight to the situation that would take us farthest from the lives we now lead," Jimmy continued. "This is strictly a 'what-if?' example. Dig?"

"Understood. Fire away," Blondie replied.

"In this 'what-if?' picture, we *do* somehow cop a recording date. Our record becomes a hit. What's next?" Jimmy said.

"We'd do what anyone with a hit would," Lou answered. "Strike while the iron is hot, go on a road tour…"

"How big a hit it is would determine the extent of the tour," Blondie added.

"Exactly," Deuce jumped in, "and that means dealin with a manager, the folks at the record company, club owners—*all* who're gonna try and stiff us from the money we got *legitimately* comin to us."

Mercy! Mister Sam, Mister Swampcat—everybody keeps harping on that, Lou thought.

"Aw, come on—not *all* of them—"

"Let us finish," Jimmy interrupted Blondie's interruption. "Goin on the road—even for just a few weeks—means we'll be away from our wives, kids, and jobs."

"Oh. We forgot somethin," Deuce sniffed, "Lou and Blondie don't *have* those commitments. So easy for *them* to just up and hit the road!"

"Look. If it's just a matter of weeks, you can get a leave of absence—"

"Blondie, not everyone works for his daddy's hauling business or his cousin's construction firm," Jimmy said softly.

"Besides, we hit up our bosses for a leave, nearly four years ago," Deuce added. "We already *been* where you cats think you wanna go with this recordin and tourin razzmatazz. Dealt with record folks, managers, the whole shot."

"Is that a fact?" Lou croaked as he and Blondie swapped a puzzled look. Their expressions and postures challenged: *Okay. Tell us all about it...*

"Here we go, boys. Tighten your chin straps," Deuce began as he and Jimmy relayed their saga of the summer of '51:

Before the Jimmy Jameson Quartet there was the Smokers, a blues-jazz combo Jimmy and Deuce organized in late 1950. Like the Quartet, they played joints in the surrounding counties and at Knoxville's three bucket-of-blood colored nightspots—Kelbert Mullins had yet to open his Full Moon Lounge.

It was the top of the summer of 1951, and "Highway Rocket" by Mike Turner and his Monarchs of Rhythm drenched the airwaves. The Williams Brothers Blues Wonders, a band popular throughout the South, blew into Knoxville. Headed by the twins Lex and Rex, the band needed replacements on the piano and stand-up bass. The twins caught the Smokers at Red Hogan's after-hours joint one night, and offered Jimmy and Deuce jobs on the spot. Musicians that they were, *of course* Deuce and Jimmy wanted to accept. Husbands, fathers, and breadwinners that they were, they had day-to-day obligations. Negotiations were in order...

Jewelle, Jimmy's wife of eight years, and Christine, two years married to Deuce, understood their dreams. After all, the wives—first cousins and best friends—had met their future husbands after seeing them perform several times. Jimmy and Deuce's artistic bents were part of their allure. Jewelle and Christine had two major concerns: that their husbands would wind up in other women's beds, and that the money they earned on the road would not match their square-job wages.

Less understanding were their bosses. Just weeks earlier, Jimmy was named foreman over the Negro workers at the Alcoa aluminum plant. Deuce was starting his third month in the cushiest tour of duty of the five turnkeys in the colored wing of the Knox County jail. Begrudgingly, their supervisors granted them leave until shortly after Labor Day. "But only this one time. And be back on time. If you want to choose this music thing, then do it all now. Don't come running back, following your music dreams in dribs and drabs, thinking this is some safe harbor where we'll take you back when things are slow in that life," Jimmy's boss told him. Deuce's supervisor stated likewise, in so many words.

Two, three, four weeks onto the road, they had received no pay. The Williams twins paid the room and board for the five other band members—along with a stately one-dollar *per diem* of walking-around money. The twins—glib, handsome, and talented musicians—were utterly convincing when they promised everyone that they would receive a princely lump sum at the tour's end. Jimmy, Deuce, and the three other non-Williams musicians *knew* they were raking in healthy receipts from the nightly overflow crowds. And no town was too small or too off the beaten track, no joint too blood-letting for Lex and Rex to book them into.

Never mind the soupy Southern summer heat, the bottle-dodging joints, roach-ridden rooms, greasy, starchy, hurriedly-scarfed meals—and still no wages—these were the most exhilarating times of their lives. They were professional musicians. To keep their wives appeased, they wired home their one-dollar *per-diem* money and whatever pass-the-hat tips they could scrounge. They half-promised the Williams twins they would stay on past Labor Day—their square-world jobs be damned.

Then, Dallas.

In the last, excruciatingly hot week of August, after a week of playing every joint in the club-rich sister cities of Dallas and Fort Worth, Lex—no, it was Rex, Jimmy corrected Deuce—burst into the fleabag hotel room shared by the five non-Williams musicians. Everyone thought Rex was pulling a perverse practical joke as he shrieked that Lex had vanished with *all* their money—thousands of dollars secreted in a special suitcase. After ten minutes, the others realized Rex's hysteria was real.

Deuce was the calmest in the room. "He couldn't have got too far," he said, then asked what was the next big city in the direction *opposite* from where they had come.

Austin.

Sure enough, two days later, they tracked down Lex there, with the town's most beautiful whore, a nineteen-year-old girl of Mexican, Comanche, and Negro ancestry. They beat Lex nearly to death, with Rex doing the most damage. Lex, though, had already spent half the summer's take on the whore and her sisters—of the blood and of the profession—and lost the other half gambling.

There was nothing to do but cut their losses, return home, and prepare for tongue-lashings from the wives—an immediate one, and a lifetime of snide remarks over their stupidity of that summer of 1951.

"Daaaag," Blondie growled sympathetically. "That's mucked up..."

"There's more," Jimmy said. "Remember the song 'She Wrecked the Rocket?'"

"Heck, yes," Lou replied, "an 'answer song' to Mike Turner's 'Highway Rocket,' late '51, by Mackie Preston, top five on the *Cashboard* R & B..."

Deuce vigorously shook his head. "Mackie Preston was really the Williams Brothers Blues Wonders."

"Naw!"

"Yep. We were 'tightening up' the song in a rehearsal spot in Birmingham—that turned out to be a recordin studio. Lex had the tape runnin on the sly. Weeks after he pissed away the whole summer's take, he put out the record under the name Mackie Preston," Jimmy said.

"And cleaned up," Deuce added. "Must of sold a third of a million copies. We haven't seen a penny from it—and hide nor hair of Lex Williams since."

"We learnt the record was cut on an independent label out of Birmingham, which sold the masters to Phil Samuels at Moon Records in Nashville," Jimmy explained. "Before we did anything stupid, we got with a bunch of lawyers. All the mouthpieces said the same thing: we had absolutely no legal right to a penny of the royalties, 'cause we didn't sign no contracts."

Lou whistled. "I see why you boys've got such a sour taste about touring and recording."

"You better know it," Deuce said, simply and sadly.

Silence.

"That was then. Four years ago. You're older, wiser, won't get burnt again," Lou said.

"Different shift, same shit," Deuce moaned.

"Not necessarily," Blondie argued. "I doubt the Williams Brothers Blues Wonders had anywhere near as solid, as unique a *sound* as we got!"

"That's right," Lou concurred. "*Sound*. That's what everyone who digs us raves about—our sound. That makes us like a house of cards: you remove one and it all comes tumbling down. Am I right or what?" Jimmy and Deuce nodded, so Lou continued. "And if we do give it a go, we'll be infinitely more careful in terms of who does what for us."

"Oh, yeah—like *we're* in the position to pick and choose," Jimmy snapped, "and not the fat cats in the fancy suits behind the big desks in the big cities. Four unknown dudes from Knoxville approach them, they'd look at us like dust balls on their carpet."

"People like that come with the territory, but aren't automatically the territory," Lou said with some impatience.

"Easy for you to say," Deuce snorted benignly.

Blondie spoke up. "Jimmy, Deuce, yawl don't realize how friggin *good* we are—"

"Oh, we *realize* it!" Jimmy cut in. "It's gettin reputable folks to take us seriously that's the kicker. Gettin them to even *listen* to us is close to impossible."

"We don't have the *time* to search out the few fair ones, even if we was as gung-ho as you two," Deuce added.

"Blondie and I have the time and energy," Lou said simply, firmly. Deuce and Jimmy eyed each other, then Lou and Blondie, then Lou alone. That they said nothing encouraged Lou. He continued. "We'll take it slowly, step by step. *I'll* make the calls. Any nibbles I get, I'll clear it with you two before we make the next move."

Jimmy half-smiled, half-grimaced. "I hear what you're sayin, Lou, but I repeat: we're not the ones holdin the aces here..."

Lou nodded deferentially to the older men before he spoke. "You two will make all the final decisions. If we can't come up with the right folks, then the search is over, case closed. That way, we can't lose; we can only win."

Jimmy and Deuce mulled over that for a long count.

"But if we *do* unearth something worthwhile," Blondie said, "then let's follow it up. Common sense: if we find some big wheels willing to take a chance on us, *we* gotta take some risks."

"And if a genuine hotshot thinks we're worthy—what's that say about our chances for success?" Lou added.

"I smell a promise to a commitment," Deuce said after a brief silence.

"Let's give it a year," Lou said. "Just a year. I know your bosses said they'd never give you another leave, but if we make the right connections, you've *got* to risk your jobs."

"And if things don't quite pan out, it's not as if you cats can't get other decent jobs," Blondie added. "You're smart, popular—and where does it say you gotta work for somebody else? Shit, yawl can start your own businesses…"

C'mon. You cats know *you want to do this, have long since wanted to take another shot—just needed this prod from us youngbloods…*

The senior members mulled over Blondie's words, then Deuce spoke. "What the hell is a year? We can fix anything that gets broke in our lives in that short-a time."

Lou's spirits rose, but he did not let on.

Jimmy looked around, then lowered his voice as he spoke. "Hell, time away from my ol' lady would do us both a world of good. And I'm crazy about my three crumb-crushers, but boy, they do a job on my nerves…"

Lou's spirits rose yet higher, but he did not let on. "How about it?" he asked. "A year?"

C'mon. You cats know *you want to do this, have long since wanted to take another shot—just needed this prod from us youngbloods…*

Jimmy and Deuce first made an eyeball consultation. "A year," Jimmy said, softly.

"A year," Deuce echoed. "And Lou does the brunt of the leg-work."

Lou choked back a smile. "I'll make a flurry of calls tomorrow. Let's shake on it."

They did.

Jimmy pulled out a notepad. "That settled, about this past week-end's performances…"

* * * * *

The next day, Wednesday, found Tommy Lovelace, Lou, and three others setting the foundation for a future office building on Main Street. At lunchtime, Lou asked for the rest of the day off.

Tommy, a short, muscular, brown-skinned man, was Lou's first cousin on Florence's side and eight years his senior. Tommy looked away and muttered, "Go on."

Within minutes, Lou was home and began a series of phone calls. He first reached Ocean Records in New York, for whom Claude McPatter & the Wanderers, Ruth White, LaVelle Barker, and the Urbans recorded. To his relief, he reached Des Claver, Ocean's head writer and producer.

"Good afternoon, sir. My name is Lou Cannon; I represent a rhythm-and-blues band. I'm calling from Knoxville—"

"?—Knoxville—?"

"Yes, sir. That's in Tennessee—"

"?—Tennessee—?"

"Yes, sir—the South—"

"*That* I know. If you're calling about an audition, we only handle New York-area talent."

"But, sir—believe me, we are *quite* good—"

"I'm sure you are, and I'm sure everyone down in Kentucky—"

"—*Tennessee*—"

"—*Tennessee* thinks you're the hottest thing since cold beer. But this is the big leagues—"

"All we're asking for is an audition." Lou struggled to keep an even tone.

"Second verse, same as the first. We only handle New York talent. Slick, polished New York talent. No offense, but how *hip* can you Tennessee boys be?"

"Thank you, sir. Sorry for taking up your time." Lou hung up and next called Moon Records in Nashville. Expecting a secretary, Lou was taken aback when the company's owner, Phil Samuels, answered. "Mister Samuels?" Lou croaked.

"Speaking. Who's this?" drawled the young, but already legendary producer. Before Lou could say much, Samuels stopped him. "Son, you're colored, aren't you?"

"Uh—yes, sir, but—"

"Perhaps you'd be better served by an R & B label—"

"But, sir, you've got *several* colored bluesmen on your—"

"A handful, yeah, but I'm not in the market for more, right now."

"Sir, if you would just give us a listen," Lou struggled not to sound desperate. "We're only a short drive away. We could—"

"Call Jay-Vee Records or the Hess Brothers in Chicago, or Des Claver with Ocean, or Jim Powers with Monarch Records up in Cinci—"

"Thank you, sir. Sorry for taking up your time." Battling to maintain a confident tone, Lou next called Crescent and Unique Records, both New Orleans labels. He found the former to be rude and the latter unprofessional. He ruled out three West Coast outfits: too far away. Jim Powers of Monarch repeated the doubt that any unknown band from Knoxville could be any good.

Fighting frustration, Lou forged on. He reached Jay-Vee in Chicago, a well-respected colored company run by a husband-and-wife team. Though the label was only three years old, their Coup de Villes, Five Fevers, and Marigolds were steady dwellers in the R & B top ten. Lou spoke to the co-owner, Janice Breckenridge, who seemed interested. She and Lou thought they had a deal until she told him the quartet would have to pay its own expenses to and while in Chicago, and foot the bill for the recording session. Lou thanked her and hung up.

By now it was three p.m. Lou decided he had suffered enough rejection for one day, but would call Swampcat Newsome later that evening.

As always when his spirits were low, Lou secluded himself and worked on some songs. He made encoded musical notes for the melodies, and jotted down lyrics in a notepad. After two hours he had recharged his batteries. He told his mother he would have dinner later, then took a stroll along Bethel Avenue, humming his revamped tunes.

At eight sharp, he rang Swampcat at RICKY.

"Swampcat here. It's your dime, but my time. Talk to me."

Lou slathered his voice with all his remaining confidence. "Hi, Mister Swampcat. This is Lou Cannon from the—"

"Hey, Big Time! What's cookin?"

Swampcat's energy further rallied Lou's spirits. He told Swampcat about the series of fruitless calls. "You boys've got too much on the ball to go unheard," Swampcat reassured him. "Still, this is one tough business to get a foothold in—"

"Mister Swampcat, isn't there *anyone* else *you* can talk to?" Lou let his desperation fly. He did not breathe during the long silence from the other end.

Finally, Swampcat spoke. "There *is* one call I can make that might do some good. Tonight is what—Wednesday?—I *may* be able to reach this cat later tonight—maybe!"

"Gee, thanks, Mr. Swampcat, if you would—"

"Again, I cain't promise anything. But a try beats a wish any day."

"Thanks again, sir!" They hung up. Lou stared ahead, seeing nothing. *Careful, bud...don't get your hopes up too high, or put all your coal in one wagon . . .*

CHAPTER FOUR

Wednesday, April 13, 1955; 5:13 p.m.
New York City. Columbus Circle.

Claiborne "Cootie the Cutie" Coutrere strode briskly, less than four blocks from his destination. He preferred to walk—or run—the nearly one hundred blocks from Willa McAshan's Harlem brownstone. His gait was light, long, and liquid, a holdover from his days as a high school state champion half-miler just seven years ago.

He delighted in the recognition from passers-by. That he was on the cover of the current issue of *Ebony* attracted even more notice. He was especially proud of the cover: the caption "Claiborne 'Cootie the Cutie' Coutrere—the Most Influential Negro Disk Jockey on the Radio?" blared in bright red letters above his smiling face.

He caught a mature, long-haired, olive-skinned woman sliding him a glance and his thoughts drifted to Willa. Many assumed a youngster like him would be attracted to an older woman like her largely because she was a successful businesswoman who owned a house on a ritzy block. However, that was hardly the reason she had taken over a major role in his life the last three months.

As he walked through Harlem, many people stopped him and expressed how they adored his show. After just six months on the New York airwaves, he was becoming as popular uptown as Joe Louis, Ray Robinson, Willie Mays, and Harlem's beloved congressman-minister.

In the thirteen weeks he had spent more nights at Willa's than in his own apartment, Cootie ran the five miles from Convent Avenue to the midtown studio at least three times a week, regardless of the weather. He had to be careful, bundled in a hooded woolen sweatsuit, sniffing hard and firing punches as he loped down Broadway, Riverside Drive, or Central Park West. It was better that people mistook him for a prizefighter in training than a criminal on the short lam.

The walks and runs cleared his head, and gave him ideas for the hip rhymes and phrases that were his stock in trade. Since he was responsible for selling commercial time on his seven-to-midnight spot, he composed the ditties and scenarios as he legged it. He kept a notepad and stopped to jot down ideas when he could.

As he eased down Broadway from black and tan Harlem into young, white Columbia University territory, fewer people stopped him. Many recognized him, but silently, or with a point and whisper. He did most of his creating in this part of his journey.

Many of his listeners still did not know—or believe—he was a Negro. After all, WPLC was a white station whose signals reached along the Atlantic Seaboard. The buzz was that such a juggernaut would not entrust a colored jockey with its most important time slot; this Coutrere had to be some white hepcat who only *sounded* like a Negro. That scuttlebutt amused Cootie greatly, and buttressed his not immodest belief he was, like the *Ebony* caption hinted, the hottest colored platter-pusher in the U.S. Nationally, only one other deejay had more sway over whether a record flamed or flopped: Adam Freeman, a good buddy of his. Freeman spun the wax on WCIL, a Chicago station which, like WPLC, blasted out the legal limit of 50,000 watts.

Cootie stopped at 56th and Broadway and gazed down the block at the dozen teenage girls in front of the skyscraper that housed the WPLC studios. They waved placards declaring them as members of "The First and Official Cootie the Cutie Fan Club." Cootie smiled; that's what he paid them to do. He turned right to use one of the service elevators on the south side of 56th, between Broadway and Eighth Avenue.

Before he boarded one, a stocky brown-skinned man intercepted him. He was of medium height and pushing fifty. He wore a lime-green zoot suit, imitation alligator shoes, and a hot pink silk shirt open at the collar, despite the April chill. Clashing odors of cheap cologne and house-brand bourbon radiated from him. *Damn*, Cootie thought. *Nothing sadder than an over-the-hill hipster. Looks like he plucked those vines out of Cab Calloway's trash pile—ten years ago. And that process has taken a recess...*

The man was flanked by a willowy, honey-colored lass in a long trench coat. He flashed a row of gold-capped teeth as he stuck out his right hand; in his left he brandished a stack of 45 rpm records. "Joe Jenkins, Hotsmash Records. Got a killer tune out on Little Tiny Smalls—"

"Never heard of him."

As if he had not heard Cootie, Jenkins pressed the 45's into his hand. "Play this, your phones'll light up like a Christmas tree!"

Cootie looked at the records, then used them to scratch the palm of his free hand.

Jenkins smiled weakly, looked away from Cootie's gesture, recovered his bluster and nodded toward the pretty girl. "By the way, this is my cousin...uh..."

"Rhonda," she snipped. She opened her trench coat. All she had on beneath was scanty, see-through underwear.

Jenkins found encouragement in Cootie's admiring gawk. "If you wanna go up, play the record, get friendly with my cousin Wanda—"

"Rhonda!"

"Whatever."

Cootie savored a long look at Rhonda and headed for an opening elevator door. "Thanks, but no thanks."

"?...But...?"

Cootie swooped past them and vaulted into the freight elevator. "Hey, Rhonda—try not to catch cold!" He slammed the door and ascended to the seventh-floor studios.

The receptionist stopped him before he passed her. "Mister Sherman wants to see you when he gets out of his meeting."

"Must be about all that commercial time I sold in the past two weeks." Cootie winked, made a "ka-ching" sound and mimed the shutting of a cash register door. He went to his cubicle, fixed his elixir of tea, honey, lemon, and bitter ginger, then began his vocal warm-up exercises. He pulled a handful of discs from the mountain of 78's and 45's sent in from producers, deejays, and the artists themselves. He would listen to as many as he could in the ninety minutes until show-time. Within twenty seconds he could tell if a record had any legs.

Some he dismissed as too crudely produced. Some he vetoed because the lyrics were too banal or smutty. He scrapped a few he liked because he knew WPLC's board of directors would consider them too gutbucket and yank them from the playlist. Not that *he* had qualms about records by Negro artists that sounded too "colored"; he had slipped several onto his show. Still, he realized some of the better R & B discs were too gritty for even his hippest white fans—and some black listeners, also.

He decided on three he would try out on the last hour of his show, which he dubbed "The Late, Late Ride." He then studied a road map for next week's trip to his native New Orleans.

Harry Sherman, the station's business manager and program director entered. "Coutrere—about that commercial time you've recently sold—"

"Yes, sir! Almost twenty-five percent more than before!"

"Uh—yes—right." Sherman removed his horn-rimmed glasses and ran his fingers through his thick, wavy, steel-gray hair. "On one hand, it's good—but—all the product you've brought on board is geared toward colored folks. 'Duke Pomade.' 'Danilona Skin Cream.' The Harlem restaurants, nightspots, barbershops—"

"Of course—Negroes make up a large segment of my audience."

"But—still—this is a 'white' station, and a lot of your white listeners are—"

"Chances are most of my white fans don't think of me, or anything about my show in terms of black and white—"

"Don't get me wrong, Coutrere. We appreciate your hustling down revenue. Let's make a deal: you play the commercials like you do your race records—the later into your set, the more of them you play, until after eleven you can do pretty much what you want. Capeesh?"

"Oo-papa-dedic, that's copasetic, Daddy-o."

Sherman started to leave, but wheeled around. "Two more minor complaints. 'Hot Lana From Atlanta' by that Little Raymond—"

"—Little *Robert*—"

"—Try not to play it *before* nine. My grandmother—eighty-five years old, *loves* your show—heard it last night and thought the Mau Maus had taken over the station."

"Whatever you say, boss." Cootie rolled his eyes just enough so Sherman would notice.

Sherman shot him an "I'll-ignore-that" look, and continued. "And didn't you promise *not* to play 'Bunny's Got a Bun in the Oven' until after eleven? If it weren't such a great-*sounding* record, I wouldn't let anything with lyrics that suggestive on the air."

"I get a ska-zillion requests for that—"

"*After* eleven, Coutrere."

Cootie struggled to keep a straight face. "Yes, sir! Wouldn't want to seduce any innocent, impressionable kids with that vinyl voodoo, now would we?"

"Nobody likes a smart-ass, my friend. And this is *still* a pop music station. Give the new Perry Martin and Frank Maggio tunes more of a push."

Cootie sighed. "Yeah—at bedtime; they'll put our listeners right to sleep—"

"Coutrere, don't muck with me!"

"Okay! Martin and Maggio!" Though he had never told Sherman, Cootie was as big a fan of the crooners as anyone.

"Before then, once every hour for both of them."

"It's your world; I'm just hitchhiking on through."

"Ciao." Sherman left; Cootie had fifteen minutes to airtime. He decided where he would insert the new commercials. When the "On the Air" sign flashed, he dived into his duty...

Keeping his agreement, in the first two hours he mixed standard pop tunes with the more genteel R & B sides. Between nine and ten, he played the grittier colored and country-tinted white records, tossing in a couple of dirt-down hillbilly ravers. By ten, he was mostly spinning the slick, hard-driving, blues-based sounds many now called "rock-n-roll."

At eleven he pulled out all the stops. In this last hour, he played the gutbucket Negro sides one would not expect to hear on a major 'white' station. Many listeners were aghast at—and drawn to—the sheer earthiness of the rhythms and ribald imagery in the lyrics, although Cootie drew the line at anything *too* explicit.

The "jump" tunes featured bass lines that thrummed with a life of their own; grunting, throaty baritone saxophones that called to responding soprano and alto horns; screeching, beseeching guitars; and vocal gymnastics from the lead singer and back-up crew. Sometimes piano notes slithered subtly around it all; sometimes the sound from the eighty-eights was behind the wheel. Incessant percussion buttressed every tune, the heartbeat of the music.

The slow tunes highlighted love lost, love miraculously found, love pursued, love un-requited. These recordings seldom had—or needed—more than a loping piano, sighing guitars, and ponderous drum-thumps. The lead singers, invariably falsetto or first tenor, church-trained and silver-throated, turned even the most banal lyric into a gem for the ears, hitting it with crisp enunciation. Every doo-wop, shoo-bop, and walla-walla-womp-womp painted the perfect backdrop to the lead narrative, never imposing, always underscoring.

A rash of requests for "The Honey With the Money" by Claude McPatter & the Wanderers prompted Cootie to spin it for the fourth time in less than three hours. A janitor slid into his booth and whispered, "Miss McAshan's on line three." Cootie nodded, picked up the receiver, and pressed the lighted button.

"Hey, sexy, whatcha know good?" he purred.

"I've *finally* gotten feedback from everyone at our January meeting," she began in her deep, smoky voice.

"?...And...?"

"Some are thrilled, some aren't so gassed, but nobody's got a *major* problem with it, as long as we deliver our end of the bargain."

"Look out! Soon we'll be rollin like a big wheel through a Texas cotton field!"

"Don't get your hopes up too high. Never can tell with these risk-fearing Negro businessmen. Regardless, we'll set another meeting in the next few weeks." She paused. "By the way, pay more attention to what you're doing. You've got a tendency to play Louisiana Fats, the Moonlighters, Little Robert, Moanin' Lisa, and the Philadelphia Belles all in a row. Keep doing that, some folks might get suspicious."

Cootie looked at the pile of wax he would play next. Indeed, the platters by those artists were stacked together. "Got it. I'll be more careful from now on."

"You coming by tonight?" she asked.

"Naw, can't make it. Got a promotional bit at Times Square at nine in the yawning," he replied. The mere thought of getting up that early was enough to keep him awake all night. "But I'll shoot by your office about two in the p.m. We can have lunch together."

"Sounds like a winner. Be good," she said, then hung up.

Cootie had not moved in with Willa. Not yet, anyway. He maintained the modest, one-bedroom fourth-floor walk-up on West 49th Street that WPLC'S management had found for him when he moved to New York the previous October. It was a ten-minute walk from the studio. And living with a woman whose name was on the lease or mortgage when his was not could be a tricky proposition, he knew. Twice he had lived with women, this time last year in Chicago, and in Washington, shortly after graduating from Howard University. Both arrangements ended the same way—arriving home one night, he found the locks changed and his possessions piled outside. He would take great care that his relationship with Willa would not end on such a melodramatic note, but a guy never knew.

Like everyone he allowed into his personal orbit, Willa served a specific purpose. His plans went far beyond wailing into a microphone, pimping other people's creations. Never mind that naysayers put down his ambitions as far too lofty for such a young colored man. Willa had the connections he needed to grease his path toward his objectives.

He had learned—was still learning—that this business was a relentless you-wash-my-car-I'll-mow-your-lawn tango. Everyone who stepped onto the floor did so with a concrete agenda; Willa's game plan was the perfect complement to his.

That they shared a physical attraction was a different matter. Each saw it as a delightful bonus. Both hoped being lovers would never stand in the way of their business dealings. Cootie did not know how their relationship would fare after he—they—achieved most of their goals, but for now he needed her far more than she needed him.

Cootie, Freeman, and the handful of jockeys whose popularity cut across color lines waged an undeclared competition to find the new artist with the new sound that would thrust this rhythm-and-blues/rock-n-roll to its widest possibilities. Though the smarter, slickly-produced R & B sides were catching on with white listeners, much of that popularity lay in their production values and promotion. Fresher, cleaner, lighter musically, it was still boogie-woogie jump-blues for a younger, more urban audience.

What Cootie and the other jocks sought was a sound that expanded upon that. That new sound, of course, would incorporate elements from other music genres—but how much, and to what degree? The artist who could strike that delicate balance would launch a revolution, if only in the self-contained world of youth-targeted popular music...

...And the jockey who discovered that artist would have great power in that universe. Like his friendly competitors, Cootie kept his eyes open and ears peeled for that new artist, that new-and-improved sound...

He had just placed Moanin' Lisa's "Twelve-Inch Ruler" on the turntable when the phone caterwauled again, at 11:25.

"WPLC! The station with more hits than a Giants-Dodgers doubleheader!"

"Hey, Big City! Swampcat here! What's shakin, babes?"

"Nothin but the leaves in the trees, and they wouldn't be if it wasn't for the breeze! Whatcha know good, Swamp?"

"Heard you was shootin down to Nawlins next week for your sister's weddin!"

"Yes, indeed! Like, uh-ruh—next Friday!"

"Do yourself a favor, Coot. Detour through Knoxville—"

"But that's damn near two hundred miles out the way—"

"It'll be worth it! There's this boy there—you gotta see him to believe him! Throws all kinds-a music together—and it works!"

"Knoxville? What kind of killer musicians can there be in—Knoxville?"

"Don't play 'em cheap 'cause-a where they had the small misfortune of bein *born*! Just go and see for yourself, nigro! You think I'd be this hyped up over a bunch-a *stiffs*?"

Cootie's scalp tingled, and he took that as some sort of sign. "You say this cat throws all sorts of music together?"

"Like a rhythm stew!"

"Blues? R & B? More toward what they're calling rock-n-roll?"

"I'm tellin you, you cain't *label* their sound! And I cain't explain it over the phone! Git your high-yaller ass down here to see 'em!"

Something was causing Cootie's heartbeat to pick up. "These studs got a name, Swamp?"

"The Jimmy Jameson Quartet. The vocalist and star, though, is a good-lookin brown boy, Lou Cannon. Plays a guitar just like he's ringin a bell. The cats on piano, drums, and bass can burn, too! The band's as good as Little Robert's Go-Getters—!"

"Whoa, Swamp! You aren't bullshitting me, are you? As good as the Go-Getters?"

"Well, them cats can *play* as good, but they ain't as slick with their stage act—yet," Swampcat backpedaled.

A light electrical current raced through Cootie. The room was suddenly warmer. *These could be the cats with the sound that's conventional enough to be popular—yet distinct enough to break the mold and create a new set of rules...*

"Coot...you still there, brother...?"

"Still here, Swamp. Give a man time to think, why don'tcha? Springing this on me, out of the clear blue..."

Cootie heard a grand sigh from the other end. "You know I love you, Coot, but these boys is too friggin good to go unheard much longer," Swampcat said. "If you pass on 'em, I'm-a hafta give Adam Freeman a buzz..."

"Take it easy, Swamp. Hold on. I gotta put on a new side." As Moanin' Lisa's tune faded out, Cootie spun "Please Take Me to the Prom" by the Philadelphia Belles. *What the hell? What's to lose but a few hours and five, ten bucks in gas money? And if these cats are as hot as Swamp says they are...*

My ticket to the catbird's seat might be tucked away in the hills of East Tennessee...

"Hey, Swamp—it's a go!"

"Now you talkin!"

Cootie did a flash study of his road map. *Catch 75 out of Knoxville, shoot down to Chattanooga, pick up 59 there and I'm back in business.* "I'm putting a lot of faith in your judgment, Swamp. Only because of your rave review am I going..."

"You can whup my ass *personally* the next time you see me if you don't dig 'em."

Cootie laughed. "That won't be necessary. Just give me the particulars..." He jotted down the instructions. *Yeah, at worst, time and gas money down the commode...at best...*

His scalp tingled again, for a long moment.

CHAPTER FIVE

Thursday, April 14, 1955; 11:15 p.m.
Asheville Highway, near the Knoxville City Limits.

Tennessee State Highway patrolman Lester J. Nuxhall was three speeding tickets shy of his weekly quota and determined to fill it before his shift ended. He had been parked behind a cluster of oak trees for ten minutes when he got his first nibble. A navy-blue, late-model Lincoln Continental zoomed by like nobody's business. "Welcome to my web, said the spider to the fly," Lester chuckled as he goosed the gas and blared his siren. *Looks like some big shot's car, but a man's gotta do his job...*

Senator Theophilis Briscoe mumbled a mild curse when he heard the siren, then slowed down. He had driven this same route from Washington, D.C., to his home state's capital at least four times a year for the past two decades. A man who lived by the clock, he was forced to leave Washington two hours later than usual because of an extended meeting. Usually by this time, he was in northeast Alabama on Highway 59. *Just goes to show what happens when your schedule gets thrown even the slightest out of whack,* he mused. A hawk-faced patrolman eased his vehicle abreast Theo's and motioned for him to pull to the side of the road.

Theo complied, cleared his throat and tacked on his winningest smile. The patrolman uncoiled his lanky frame from his car. As the officer approached, Theo rolled down his window. His hand shot upward when the trooper indelicately beamed a flashlight into his face.

"Okay, doctor—where's the fire?" The trooper's words clattered out in a metallic East Tennessee twang. In half a heartbeat the flashlight was on the ground, and the patrolman was bug-eyed with disbelief. "Senator Theophilis Briscoe!" Lester Nuxhall croaked wildly.

"I'm afraid so."

Lester reached through the window and pumped Theo's hand. "It is an honor and a pleasure! Mercy! Never in my wildest dreams!"

Theo merely smiled. "You hungry, sir?" Lester asked.

"I could stand a bite," Theo replied. He usually stopped at a diner outside Gadsden, Alabama, for a midnight refueling, but the late start had played tricks on his stomach.

"Follow me," said Lester. Minutes later, they pulled into the parking lot to Myrtle's Diner. The eatery was a Louisville & Nashville Railroad dining car that had been retired, relocated, remodeled, and resurrected about thirty yards from the highway.

"Nothin fancy, but it's the last thing open between daylight and Georgia," said Lester as he yanked Theo's door open. They stepped carefully through the gravel-and-dirt lot.

"Long as the coffee's hot and plentiful." Lester made a big show of opening the front door for the senator. The dozen late-night regulars froze when the two entered. All stared at the tall, portly man with Lester.

"If'n I didn't know no better, Lester, I'd *swear* that was Senator Briscoe taggin 'long with you," said a woman about forty who *had* to be Myrtle, as she squinted hopefully at the stranger.

"It *is* me, ma'am," Theo modestly replied. *She looks like the first runner-up in a Dale Evans look-alike contest.*

"Lordgawdamighty! I'd've known that pretty silver hair of yours anywhere! You're even better-lookin in person!" gushed Myrtle. Her customers shook off their initial shock and crowded around Theo to shake his hand and pat him on the back.

"You're the best thang the South's got goin for it in Warshintin City, sir!" crooned a man as he touched the hem of Theo's seersucker suit. "If it wasn't for true Sons of the South like you, the spearchuckers would run amuck!"

"They'd turn this country into one big Africa or Harlem if our Dixiecrat senators didn't keep 'em in check, yessirree, bob!" a grandmotherly-looking woman chimed in.

"A man should do what he's elected to do," shrugged Theo.

"You really gave 'em what-for on *Face America* t'other day!" said a tiny blond woman of about thirty. "Cain't *nobody* match wits with you in a debate."

"You explained where you stand on those jungle bunnies—but good!" Lester added.

Theo frowned. "I gotta keep reminding our people not to make the mistake of *hating* Negroes. If anything, they're to be pitied—a troubled, childlike race." He looked Lester squarely in the eye. "You'd never go out your way to pick a fight with an invalid or a reetard, would you?"

"Oh, no, sir!" Lester rapidly replied.

"Same holds true for colored folks…as long as they know their place."

"Plus, how much can you expect of 'em, only three, four, five generations outta slavery?" Myrtle asked.

"Still, they don't help their own cause, with all the cutting and shooting they do of each other, and breeding like they're still on the plantation, under massa's care. Mind you, it's only a certain element of nigras that carries on like that—but the sad part is, instead of the smart, decent Negroes policing the nigger trash, cutting 'em out like the cancer they are, all the good Negroes do is make excuses for 'em," Theo stated. "When the decent black folks decide to do something about those who bring disgrace to the whole race, only *then* will they be respected as a people."

"Amen, brother," interjected a scholarly-looking middle-aged man. "Like their own Marcus Garvey told them: 'You're not on the bottom because you're despised—you're despised because you're on the bottom."

A murmur of accord, then silence. Suddenly, Theo slapped his belly. "Mercy! I'm 'bout hongry as a starvin yard-dawg, don'tcha know," he announced.

Myrtle blushed. "Lord, here I am forgettin my manners *and* obligations as a hostess. Whatcha havin, sir? It's on the house—of course!" Theo ordered steak, fries, cole slaw, and ice tea.

A thin, balding man at the threshold of middle age identified himself as Walter Joe Sparks and asked, "Senator, what's the latest on Capital Hill?" His tone was that of a child requesting a bedtime story from his daddy. The others hunched forward in their seats. Theo did not disappoint as he recounted a recent lobbying session between Dixiecrats and Cuban tobacco plantation owners.

Cleon, the ancient colored man who cleaned the restaurant nightly, trickled in. As always, he went straight to the jukebox. He punched up Louisiana Fats' latest, the dreamy "Louisiana Moon," and disappeared into the back.

As the customers listened to Theo's story, they patted their feet to the haunting melody and Fats' plaintive warbling. Theo's tale concluded before the song ended. Everyone's attention shifted to Fats's lament. "Damn!" Lester hissed, "that li'l fat jig's got hisself *another* big hit!"

"That boy could sing a grocery list and it'd make the Top Ten!"

Caught up in the song, no one noticed that Theo's face had clouded over and gotten redder by the second.

The bluesy ballad was whisking dirt off memories he had long since tried to bury:

>He was twenty-two and had just graduated from State and would be going off to law school in a few weeks and was trying to get his girl Peggy to go all the way and they were parked by the Southern Railways tracks that separated Theo's working-class white neighborhood from jigtown and he was telling Peggy this might be the last chance she would have for a while to prove she truly loved him and she kept pushing him off and then the sound of jump blues from a nigger roadhouse began to fill the air and the music was like a magnet that pulled Peggy and she sprinted across the tracks and over to the tin-roofed shack and of course he had to follow her and she stopped at the door knowing full well a white gal couldn't go into a colored joint but a buxom colored woman said c'mon in white folks we ain't gonna bite so Peggy floated in and followed the music and of course he had to go in with her and on stage singing those blues was the prettiest colored man Theo had ever seen and obviously the prettiest Peggy had too because she couldn't take her eyes off him and the Choctaw Indian-looking chocolate-skinned smoothie who the sign outside said was named Dion Eason noticed Peggy staring at him and Dion winked at her and she blushed and Theo would have *loved* to have had that nigger's nuts in his pocket but this was after all a dinge joint so he would have to grin and bear it so he did all he could under the circumstance which was yank Peggy the hell away from there and cast a look back at Dion which told the pretty-boy I'll see you later nigger under a different set of rules and he pulled Peggy back into the street and when he started to give her what-for for making eyes at a jig she dummied up on him and for the first time ever he slapped her but instead of her crying or even showing anger she laughed and told him in the cruelest tone I'll make you sorrier sorrier sorrier than you've ever been in your life for that and his blood ran cold as something told him she would do just that...

"TURN OFF THAT GODDAMN NIGGER MUSIC!!" Theo roared. Everyone recoiled. Myrtle sidestepped to the juke and pulled the plug.

"Yes, sir, if it upsets you…"

Everyone stared, gape-mouthed. The cleaner materialized from the back, leaning on a push-broom, the calmest person in the place. "Coon music's for coon joints," snorted Theo. The stares remained in place. Theo flipped the colored man a half-dollar piece. "Play somethin else—*somewheres* else, uncle." He turned to Myrtle. "You got any Hank Williams on that box?"

"Of *course* we got ol' Hank. What kind-a place you think I'm runnin here?" she replied in mock indignation.

After spins of "Your Cheatin' Heart" and "Hey, Good Lookin,'" it was as if Theo's thunderclap never happened. He finished his meal, then held court for another fifteen minutes. When it was time for him to hit the highway, Myrtle packed him several sandwiches, some cake slices and a thermos of coffee. He glad-handed his fans and vowed to keep up the good fight in Congress.

As he bid them adieu, Theo peeled out of the parking lot and onto the road. At the last possible moment, he saw the other car hurtling down Asheville Highway. He slammed on his brakes; the other driver jerked his vehicle to the right. The cars missed colliding by a yard. Theo catapulted from his car; the other driver rolled down his window. He was a young Negro—and in the dim light resembled Dion Eason. "Goddamn it, nigger—watch where you're goin!" Theo screamed.

The Dion Eason-looking Negro hollered: "Fuck you, redneck motherfucker! *You're* the motherfucker that can't drive!" With that the aqua-marine Oldsmobile screeched away.

Lester was more aghast than Theo. He rushed to the senator's car. "Y'hear how he *cussed* you, sir? You want, I can call someone further up the highway and—"

"Naw, that's okay, Lester. Niggers like that already have a rope with their name on it. I don't have to be the one to yank it. He'll get his." Myrtle and company assured Theo that most Knoxville Negroes knew their place—those that did not had better haul ass up North. For the second time, Theo backed onto Asheville Highway. This time he went much slower…

Still shaking and seething, Lou hung a quick left on Kirkwood and then a right onto McCalla. He didn't know if he was more frightened from having avoided a nasty wreck, or angry at the sheer gall of the silver-haired man in the Lincoln. Lou had never called anyone *that* name before; he hated the word and its implications. His heart pounding, he glanced often into his rear-view mirror. After a few minutes, when no siren-screaming police cars had raced after him, he felt the danger was over—for the time being. He realized someone could have gotten his license plate number, and the thought made his stomach queasy.

He scolded himself for not just dropping off the package, telling his grandmother he had endured a long day at work and had another facing him, then beat a hasty exit. Instead, he let her bend his ear past midnight. She retold the story—for at least the thirtieth time—about how *her* grandparents had been free people of color long before the Emancipation. Still, Lou never tired of hearing it—and Mother Cannon could tell a story with the best of them. Yet, an inner voice had told Lou to leave quickly this evening. As he reached Five Points and turned onto Vine, his hands *still* shaking, he wished he had obeyed that warning.

Suddenly, the realization of who the silver-haired man looked like—might even *be*—struck him. *Senator Theophilis Briscoe. Saw him on television—what—four days ago?* However, that possibility fled his mind as quickly as it entered. *Nah, the world is not that small. You've got Briscoe on the brain because you saw him the other day on television...that was just someone who looked a lot like him...*

Lou turned left off Vine. *Nah...the world is not that small...*

CHAPTER SIX

Friday, April 22, 1955; 3:10 p.m.
Convent Avenue, Harlem, New York.

Cootie had spread everything he needed for his trip on the kitchen table. The items were lined up like battleships poised to strike: the directions for the quickest routes from the highway to certain address-es in Philadelphia and Baltimore; the contents from his shaving kit; walking-around money; and a small-caliber pistol he would hide where even the most expert lawman could not detect it during a pat-down.

He eyed what might be the most important item he would need: a standard contract from the Felder Brothers, Abraham and Solomon, of .30/.30 Winchester records—in case this Knoxville band was as good as Swampcat claimed.

He had already stashed two big suitcases and several presents for his sister and soon-to-be brother-in-law into the trunk of the car he would be driving. Satisfied he had everything, he was ready to roll. He crossed into the parlor, where Willa was performing yoga exercis-es. Clad in a leotard, she sat on a plush throw-rug, her long legs jack-knifed beneath her, back high and straight, head tilted slightly, eyes closed. Seated amid the room's African-art motif, she looked endear-ingly exotic to him. Not wanting to shock her from whatever state she was in, he whispered her name. She slowly opened her eyes, but quickly regained her bearings. "I'm ready to scat," he told her.

She rose from her lotus position in one fluid, eye-blink move-ment. "You sure you don't want me to fix you a snack, Clai?"

"Nope. I'll be okay between here and D.C. I'll throw a lunch together in Washington before I leave there." Actually, he had plenty of food for his long drive. Mrs. Miller, the next-door neighbor, had filled a shopping bag with bologna sandwiches, fruit, pound cake, and the obligatory fried chicken. Cootie saw Willa as a woman of many talents, but down-home cooking was not one. In the months he had been spending most of his nights at her place, he had yet to accustom himself to her typical fare of broiled fish, fowl, or the leanest meats, steamed vegetables, and fruit salads. Bacon and sausage never sullied her skillets. It would take some time for him to jump onto that health-nut bandwagon. Navigating Southern highways was tough work; he needed the kind of food that left grease stains on paper sacks.

He placed an arm around her wasp-like waist. The muscles in her midsection felt like small steel cables. *Mercy*, he thought. Aloud, he said, "*Donne moi une* hug!" She smiled wanly, rolled her eyes slightly, and hugged him. Was it his imagination, or was she still miffed at him? He kissed her on her freckled, banana-colored nose; she was just four inches shy of his own six-feet-one. He clutched her tighter; she responded in kind.

"Gonna miss me?" He punctuated the rhetorical question by nuzzling her neck.

"Of course, in between all the work ahead of me."

"Maybe I'll find you some more between here and the Voodoo City," he said as he kissed her thick, neat, arching eyebrows.

"You do that." She eased out of the embrace and pushed him away, gently.

He looked at her. "Okay, sweets. What's wrong?"

"Wrong? Nothing's wrong. What makes you think that?"

"I know you still got a burr under your saddle because my parents didn't *officially* invite you to Desiree's wedding—"

She flung up her right hand. "Stop right there! If you think *I'm* upset because *your* parents have a problem with the nature of our relationship, guess again."

"I mean, they never said you *weren't* welcome," Cootie side-stepped, "it's just that since they never met you—and *I* haven't known you for too awful long—"

"Quit making excuses for them! They don't like that I'm so much older than you—"

"By seven measly years."

"*Eight*—and, that in their eyes, we're 'living in sin'—"

"Like I've said, my parents are Catholic as all get-out. But after I told them how much we mean to each other, they *did* say you were welcome to come down for the wedding—"

"Yes, as long as we didn't share a room—not in *their* house," she sniffed.

He embraced her again. "Aw, don't stay upset over that…"

She slid from his grasp. "*You're* the one who brought up the issue—again! *I* could care less about the images your parents must have of this twice-divorced older woman corrupting their son! I've got too many people depending on me for their livelihoods—"

"I know; I'm one of them."

"With all due respect, your parents sound like they'd prefer you with someone who'll jump at your every beck and call. I'll bet right now their scouring New Orleans for some nineteen-year old without a working brain cell in her pretty, long-haired head, who'll worship the ground you walk on and give them a new grandchild every year—"

"Girl, puh-leeeze!" Cootie cut her off. "I'm sure once they meet you, they'll love you as much as I do. In fact, when I told them you were a lawyer, they were *quite* impressed."

Willa stared at him. "A—lawyer? That's *all* you told them I was? Lord." She shook her head, breezed into the kitchen, and lit the flame under the teakettle.

"Well, you are, aren't you," Cootie hedged. "My mama said: 'Oh, my! Cain't be too awful many colored woman attorneys in Noo Yawk, now can there?'"

Willa pulled teabags, honey, and coffee mugs from a cabinet shelf. "Why didn't you tell them what I've *really* been doing for the last year and a half?" she demanded.

Cootie shook his head. "Honey, they're Good New Orleans Creole Mulatto Catholics. They wouldn't understand."

"Why? Is there something—dishonorable—about what I do?"

"Of course not."

"They wouldn't think my work is suitable for a woman, is that it?"

"Like I've told you, they're so old-fashioned—"

"Tell me about it." She thought of how her own parents still had doubts about the detour she had chosen in her legal career.

"They weren't too thrilled about me trading law school for a microphone, but they got over it," he lied. In truth, his parents had yet to resolve his decision to become a disk jockey. Despite his rapid climb up the radio ladder, they desperately hoped he would return to his senses and enroll in Howard Law School, as mapped out since he was ten years old. His father and other male relatives promised to match his current salary *and* pay his law-school tuition if he would forsake the airwaves.

"They'll get over us," he added, softly.

"They'd better." The teakettle whistled.

"And I'd better get a move on. Gimme smoochee." They embraced.

"Clai, be sure you stay overnight in D.C., you hear me? I know you'll want to drive straight through—"

"I'll save a ton of time that way—"

"—But you're not used to those dangerous highways winding through the Virginia mountains, and I don't want you to fall asleep at the wheel and—"

"Yes, Mommy," he cooed, "I promise I'll spend the night in D.C." He paused, then smiled wickedly. "Probably shack up with one of my old girlfriends from Howard—"

She punched him on his shoulder. "Don't mess with me," she said, laughing.

Mercy. For a tall, thin woman, she packs a wallop. "Okay," he said as he rubbed his shoulder. He kissed her long on the lips. "Gotta roll," he sighed reluctantly.

Willa walked him to the door; it was too cold for her to go outside in just her leotard. "When you get to Washington, call me," she said as he ambled down the sidewalk.

"Like, yeah."

"Clai." He turned to her. She blew him a kiss. He pretended to track it down like Willie Mays hawking a fly ball in centerfield. He feigned losing it in the sun, then sighted it again and made an over-the-shoulder catch. He gently massaged the kiss above his heart.

Willa laughed. "Go South, young man," she said, and watched as he plopped his load into the trunk of the 1952 Studebaker sedan parked out front. Cootie had borrowed it from a friend. He had learned the hard way what happened once he got south of Washington. He knew if he drove his coffee-colored '55 Coup de Ville, he would be stopped by every redneck with a badge and a hard-on for any high-class set of wheels with Northern plates. That he was a sharply-dressed, well-set smoothie would rattle their cages all the more.

The Studebaker was properly unremarkable. Other than its color, which Cootie felt was too close to Marine Corps olive-drab, he had no qualms about the car. He took one last look at the house, saw Willa waving at him from behind the door, honked, and was off.

As he waited out a red light at 145th and St. Nicholas, he watched the battle of the singing groups. As always on Friday afternoons, a doo-wop group was stationed on each corner of the intersection. They warbled away, each trying to outperform the others. The competition was fierce; three groups that had recently scored R & B hits were discovered in this fashion. Nearly all used it as a stepping stone to the Wednesday Amateur Night at the Apollo.

Any group other than a male quintet was rare. Sometimes a female or two popped up in a group—but all-female groups were out of the question on *these* corners. The singers honored a gentlemen's agreement: one hour on a corner, then beat it. The groups policed themselves against outsiders and mavericks.

The battle of the groups began shortly after school let out on Friday, until around midnight, then resumed the next day from roughly noon to midnight. Each group set up a bucket for collecting tips. People came from all around for the free show; those who lived in the nearby buildings seldom complained.

Both times when Cootie had gone to see the show up close, the singers mobbed him. Some camped outside the house on Convent and chirped away, but Willa put a stop to that. Persistence had its limits. She spread the word that her pals on the police force would not tolerate such behavior, thank you very much.

Cootie's eyes swiveled to soak in the action on the four corners, wanting the green light to take its time. Five clean-cut teenagers on the southeast corner hooked him as they performed a lively rendition of the Five Fevers's "On My Front Porch." His focus kept returning to the smallest and youngest. Though the lad was not the lead singer, he had the most energy, was the smoothest dancer, and his bell-clear soprano rang above the other voices. His baby face was an adorable brown moon; he was probably all of thirteen. Cootie noted how the females—from five to eighty-five—giggled, smiled, pointed at, sighed over, and cheered on the cute brown boy's every move.

A cacophony of horns snatched Cootie's attention from the sideshow. He wondered if the group with the moon-faced kid had done Amateur Night yet. Since he was on the air Wednesdays, he seldom got to make that event...

Two hours later, Cootie dropped in on Herman Drexel of Freedom Records in his North Philadelphia office. Drexel, a rumpled, grandfatherly man, thanked Cootie for being the first to give wide airplay to several high-charting Freedom sides. Drexel wished Desiree Coutrere well, then handed Cootie an envelope.

"I don't know your sister, but I'm sure she's a wonderful girl," said Herman. "A little present for her." Cootie whistled when he felt the envelope's thickness. "Go ahead, look inside," Drexel nudged.

It was stuffed with twenty-dollar bills. "Mister Drexel, for someone whom you've never met—this is one helluva wedding gift."

"Is that too much to give a stranger? Bad manners? Breach of protocol? Look. She's *your* sister—and remember: *she* never rode any of my records into the Top Ten. *You* did. Four times. You decide what to give her, and what to keep for yourself."

"Sir, you are too kind. I assure you I will *not* insult my sister by giving her an overgenerous gift from a stranger." Cootie set aside the one hundred dollars he would give the newlyweds in one part of his suitcase, the rest in another compartment, and headed across town.

Toby Camble of Filly Records had yet a larger gift for the couple he did not know.

"Coot, be sure to pluck out a nice carrier's fee. Take what you want," Toby said.

"I like it like that!"

Next was Baltimore, and the home of Cool Daddy Flakes, the kingpin of Colt Records. Cool Daddy counted out thirty crisp one-hundred dollar bills. "Damn, Cool Daddy, don't you have anything *not* consecutively numbered?" Cootie groused. Cool Daddy frowned, waddled to a wall safe, opened it, extracted the same amount in well-traveled bills, and tossed them to Cootie.

"This is between you and your sis. You know what to do."

"Like, yeah. Later, skater." Cootie scurried to make two similar visits in Washington. The record moguls there were as generous as the others. Cootie then spent the night at the home of an Omega Psi Phi fraternity brother. He arose at daylight and set out for Knoxville.

* * * * *

Cootie examined himself from head to toe in the Davis's full-length mirror. His royal-blue two-button silk suit was wrinkle-free. He straightened his scarlet tie, wishing it were a closer shade to his wine-colored alligator shoes and matching socks. He had just changed from a hot-pink silk shirt into a cotton powder-blue number; he was not in a silk-on-silk mood. He admired his matching pearl cufflinks, pinkie ring, and tie pin.

Last came the wide-brimmed, specially-made Stetson hat that matched his suit. He had to decide between the small or medium-sized Columbia-blue turkey feather in the hat's two-inch scarlet band; this being Knoxville, he chose the small one.

Just twenty minutes until the eleven o'clock show, Cootie realized as he checked his watch. Fred Davis had told him the Full Moon Lounge was a ten-minute drive away, and easy to find. Satisfied with his self-inspection, he ambled out of the Davis's guest room.

Swampcat Newsome, assuming neither of Knoxville's two colored hotels met Cootie's standards, had arranged for him to stay with Fred and Ella Davis, his life-long friends. Cootie had rolled up to their home on Wilson Avenue shortly after seven that evening; the drive through the Virginia mountains *had* been rough, as Willa had warned. He had eaten a snack, taken a two-hour nap, and awoke, ready to see if this band was the cat's meow, as promised.

He knew he was keeping his hosts up. Out of protocol, he asked the Davises, who had to be well into their fifties, if they wanted to make the Full Moon scene with him—his treat, of course. Fred, a pleasant-faced, rotund, dark-brown man chuckled and replied, "No, thanks, sonny-boy. Our blues-club days are behind us."

"We're of the Church, now," Ella, a pleasingly-plump dark woman chimed in.

"But that doesn't mean it's wrong for a youngblood like you to go out and rip it up on a Saturday night," Fred added.

Cootie strolled into the kitchen, where they were waiting, so they could let him out and finally go to bed. They did not seem overly impressed with his celebrity; after all, Swampcat himself was no small shakes in these parts.

"Sonny-boy, you look real—" Ella began, as she eyed his outfit " —like the big city wheel you are," she finished. Cootie bade them goodnight and headed for their yard, the keys to their '54 Chrysler in hand. He had convinced them to loan it to him; he preferred it to the Studebaker squaremobile. He jumped in, was off, and found the club in a matter of minutes. Cars overspilled from the parking lot—he took that as a good sign—so he parked on a sidestreet two blocks away. As he walked to the Full Moon, he felt great spring in his step, despite the long drive and short nap. He sensed something big was in the air tonight, that he had done right to make this detour.

He took in everything without focusing on anything as he joined the crowd milling to get in. Glances—from males and females, colored and white, furtive and downright gawking—rained on him. He knew *some* had to recognize him from the *Ebony* cover; he also realized much of the attention was because he was a hotshot-looking visitor to an off-track Southern burg. *I feel like the mysterious stranger in the cowboy flickers as he rides into town, everyone staring, knowing he's come either to save the place or destroy it...*

Careful not to lock eyes with any one person, he glided through the masses with practiced reserve. He studied the one-story, cinderblock building, and was impressed with its size. He waited on the line leading to the cashier's table just inside the door, and savored the clean, crisp mountain air.

It was his turn to pay. The squat, brown-skinned cashier did not look up. "What's the damage, Sweetie Pie?" he asked in his creamiest chocolaty baritone.

"One dollar," she droned, but still had not looked up.

Cootie wanted her to look up. "Here you go," he said as he handed her a twenty.

She studied the bill and frowned. "Hunny, I *know* you got some-thin smaller—" She looked up and her mild belligerence vanished. "Hey! I know you! You on this month's *Ebony*-book cover!"

"I'm afraid that's true," he said as he grinned and reclaimed his twenty from her loosened grasp, and returned it to his wallet. He start-ed past her, and into the club.

"Hold on, Mister Im-por-tant: magazine cover and all, you *still* gots to pay!" she snipped. Cootie peeled off a five, told her to keep the change, and waltzed inside. He planted himself in the back and surveyed the scene. *Big fuckin place—must've been a warehouse or a garage in another life.* With five minutes to showtime—though these places *never* started on time—the crowd was large and, he sensed, lively. Moreover, a goodly number of white folks had made the scene. From their relaxed interactions with the Negro patrons, Cootie could tell they were not strangers to this place. *White folks dig these cats. Good sign—for what I got in mind for them...if they can cut the mustard...*

A low-slung waitress who looked like Marilyn Monroe's honey-colored half-sister sidled up to him. Her perfect, pearly teeth were frozen in a smile behind her generous, purple-painted lips. "Hi! I'm Margie! I *know* who you are! Lemme escort you to a table! Where you wanna sit?" Her breathless delivery and steel-guitar East Tennessee twang forced Cootie to listen hard to filter her words.

He pointed to a table near a corner, where he could have a good view of both the bandstand and the audience...but not be seen well by the band on stage. "That'll do just fine, Honey Pot," he drawled. She loosed a high-pitched giggle and led him across the room.

"That's right, girl! Pump that extra swang in them hips!" a female voice hooted. Margie giggled again and smiled coyly at Cootie.

He sat. She hovered above him, still grinning uncontrollably. "What can I get you, Mister Disk Jockey Man?" she cooed, staring into his eyes. "I mean...here and now?"

"Double Jack, rocks, and a Heineken chaser." She frowned blankly at the latter. "Falstaff, then," he amended. He nodded to a jukebox across the room. "That thing working?"

"Far as I know, yeah."

He fished a handful of change from his pocket, and told her to punch up the latest by Louisiana Fats, Little Robert, Moanin' Lisa, the Moonlighters, and the Philadelphia Belles. "Got that, Hotstuff?" he asked. She nodded affirmatively. "And if they play out before the show starts, hit 'em all again."

"Yes, sir, Mister Radio Man, sir," she saluted and wiggled off. He leaned back to observe the crowd, many of whom were observing him. He judged most of them to be what passed for well-dressed in this town. Good. He was hardly in the mood for any countryfied riffraff. He smiled when he realized how closely the Full Moon and its ambiance resembled the Drop On Inn in New Orleans, where he had discovered Little Robert on New Year's Eve past—except the Full Moon was three or four times larger than the Orleans Avenue joint.

Word soon spread about who he was. He deflected the envious glares from many of the men; by now he was accustomed to such. The Bronze Marilyn returned with his drinks. Louisiana Fats warbled on the juke. "Ennythang else?" she exhaled in a pregnant tone.

"When I need you, I'll make you know it," he replied, coquettishly. She sashayed away, dangerously swishing her shapely hips. *Pretty as her face is,* Cootie marveled silently, *she looks even better departing.* He saw she had written her name and telephone number on a napkin; he would have been surprised—and insulted—had she *not.*

Yet, he thought of Willa, and remembered who needed who more in their relationship. He took a quick look around, then crumpled the napkin.

People from nearby tables began to whisper just loud enough for him to overhear:

"That's the guy on the *Ebony*-book. Ain't he fiiiine?"

"He one-a them snotty-ass Noo Orlins Cree-yoals. Think they white."

"He *is* tall. Lotta them famous guys is short. Compensation, or somethin."

"He ain't all *that* good-lookin. Just bright-skinned, is all."

"Girl, you change your mind if he park his bathrobe on *your* bedpost, now what you wanna bet, child!"

"What the hell that bigshot doin in Knoxville?"

"What the hell you think? He's here to give Lou and the boys a look-see."

"No shit? Them niggers is *that* good?"

"That's what Mister Important is here to *determine,* fool!"

"Go axe him for his autograph!"

"*You* go!"

"I'll go if you go...first."

"Aw, too late—show's about to start. Maybe afterwards."

A portly middle-aged man bounced onto the tiny bandstand and up to the microphone. Dozens screamed Moon's name, and tossed good-natured barbs at him. Moon grinned, held up his hands, and waved them wildly. Behind him four young men eased into their places on stage. "Heeeey, yawl! How we doin t'night?" Moon shrieked. The jam-packed audience responded enthusiastically. The band slid into a standard blues groove. Moon made a proud, paternal, sweeping gesture to them and bellowed, "I know what yawl's here for, so Katie bar the door! Brace yourself, K-town: here's the Jimmy Jameson Quartet, Featuring Lou Cannon on Vocals!"

The crowd went wild, then wilder still when the vocalist caressed the microphone, leaned into it as if to give it a French kiss, and growled, "You left me pretty baby..."

The frenetic response drowned out his next two lines. "'Cigarette Blues!' That's *my* song!" a heavyset woman in a lavender dress screamed. Within seconds, the entire joint was vibrating. Half the audience members joined in the song at key spots.

Before Cootie realized it, he was caught in the tide. *Where've these boys been all my life? This cat's barely opened his mouth and the chicks are creaming like crazy!*

He had to remind himself he was here on business. He tuned out the bouncing blues and sized up the lead singer. Like Cootie had observed about many people in his short time in this town, Cannon had Negro coloring stretched over distinctly Indian features. The vocalist was tall, angular, and loose-limbed. Cannon also had skin the color and texture of chocolate candy, Cootie noted, similar to the R & B wailers who had recently clicked with young whites, Louisiana Fats and Little Robert. Cootie looked at his own caramel complexion, and wondered why so many Colored Creoles detested the beautiful deep brown tone of people like Lou Cannon and Fats.

Almost as striking-looking was the drummer, a beige Negro with wavy hair the color of a paper sack. On stand-up bass was a pleasant-faced guy who looked like a pro football tackle. At the piano was a chunky man with delightfully oversized eyes. His impassive face belied the dexterous manner in which his piano licks snaked around the drummer's backbeat and in and out of the young giant's bass notes.

As "Cigarette Blues" wound to an end, Cootie made a mental note. *Look good together, sound good together.* He doubted the song could sell big to general audiences, but with a hard ride, it could crack the R & B top ten.

Next came a blues ballad, "Late, Late at Night." The Cannon kid had a fine voice, Cootie judged; he's a good actor and can sell a song. Intermittent shrieks rose from the women. Cootie glanced at the corner that about fifty whites had commandeered; the women did not— or could not—disguise their attraction to the handsome singer.

That was both a good and potentially worrisome sign.

After the slow blues, the band swung into a lively rendition of "Good Morning, Blues." *Leadbelly. Look out! These cats have done their homework.* Next came a jump boogie-woogie version of Duke Ellington's "Don't Get Around Much Anymore." The people in the audience clapped, swayed, and chanted along, willfully mesmerized. Between songs, the vocalist bantered with his bandmates, the audience, and Moon. *This dude was born to be on stage,* Cootie thought, adding another plus to his mental list. Then, like a sudden thunderclap on a hot summer night, the band ripped into "Jambalaya" and sent the crowd into its wildest frenzy of the night. *Mercy! This is enough to make Hank Williams pull a Lazarus, grab a git-box, and join in!*

An instrumental break found the vocalist on the edge of the bandstand, waving the head of his guitar inches away from the full, pouty lips of a young woman in the front row. "Lou Cannon, if you *don't* git that big, long, hard thang away from my mouth, you better!" she cried.

"Aw, hunny hush!" chimed in a girlfriend. "You knooooow you like it like that!"

The lead singer then hunkered into a deep-knee bend and walked back and forth across the stage in that position, bobbing his head like a turkey. "Yeah, Lou—do that Turkey Wobble!" squealed the pouty-lipped girl. The crowd bellowed its approval.

The band rocked on. Cootie admired their eclectic repertoire: they played blues and jazz standards with arrangements so fresh it took a few moments to recognize them; Cootie counted at least four songs that had to be originals. Swampcat had told him that Cannon wrote songs for the band; Cootie judged the storytelling lyrics as clever as any by recent wordsmiths, even Hal Dillard, and in the tradition of Hank Williams, Louis Jordan, and Big Joe Turner.

Cootie checked his watch. Seventy-five minutes had stolen by like fifteen. He knew the audience could not stand much more of this.

Suddenly, a derringer-sized woman stood in a chair and fired a shotgun blast of a voice: "Hey, Lou! Time for that hillbilly goof!"

Cootie's ears prickled. *This* was the one Swampcat had harped as the killer tune.

The handsome lead singer smiled sweetly. "Cain't stay here all night, got to go home *sometime*," he demurred. This only caused more people to demand it. He grinned, tilted his head toward the crowd, cupped his left hand to his ear, and waited. The crowd gave him the response he wanted: a chant began for "the hillbilly goof."

"Oh, puh-leeeeeze...not *again!*" whimpered the lead singer.

"Hillbilly goof! Hillbilly goof!" The chant spread and grew in volume.

He blinked innocently at his audience. "It won't hurt, will it?" he whispered, yet seemingly resolved to suffer the pain.

"Ooooohhh, nooooooo!" the crowd chanted in reply.

"Promise you won't tell anyone we did—it?" he asked, as he swallowed hard.

"Ooooohhh, nooooooo!"

"If I do—it—with you tonight, will you come to see me next week?" Lou Cannon continued his coy schoolgirl act.

"Oooooohhh, yyyeeeeeesss!"

He placed his hands on his hips and glared into the audience. "If you're lying, I'll never never never speak to any any any of you ever ever ever again!" he lisped. The audience roared. Lou turned to his bandmates. "Five, six, seven, and..."

Claiborne Coutrere, who pimped hot wax for a living, knew a chartbuster when he heard one. Twenty seconds into "that hillbilly goof" he smelled a smash. He closed his eyes and listened to the song as if it were on a turntable in his radio studio.

As the second verse ended, Cootie was lost in another realm. On the surface, "Cora Ann" was a musical mulatto of Negro jump blues and white hillbilly rhythms. Upon closer inspection, however, the song represented a conscious, skillful blend of every brand of American popular music from the past twenty years.

If you were a blues or R & B fan, that's what you heard. "Cora Ann" was as country as an Arkansas outhouse. With Cannon's crystal-clear phrasing, many would swear he was white. And though the band had only four musicians, each played with such crisp distinction that jazz buffs could appreciate this song. Then, Cootie could not contain a laugh when he suddenly recognized the melody from which Cannon had heavily borrowed for "Cora Ann": the Leadbelly/Blind Lemon Jefferson duet, "Silver City Bound," from the 1910's...

By the time the final stanza rolled around, Cootie felt as if his spirit was floating above the audience while the rest of him stayed glued to his chair. *THIS IS IT!* he wanted to jump up and scream, and looked around to make sure he had not. His face was petrified into a wild grin; sweat streamed from his brow and armpits; he was breathing twice as hard as when he had smashed the state half-mile record seven years ago. The band looked, felt, and sounded as if playing from far away, as if in another dimension of time and space, like in the spooky movies.

Now this *is what Freeman and those other cats have in mind when they talk about rock-and-roll—even though they've never heard these studs. The other musicians, colored and white, have been hammering around this sound, barely missing it. Cannon and his boys have nailed it dead-fucking-center,* Cootie gloated silently.

Ol' Swampcat steered me toward the Sweepstakes winners here, boy! We get these cats in our fold, and Mister Rhythm-and-Blues vaults to the top of the deejay class!

He reined in his high hopes. *Now, all I've gotta do is get these studs under contract, into the studio, on the airwaves, and convince every hip kid in America that* this *is the sound that sets the standard for rock-n-roll.*

Not exactly a stroll on the beach.

The band finished the song and the crowd cried out for more. The musicians played a brief instrumental reprise, collected their instruments and raced offstage, with their fans still clamoring for more. *Good showmanship. Always leave 'em wanting that one more.* Cootie looked around as the audience stood, stomped, cheered, and whistled. The proprietor stepped out and raised his arms for quiet. When he got it a half-minute later, he spoke.

"That's all and there ain't no more. Hit yourself in the butt with the door. Yawl ain't gotta go home, but you sure gotta shake *this* place. See ya same time, same channel next week for Knoxville's own, Knoxville-grown—the Jimmy Jameson Quartet, Featuring Lou Cannon on Vocals!" The house lights blinked demonically, and from the jukebox the Bassets moaned their classic gotta-call-it-a-night lament, "Goodnight, My Darling, Goodnight."

Cootie was so overcome that it took him a while to remember he had work to do. He swam against the tide of the departing crowd, blind to autograph requests, missing the Mulatto Marilyn's wet-eyed, take-me-home look. Somehow he made it to the bandstand. He spied a short, narrow corridor and followed it to a pair of closed doors. From behind one he heard joyful, masculine banter. He sucked in a deep breath, then burst into the tiny afterthought of a dressing room. The vocalist and drummer were shirtless, their lean torsos glittering with sweat. The pop-eyed piano player stopped in the middle of lighting a king-sized cigar and gawked at him.

"Man, when Swampcat told me you studs were hotter than Alabama in August, he was not lying!" Cootie gushed, then caught the stunned looks on their faces. In his excitement, he had forgotten the first rule of backstage etiquette—especially when dealing with strangers. *Oh, shit! Forgot to knock; wasn't invited; they look like they got a yen to kick my—*

"HEY, MAN! YOU'RE—YOU!" the almost-white drummer erupted, his green-flecked gray eyes threatening to explode from their sockets.

The lead singer catapulted from his seat like Bill Russell going up for a rebound. "I DON'T BELIEVE IT! NOT HERE! NOT WITH—US!"

The bass man scrinched his eyes at Cootie as if peering at a ghost or a Martian. "Mister Rhythm-and-Blues?" he said, half-question, half-demand.

"YOU'RE MY IDOL, MAN! YOU REALLY ARE!" the vocalist squealed, though he did not brave a move closer to Cootie. He then realized how he sounded, and looked around sheepishly. "I mean, you know—"

"Yeah, I know," Cootie replied with a reassuring chuckle.

The piano player remained silent, all the while fixing a skeptical glare on Cootie.

"Wow! Cootie the Cutie! The *main* brain!" sang the blond boy. "What brings—?"

"How'd you hear about—?"

"What'd you think of our—?"

"Fellas, fellas, *fellas!*" Cootie cried as he laughed and threw up his hands. "Let's get some names, then down to the nitty gritty." The four introduced themselves. Cootie told of Swampcat's rave reference. That out of the way, Cootie began in his weariest, seen-it-all tone, "Okay. Fasten your seat-belts. Here's the *real* scoop..." He told them how wonderful *he* thought they were, and that some of their original tunes, particularly "Cora Ann," had potential. He vowed once they had something on wax, he would give it the big, *big* push. He did not have to remind them that most R & B jocks followed his lead.

"We gotta *cut* a record first," Jimmy finally spoke, but retained his fish-eyed look at Cootie. "What kinda clout you got in that area?" he asked, challengingly.

Cootie smiled as he withdrew the blank contract from his jacket pocket. "I'm way ahead of it. Since Swamp praised you studs to high heaven, I took the liberty of..." He spread the contract before them on a table. "Trust me. It's standard." He was not surprised when Jimmy and Deuce arched their eyebrows suspiciously.

The four read it—or tried to. "This damn thing is in legalese," Deuce moaned.

"And it'll be a while before we can have a mouthpiece go over it," Jimmy said.

Lou swept his mates with a glance, then said: "Mister Cootie, if you would, please..." He nodded toward the door.

"Of course." He went out, and tried to listen through the thin wall. They must have anticipated this; they kept their voices low. Several minutes later, the lead singer emerged.

"Mister Cootie—"

"Please—Cootie will do just fine, thank you."

"Cootie, if you'll allow me to make a phone call first, then just follow us..."

Lou led the five-car caravan on a one-mile journey from the Full Moon. Lou turned up the driveway to a large white two-story house atop a hill on Bethel Avenue. The others parked on the street, which was silent, save for the random yapping of dogs in the near distance. As Cootie began the climb up the concrete stairs, an amber porch light snapped on, followed by the front door opening and framed by the silhouette of a man, tall and well-fed. From twenty feet away, Cootie could sense the man's irritation at being roused at such an hour. He reached the porch and took a deep breath before following the musicians inside.

The man, an older, thicker version of Lou, gave Cootie a head-to-toe inspection, his large brown face emotionless. A sharp-featured woman materialized. She struggled to contain her joy. Lou gestured to them. "Cootie, these are my—"

"The Reverend and Missuz Cannon," Cootie said as he swept past Lou, his hand extended, smiling extravagantly. "Sir, I've heard *so* much about you!" He pumped the reverend's hand, and turned to the woman. "And it's plain to see why Lou is *such* a fine-looking boy," he said as he gently squeezed her hand. "Has anyone ever told you that you look *just like* the lovely and talented dancer, Miss Katherine Dunham?"

"Oh, hunny—hush! But yes, I've heard that a few times!" she replied. "And you look just like *yourself!*" Cootie smiled. The reverend grinned thinly.

Cootie squeezed her hand again. "*So* pretty," he whispered, then turned to the reverend. "Sorry to have to get you up on a night before you have to preach—"

"Then let's get down to business," Reverend Cannon said plainly. He led them past several well-appointed rooms and into a kitchen with a fresh canary-yellow paint job. The six men plopped at the table. Florence, still smiling broadly, bustled among them, pouring coffee into cups already in place.

"How do you take your coffee, Mister Cootie?" Florence trilled. "I've got regular milk, heavy cream, Pet canned evaporated milk—"

"The first thing you come across will be fine," Cootie baritoned.

Lou pinched his mother on her thigh, then glared mildly at her. *Mama! Stop fawning!* Florence ignored him, kept smiling, and delicately tilted a bottle of cream over Cootie's cup.

"Say when, honey." Cootie nodded when it was time for her to stop.

Reverend Cannon cocked his head toward Cootie. "Okay, son..."

Cootie placed the contract before the reverend, and explained how he felt the group *already* had several hits in them and—

"You *work* for these .30/.30 Records folks, son?" the reverend cut him off.

Cootie's gaze dodged the reverend's. "Since I'm a disk jockey, I can't work *for* any record company." He saw how they caught the hedge in his voice.

"But you just—happen—to have one of *their* contracts with you," Jimmy said, as he narrowed his froggish eyes.

"A—standard—one," Deuce said, dipping the middle word in gun oil.

Cootie exhaled nervously. "I work within a tiny, self-contained universe. If a record producer pops a piece of gum in his mouth uptown, five minutes later all the jockeys and songwriters downtown can tell you whether it's Spearmint or Dentyne. Let's just say—we look out for one another. We *have* to."

"You loan me your car, I'll mow your lawn, that how it works?" Jimmy asked.

"Something like that." Cootie explained how Swampcat's description of the quartet and its music made them a likely fit with the Felder brothers at .30/.30 Records—and tonight's show had verified it.

"You get a kickback or something for finding them talent?" the blond lad asked.

Cootie shifted his weight from his right hip to his left. "They have ways of compensating me," he replied as he swept them with a look: *you know exactly what I mean.*

An explosion rocked the house.

"IT'S—HIM!"

Cootie looked up; two slightly younger, pretty-girl versions of Lou held on to the doorway, clad in long flannel nightgowns, their faces aglow in stunned pleasure.

"Hey!" Lou snapped. "We're in here doing business!"

"Don't you *dare* pinch me, girl! Let this dream go on and on!" shrieked the taller and older-looking.

"*Nobody's* gonna believe he was here, in *our* house!" sang the younger one.

"Everybody's got to be *somewhere*, girls," Cootie said with a toothpaste-commercial smile and in his deepest, oiliest voice. "I just happen to be right here, right now."

"Oh!" the taller girl gasped. "So profound. So—poetic! *Such* a cutie-patootie!"

The smaller one was now enveloped in a joy too exquisite for words.

"Mister Cootie, these are Lou's sisters, Ruth and Sarah," Florence said.

"So fine-looking. Just like you and your husband," Cootie cooed.

Ruth and Sarah had to lean on each other to remain upright.

"Oh, brother," Lou muttered in an aside to the nearest wall.

"Girls. You've seen Mister Cootie. Now tell Mister Cootie 'good-night,' and go back to bed," Reverend Cannon dictated with benign sternness.

"Goodnight, Mister Cootie," Sarah and Ruth chanted. They clutched each other's shoulders, threw back their heads and screeched primally.

"Dah-dee," Lou whispered through clenched teeth, "will you *please* tell them to—"

"Girls! That's enough! Don't let me have to tell you again!" This time real irritation throbbed in Reverend Cannon's voice. The girls backed away slowly, not taking their eyes from Cootie until the wall came between them.

"Great googa-mooga!" Blondie whispered to Cootie. "That sorta thing happen to you *all* the time?"

"Nope. Only on the days when I leave the house," Cootie said in all seriousness.

"Lordha'mercy!" Blondie hissed.

"Question, Cootie," Jimmy said. "Do the record company folks actually *pay* you jockeys for plugging their songs?"

Cootie absently stirred his coffee. "Not flat-out, directly. We do, however, get our fair share of Christmas and birthday gifts, and so do our spouses, *if* you know what I mean." He nodded and panned them with squinting eyes. "And you *know* what I mean."

"But isn't that play-for-pay razzmatazz against the law?" Lou asked.

Cootie cleared his throat. "No—but it *is* heavily frowned upon," he admitted. He thought of the recent whispers about pushing to make it illegal. He noticed everyone staring at him. "I've kept you fine folks up long enough. Have some lawyers look it over, get back to me..."

Reverend Cannon jabbed the contract with a long, muscular fore-finger. "Son, don't take this the wrong way, but we'd all be *quite* dis-appointed if this is less than—"

"Reverend Cannon, sir," Cootie interrupted, his voice a wounded sore. "Far be it from *me* to try to bamboozle a man of the cloth—in his own kitchen—on the Lord's Day."

Reverend Cannon glared at Cootie: *Don't try that Mister Personality soft-shoe with me, bud.* Aloud, he said, "Don't think because we live in what some call the boondocks that we don't know how snake-infested the music world is. We've got to tread carefully—if we tread at all."

Silence. Cootie clamped his lips, then spoke. "I understand and agree, sir. Again, take your time. Hopefully we can do business." He brushed the musicians with a smile. "You boys *do* have the goods, no doubt." He started to add more, but thought it best to end on that note. He rose and asked for directions back to the Davises' house. He wished them a good night, and fifteen minutes later was tiptoeing past his hosts' bedroom and into his own.

Six hours after that, he was headed south on Highway 75. Nine hours after leaving Wilson Avenue, he was in his parents' home on Saint Bernard Avenue, regaling a large flock of relatives with tidied-up stories of the latest in the world of R & B.

* * * * *

After the New York jockey left, Lou walked his bandmates to their cars. "You think that cat's on the up-and-up?" Blondie asked.

"My money says he's slicker than a nine-cent cheeseburger," Deuce drawled. "And don't let that pretty face and smooth talk hornswoggle you. Remember: Satan was the prettiest of Gawd's angels, 'til the Lord wised up and bounced his ass down to Hell."

"You cats don't even know the guy, and already you're putting the knock on him," Lou argued. "Me, I don't think he's the type who'd stick it to another colored man."

"You mean you *hope* he isn't," Deuce countered.

"Devil or angel, the world keeps turnin," Jimmy offered. "He cain't make us do nothin we don't want to do."

"Amen to that, brother," Blondie said. He motioned for them to do their four-way hug. The others complied, and they went their sep-arate ways into the nippy night.

CHAPTER SEVEN

Wednesday, April 27, 1955; 1:34 p.m.
Eternal Peace Cemetery, Athensboro.

Those who follow me had better care for me as well as I've cared for those I've followed, mused Senator Theophilis Briscoe. Along with a daughter, Cassandra Briscoe Rawley, he was making his semi-annual pilgrimage to the Briscoe family plot. The Eternal Peace Cemetery was on the outskirts of Theo's hometown of Athensboro, a hamlet of about ten thousand at the midpoint between the state capital and the Gulf of Mexico.

The eighty-five degrees made it feel like summer, which was still nine weeks away. Theo mopped sweat from his brow, and was glad the Delta heat was without its usual accomplice, the stifling humidity. Flanked by Cassie, who was thirty, married, and the mother of three, he began to place roses on several graves. He did it reverently, if not methodically.

Unlike many his age, such visits did not fill him with prickly thoughts of his own mortality. He had celebrated his sixtieth birthday a month ago, and felt he was in sturdy, if not tip-top condition. Yes, his physician had told him to cut back on the cigars, whisky, fatty foods, and to drop twenty or so pounds, but Theo felt he deserved *some* indulgences. Besides, he knew he carried his six-foot, one-inch, 230-pound frame far better than a man his age could expect to. Moreover, both his parents had lived into their eighties and resorted to no extremes for self-preservation. Theo assumed that alone foreshadowed his own longevity.

As always, he first placed flowers on the grave of his father, Byron. The old man had been a hardscrabble sharecropper for his first three decades, then scraped up enough money to start his own business, a general store near the town square. Byron saw to it that all seven of his children put in several hours a week in the store. The business prospered well enough to put three children through college, not counting Theo, who went to Ole State on a football scholarship.

Next was Tula, his mother. Her sunny nature balanced that of the chronically dour Byron. The older Theo got, the more he appreciated how she not only choreographed a large household, but was indispensable in the store. She kept the books and bartered down the best prices from wholesalers. Theo credited his talent for mediation—if not flat-out manipulation—to Tula.

After visiting Tula's grave, Cassie and he paid tribute to Rebecca Montgomery Briscoe, Theo's first wife and Cassie's mother. Theo had married Becky in September 1923, two months after he passed the bar exam on the first try, and a month after he landed a job with the most prestigious law firm in the state. Eighteen months after the marriage, Cassie was born. Two years after that, Becky died while delivering a stillborn male child.

Theo had planned to run for a state senate seat in the next year, 1928. Of course, Becky's death altered his plans. Temporarily.

Theo's advisors, bent on cashing in on the growing popularity of the virtually unbeatable young attorney, could not allow his momentum to slow. "You sit this election out and by the time the next one rolls around, too many folks will have forgotten you, cast their lot behind this year's Hot New Prospect," Theo's chief mentor, a former two-term governor, warned. "We'll play the aggrieved-widower-who-still-must-fight-the-good-fight angle, and get you elected."

Initially, Theo opposed the idea. He felt that would desecrate Becky's death. However, his hatred of his chief opponent—a liberal suspected of having both Catholic and Jewish blood in his background—was greater than his aversion to climbing into the office partly over his wife's tombstone. Theo relented; the sympathy angle may or may not have provided the narrow margin of victory, but he *did* win, which was what mattered most.

Six years after he won the state senate seat, Theo's mentors felt he was ready to tackle its federal counterpart. Refusing to engage in the muck-flinging dogfight his incumbent opponent tried to drag him into, Theo's taking the high ground was largely responsible for his paper-thin triumph. The election was so close that his opponent, R.D. Rodds, demanded two recounts. Theo prevailed, and assumed the seat in Washington.

That proved to be his last close political horserace. His re-election campaigns in 1940, '46, and '52 saw him win by landslides. In 1952 he ran virtually unopposed. Now, in 1955, he was the unofficial head of the Dixiecrats in Washington, based on his seniority, high visibility, and commitment to the objectives of the Sons of the Confederacy...

After he paid his respects to his late wife, Theo turned to the grave of Elverna Briscoe Garrett, the second of Byron and Tula's children, and their eldest daughter. She had succumbed to breast cancer in 1940, at the age of forty-nine. Next to her was the headstone of Theo's only other deceased sibling, Thaddeus, the baby of the family. A career army man, Thad had been killed in Normandy on D-Day, June 6, 1944. A shell had mangled his body so badly that the government could not ship his actual remains home. Thus, Thad's grave in the family plot was merely symbolic, though Theo had made it a point to see his brother's true resting place while in northern France, five years ago.

"Senator, sir..." the tentative voice nudged Theo from his thoughts.

"Yes, Vicky Sue, dawhlin?" he replied. A hurt look stained her face, and he wished he could pull back the name he called. He started to apologize, but she spoke first.

"Cassandra..." she murmured, then lowered her eyes. Theo read what she had not verbalized: *Vicky Sue is one of your* current *daughters...*

"Sunshine, dawhlin, I'm sorry—"

"That's okay—Father," she replied. Theo marveled at how much she looked like her mother, with the same waterfall of curling, red dish-blond hair, porcelain skin, and sky-blue eyes. He gave her a wan smile, and she returned it.

Cassandra knew his ritual as well as he did. She nodded to a faraway corner. "I'll go back to the car now," she said.

"Okay, honey...I'll be there directly." They went their separate ways. As he cut diagonally across the yard, careful not to step on anyone's grave, something snagged his attention.

The remains of Lindsay and Nellie Caterfield, the parents of his best boyhood friend, had been transferred from the unofficial "poor white trash" corner of the cemetery to an area where people from better-off families were laid to rest. Moreover, the Caterfields now had prominent headstones, the marble glistening starkly in newness.

Well, my ol' buddy Polk's done truly come up in the world, Theo thought. Then again, Polk had done recently what Theo did when his greater wealth allowed for it: he saw to it that his loved ones were moved to the best part of the cemetery, with classy headstones.

Polk-fuckin-Caterfield, Theo whistled the name to himself. *Who'd-a thunk that besides me, of all the yahoos I grew up with, skinny li'l ol' Polk Caterfield would become famous—or infamous, dependin on how you look at it.*

Polk-fuckin-Caterfield, Theo repeated to himself. *Biggest jackleg preacher in the South. The poor man's Billy Sunday. Lord. This world is full of gullible fools.*

He strode past the Caterfields' graves to the cemetery's southwest corner. Burial in this section did not brand one as to social class, but as someone with few, if any loved ones who kept up the grave. The markers were plain; the grass here was more unkempt than even in the white-trash quarters. Seldom were flowers placed on what was known as "Loner's Land."

Theo stopped and stared at a grave whose faded, modest-sized marble cross was the most prominent marker in this section, which was not saying much. The name on the horizontal arm of the cross read: "Margaret Hearn: 1898 - 1952."

Theo continued to stare at the grave. He tried to will tears to his eyes, but his heart would not cooperate.

Margaret Hearn.

Peggy.

Her threat made him realize he didn't love her never had only wanted to get in her pants and how he could do it without a guilty conscience still when he tried to play up to her she never had any time for him and if anyone quit anyone it would be him to quit her and he heard whispers she was fooling around with someone else but he just took them as that nobody could come up with any names dates or places and the town was so small that had she been messing around he would know more about it than from third-hand rumors but the talk kept piling up and got uglier someone told someone who told his best friend Polk Caterfield who tap-danced around when he told Theo that talk had Peggy seeing a nigger yes a nigger and of course Theo did not believe it or did not want to but something made him look into it so he followed Peggy one hot Friday night he wanted to scream when she crossed the tracks into jigtown and making herself as unseen as possible in that situation she could and she knocked on the door of a shack and the pretty blues-shouting brown Indian opened the door and looked up and down what passed for a street along the row of shacks then let her in and it was only when the lantern near a window went off did Theo even know it was on.

He checked an impulse to rush into the house and tear them both apart with his bare hands but there was no guarantee he could lick the nigger in a fair fight despite how angry he was so he thought about setting the shack on fire it would burn so fast and easy but decided against that too then his head cleared long enough to come up with what he felt was the best possible plan and worst possible punishment for them yes he would make them suffer suffer suffer and he would need help yes he would have Polk Caterfield and Clifton Clowers and two or three other boys he could trust with the secret and the nigger—and Peggy—would wish they had never been born or at least never fucked with Theophilis Briscoe by God...

It was time to go. As he drove Cassie to her house, they spoke but a few forced sentences. He returned to his sister Amanda's house, where he always lodged when in Athensboro, and placed a call home to Washington. His wife Virginia and the three girls had gone to see a ballet recital, so he left a message with the housekeeper as to his approximate time of arrival. He then took a nap. At midnight he set out for the nation's capital. As always, he made the twenty-four-hour drive straight through, save for a couple of roadside cat-naps.

However, a realization that became more evident with each passing hour gnawed at him: "race" records, previously relegated to Negro stations, had begun to infiltrate the playlists of white stations.

On his drive south, he had only half-noticed this trend. On the return trip, though, he could not miss it. Theo enjoyed country, gospel, and Frank Maggio/Perry Martin-style pop tunes; while he motored, he fished the dial for stations that played those. Now, however, a fourth flavor had been added, the R & B stations notwithstanding. He also noticed some of the jockeys called this "race" music by a new name: rock-n-roll. Some of the wax spinners seemed to think this term was novel, but Theo knew from his boyhood that it was a Negro euphemism for having sex. Moreover, this "rock-n-roll" was just a sanitized version of the barrelhouse boogie-woogie blues he had heard in overspill from the colored saloons that were literally shouting distance from his old neighborhood.

As the miles flew by, a thought struck Theo: if this new rock-n-roll was integrating the airwaves, it was because white kids were listening to it. Next would be integrated record hops...*and everyone knew what dancing was just a warm-up for*, he mused bittersweetly.

When Theo pulled over for a nap in southwest Virginia, another thought hit him: *Are my* daughters *listenin to that stuff?* At seventeen, fifteen, and twelve, they were at the ages where they might be influenced by what their friends considered trendy.

That he had no idea of what type of music they listened to underscored how little time he spent with them. Sunday was his only day away from the political arena—and more because of Virginia's insistence than his own volition. With their homework, clubs, and dance and music lessons, the girls also maintained a full plate. When he *did* spend time with his family, the five of them tiptoed within a cocoon of strained politeness.

Though he did not want his daughters listening to this rock-n-roll, Theo himself liked to listen to the blues and R & B from which it evolved. He agreed with the theory that blues and country music were but flipsides of the same coin—and Theophilis Briscoe loved country music as much as anyone. Moreover, though, he never made a big deal of it, he enjoyed the jumping tunes of Joe Turner, Louis Jordan, and Gutbucket McDaniel.

Yet, he judged that the Negro music was too suggestive for his daughters, or any well-bred white children, for that matter. The lyrics were too raunchy, and the pounding drums, mating saxophone calls, and sinuous piano chords too closely captured the sound and fury of raw, buck sex. The lyrics ranged from double entendres that were slyly sophisticated in their own way, to down-and-dirty vulgarity. He had just heard one by a blues-wailing mama, "Twelve-Inch Ruler," that left little to the imagination. And another, "Bunny's Got a Bun in the Oven," made light of an unwanted pregnancy while masquerading as a jaunty dance tune.

No, he did not want his daughters—or anyone like them—listening to that stuff. As casually as possible, he would ask them what they thought, if at all, about the colored tunes seeping onto white radio. He knew they would not actively seek out rhythm-and-blues stations…but, if they were being exposed to it in stealthful doses, he wanted to know their reactions…

Furthermore, every Negro record he had heard on his return trip, and especially the bluesier, grittier ones, rekindled memories of Peggy and her pretty black Indian. By the time he was three-quarters of the way back to Washington, he shut off the radio or changed the station whenever he heard a song by a Negro.

Probably just a trend, a bunch of smart-ass nigger-lovin white jockeys thumbin their noses at convention, Theo reasoned as the miles piled up behind him. *Surely it'll pass.*

It had better, his inner voice added with a virulence that shook him.

CHAPTER EIGHT

Thursday, May 5; 6:58 P.M. Knoxville.

"Luggage secure on top?" Lou inquired.

"Check."

"Plenty of nourishment?"

The inside of Deuce's '54 Buick Electra 225 reeked of fried chicken, ham and bologna sandwiches, bananas, apples, and pound cake. "Check," answered Deuce.

"Road maps, flashlights, flares, all that stuff?"

"Check."

"The gas tank is full. The troops are eager. Let's motorvate!" Lou announced as he stepped on the gas and propelled the car toward New York City.

Minutes later, they were past the city limits. "This is where K-town looks best," said Blondie.

"How's that?" Jimmy asked.

"In your rear-view mirror."

On Tuesday afternoon, the lawyers the reverend consulted assured him the contract was legitimate. He relayed this to the quartet, who then mapped out strategies for the trip and recording session. Later that night, Lou called Cootie to tell him everything was a go. Miraculously, Cootie had no qualms about fitting the session around Jimmy and Deuce's work schedules. They finalized the ground rules over the phone.

Rather than take up Winchester Records' offer to put them on a train, they elected to drive. All four loved being behind the wheel; they polished their songs as they motored. With punctuality a rule with the band, they set out at precisely seven p.m. However, their plan to arrive in New York early the next afternoon went awry.

They were delayed three times in Virginia for "speeding," and had to pay ten-dollar bribes to local patrolmen. Clogged traffic from multi-vehicle accidents in northern Virginia and on the outskirts of Trenton cost them an hour each.

They hit New York shortly before five that afternoon, just in time for the Friday rush hour. The directions from the New Jersey Turnpike through the Lincoln Tunnel and up the West Side Highway to Hamilton Heights were easy to follow, but the stop, crawl, lurch, stop, then crawl again pace clawed everyone's last nerve. "Man, anyone who'd *choose* to live in New York has got to be crazy," growled Deuce as he called on patience he did not know he had, weaving in and out of any openings that presented themselves.

They cheered when they reached the 125th Street exit. Minutes later they were parked in front of the address Cootie had given them. A tall, wiry, butterscotch-colored woman, her thick, black hair dangling to her waist in an elaborate braid, skittered from the brownstone.

"Welcome, fellas. I'm Willa. I *know* you must be tired." They mumbled their agreement. "Clai—Cootie—left ten minutes ago. C'mon, let's unload." She undid the straps on the roof rack and began to toss down bags. They tried not to stare at her shapely buttocks that, slender though she was, protruded eye-catchingly from the checkered wool slacks she wore.

After they hauled the luggage into the living room, Willa showed them the two spare bedrooms. "Freshen up, take a nap, let me know when you want something to eat."

"What time do we have to be at the studio?" asked Lou.

"Whenever you're ready. You're to take as much time as you need." A quick shower and twenty minutes later, the bluesmen were sleeping peacefully...

The aroma of perking coffee prodded Lou awake. He looked at his watch; it was only ten p.m. His three hours of sleep had felt like nine. He followed his nose to the kitchen, where Blondie and Deuce feasted on toast, grits, salmon croquettes, and scrambled eggs. "Sit down, Lou; she's got enough to feed the New York Giants," Deuce said. Lou dived into a plate, and Jimmy joined them minutes later.

When the meal was finished, they were ready to work. "Clai, uh, Cootie will be at the studio shortly after midnight," Willa told them. "You want to go down there and get warmed up?"

"What're we waitin on?"

They piled into a coffee-colored Coupe de Ville. Blondie, who had never been to New York before, grabbed a window seat in the back. Deuce, who had made two brief stopovers as a soldier, claimed the other back window seat. Jimmy, who knew Harlem well from visits to relatives, sat between them. Lou, who had attended a few dances at the Savoy Ballroom while stationed at nearby Fort Dix, eased into the front seat opposite Willa.

He noticed she was a few years older than Cootie. She was not the heart-stopping beauty he expected Cootie to have, but quite a handsome woman nonetheless, with a beguiling aloofness that lent her an air of mystery, Lou thought.

As she drove down Broadway, Blondie gawked in disbelief. "Past eleven, and all these people still in the streets, all these bright lights—"

"Boy, stop actin so country!" bark-whispered Jimmy.

Willa's regal bearing prompted Lou to ask: "What do you do for a living, Miss McAshan?"

"Kill the 'Miss' jazz. Call me Willa. I'm an attorney-at-law."

"Oh."

She deciphered Lou's expression. "Believe me, there are plenty of Negro women lawyers up North," she assured him. "There's even a few in the South."

"Oh, I'm sure that's true, Miss—I mean—Willa. I just haven't met any—until now." He paused. "What kind of law do you do?"

"I've done some civil and criminal, but recently I've focused on show-business law."

"Oh?"

"To better serve my clients." Lou's expression repeated "clients" and tacked a question mark behind it. "I've managed R & B artists for the last three years," she divulged.

"Oh? Which ones?" Lou felt his heartbeat step up its pace.

"Louisiana Fats, Hal Dillard & the Moonlighters, Little Robert and His Go-Getters, The Philadelphia Belles, and Moanin' Lisa, among others. I'm sure you've heard of some of them."

The three in the back froze when they heard her casually toss out such familiar names. "Of course we've heard of *all* of them," Lou said, trying to hide his delight.

"You managing them, your husband—uh—friend—Cootie pushing their records, yawl can't lose, can you?" said Blondie, who promptly received a kick in the shins from Jimmy. Lou winced.

If Willa had taken offense, she did not show it. "One hand washes the other in this game," she said as she lit a Kool. "This is the last of the six I allow myself each day," she announced with a small smile and thin veneer of triumph.

She drove past the theatre district, thick with playgoers streaming out after the final curtains. Less than a dozen blocks south of Times Square, Broadway faded into a drab strip that cut through a canyon of bland high-rise structures. Willa made a left on 30th Street, parked, and led them to a building. It was unremarkable like its neighbors, save for an oversized replica of a Winchester rifle hanging over the entrance. On the butt of the gun was the company's logo; dangling below it, on chains, was a sign: "30 West 30th Street—Home of .30/.30 Winchester Records."

"Oh, *now* I see where they got the name of the company," admitted Lou, as he smacked himself on the side of his head. "I must be slow."

"Thirty West 30th. Cute," added Jimmy.

The entrance to the building had been unlocked for them. Willa led them through the tiny lobby, up to the second floor, and past the receptionist's area. They noticed a buffet of cold cuts, soda, coffee, and delicatessen salads spread on a table. Willa nodded at the layout as if to say, "Yes, it's yours." Next, four studio technicians filed in and introduced themselves. Willa then led them into the main studio, which was stocked with the latest equipment, polished and gleaming. On instinct, Jimmy sat at the piano and tickled out some chords.

Next, Willa took them to the offices in the back where they met the firm's owners. The Felder brothers, Abe and Solomon, were kind-faced, avuncular white men in their early forties.

"Heard great things about you guys," said Abe, the older and more outgoing, as he pumped their hands.

"We'll try not to disappoint," Jimmy said. The musicians returned to the studio proper, set up their instruments, and started to tune up.

Cootie arrived at a quarter past midnight. "How you boys feel?" he asked in greeting them.

"We're ready like Freddy," chirped Lou.

"I like it like that! Let's get to rockin, then! Just remember: relax. Take all the time you need. If you flub something, don't worry. Stay relaxed. Imagine you're at the Full Moon, before your most loyal fans," Cootie advised.

The session began with "Late, Late at Night." Musically speaking, it was the simplest of the four songs they would cut that night. All felt it was a solid, if unremarkable tune; Cootie's sharp ear and memory told him Lou had modeled it after a 1944 R & B top-ten hit, "It's Dawn and You're Gone" by the great but enigmatic McKinley "Gutbucket" McDaniel. Cootie, Willa, and the Felders, watching from the control booth, decided this would serve as a future B-side, but not likely the flip for the band's first release. The taping of the track was basically a warm-up; they nailed it in three takes. Cootie came out of the booth and suggested some minor changes, to which they readily agreed.

Things picked up with "Cigarette Blues." Wildly popular in the band's live act, they laid down the mid-tempo jump tune in just four takes. Cootie, Willa, and the Felders again huddled; they felt the song was not quite strong enough to be an "A"-side, but could be the flip-side of a consciously-marketed double-sided hit. Again, Cootie came out and guided them through a few minor adjustments.

"You boys wanna take a break?" Cootie asked.

"Hell, no! We're rollin—like a big wheel through a Texas cotton field!" Blondie shouted back, and everyone laughed at his theft of one of Cootie's favorite catch-phrases.

"What's next?" Willa called from the booth.

"Something I've written since Mister Cootie saw us perform live!" Lou shouted back.

Willa and the Felders stared at Cootie. "I thought you'd worked out with them the songs they would record," Willa said, with irritation.

"On us they're testing their new material?" Solomon shrieked softly.

"Let's hear it first," Cootie replied, his voice bristling with annoyance toward his friends in the booth and the band on the floor.

"'Botheration,' take one," Jimmy announced, then launched into a breakneck barrelhouse piano introduction. Lou shouted the opening phrase:

"I cain't be bothered with the botheration—oohhh, nooooo!"

The rest of the band repeated the elongated "oh, no!" refrain. In the booth, Cootie noticed that Willa, the Felders, and the technicians were already bobbing with the beat.

Lou wailed on:

"I cain't be bothered with the botheration, ooohhh, noooooo!
Never could build up a toleration
For folks who don't have no consideration
Said I cain't be bothered with the botheration, oh, no!"

Since the song was still new to the musicians, they needed six takes to get a final product. This time Cootie engineered a dozen changes, "to make it more commercial," he explained. He returned to the booth, and again he, Willa, and the Felders locked heads.

"That's good stuff, Cootie," Solomon said in what from him was a rave. "The 'ooohhh, nooooo!' hook is to die for—simple but catchy at the same time! If that killer tune you've been gushing about is better than this..."

"We'll see," Cootie said from behind a smug smile.

"Hey!" Lou called from the floor. *"Now* we're ready to take that break."

Without anyone having to verbalize it, everyone knew that "Cora Ann," the showpiece tune, was the next, and last track they would record. Everyone filtered to the buffet table in the reception area. The band members staked out their own corner as they nibbled on sandwiches and chugged coffee. The eight who had been in the booth, knowing that true musicians receded within themselves while plying their art, left the quartet alone. Cootie smiled as he watched them communicate silently among themselves within their shared, self-induced trance. Most of the few words they uttered during the twenty-minute break contained but one syllable. *Good,* Cootie thought, *these studs are exactly where they need to be...*

Jimmy signaled the end of the respite. "We're ready."

All resumed their places. When he returned to the booth, Cootie crowed, "Grab a-holt to something solid. Here it comes."

"Clai, if this is half as good as advertised..." Willa said in half-jest, half-challenge.

"Five, six, seven, and..." Jimmy counted off.

Forty seconds later, everyone in the booth was wall-eyed with excitement, and all but Cootie in ecstatic disbelief. *Now I know what it's like to see lightning caught in a bottle,* Willa scribbled on a sheet of paper and showed it around. *Wow!* Abe Felder wrote beneath it. Under that Cootie scrawled, *I hate to say "I told you so," but...*

Solly Felder doodled dollar signs on a yellow legal pad. The four technicians twitched in time to the beat.

After the second take, Cootie emerged yet again from the booth. "Fellas, so far, so good...but you've got to tighten up those bridges." The musicians stared at him, but did not argue. Cootie went to the piano and showed them what he wanted. Next, he demonstrated a syncopated bass riff he wanted Deuce to play on the choruses. After that, he worked with Lou on how to vary the "Cora Ann! Oh, Cora Ann!" vocal refrain. Finally, he made Jimmy's crescendo ending more skittering.

"Let's do a practice run," Cootie said. They did, and when they finished, everyone was pleased with Cootie's changes.

Still, after four more tries the band had yet to cut a winning take. Cootie came out of the booth. He sensed the musicians' irritation when he called for another take; he knew how tired they *had* to be.

"That last one sounded just fine to me," Jimmy said, his drawl slower than usual. His bandmates muttered agreement.

Willa came out of the booth. "We're not saying anything was *wrong* with it. We just want to try for an even better cut." The musicians stared at her, but did not argue.

Abe Felder came out of the booth. "We're goin for the whole shot here, fellas. This can put a lot of new faces on the musical map. We're not goin for pretty good; our aim is to get as close to perfect as we can." The musicians stared at him, but did not argue.

Solly Felder came out of the booth. "What say we try a couple more takes, and if need be, we'll call it a night, and hit again after a good night's sleep."

The musicians wagged their heads in agreement. "Solid," said Deuce, "but let's try to nail this thing down before we split." Everyone concurred.

After three more tries, everyone felt they had a take as near-perfect as possible. The dozen people in the studio stood frozen for the three minutes needed to play back the tape.

Cootie was the first to speak. "Cats and kitty—from where I come from, we call that a monster lurkin to be let loose." Willa, the Felders, and the technicians grinned in relief; supportive though he was of the group, they knew Cootie would not have said that unless he felt it was absolutely true.

The musicians censored whatever joy they felt. "Well," Lou said, "that vote of confidence nourishes my spirits, but not my belly. Let's kill that buffet." Cootie broke out three bottles of champagne. Lou, who had consumed perhaps a dozen beers since his high school graduation, had three Dixie cups of the sparkling wine. Afterward, he did not know if his giddiness was because of the champagne, the excitement over the potential smash, or sheer fatigue.

He decided it was a combination of all three, and left it at that.

Daylight greeted them as they left the studio. Cootie, aware that the quartet would be pulling out early Sunday, suggested Willa and he give them a tour of the city after some sleep, so both parties could get better acquainted. The musicians readily agreed.

"Solid," Willa said as she gunned the engine and pointed the car toward Harlem.

* * * * *

Saturday began shortly after two p.m. Willa and Cootie fixed the musicians a brunch of roast chicken, steamed rice, waffles, coffee, juice, and an array of fresh fruit. Next was a drive around the island of Manhattan: up the East River Drive to the Harlem River Drive, then down the West Side Highway, back up the East River Drive and across the Brooklyn Bridge, where Willa changed onto the Long Island Expressway. They motored along, with no particular place to go, exchanging life histories.

Cootie was relieved that all four had fulfilled their military obligations. Pearl Harbor had happened just months after Jimmy's graduation from Austin High. He had been immediately drafted, and saw combat in Italy, France, and Germany. Two years younger than Jimmy, Deuce began basic training at Fort Benning, Georgia, less than forty-eight hours after receiving his high school diploma. His three-year hitch ended in 1946, then he went on to play football at Tennessee A & I. Lou had also attended A & I, but was drafted after his freshman year. He served his three years stateside; he mustered out just August past; in December he joined the Jameson Quartet. Blondie enlisted in the Army Air Corps straight out of high school. He swore he had cheated certain death in at least three firefights in Korea.

"Which means you're still around for a purpose," Willa said.

"That's what I like to think," Blondie responded.

The musicians filled Willa and Cootie in on the chronology of the band, and how each became involved. That finished, Lou fired questions at Willa about her immersion into the world of R & B. She told how her father was a still-thriving civil-case lawyer based in the Negro middle-class enclave of Fort Greene, Brooklyn. Her mother was in her tenth year as a pediatrician at Harlem Hospital. Willa was the eldest of three children; her brother was a criminal attorney in Boston, her sister was a professor of history at Lincoln University in Pennsylvania.

The musicians were surprised to learn that neither side of Willa's family had any traceable Southern roots. Her brother, Stephen, had researched their origins as far back as the late 1700's on the McAshan side, and the early 1800's on the maternal side, the Sturdevants.

Willa had spent her childhood in Fort Greene. As a teenager, she often saw Richard Wright seated on a bench in Fort Greene Park, composing what would become the classic novel *Native Son* in long-hand on yellow legal pads. She told how she earned a B.S. in Political Science at Fisk in Nashville, and her law degree from Columbia.

Lou could not help but notice Willa's reluctance toward talking about herself; she appeared to be answering their get-acquainted questions out of a sense of obligation.

For Cootie, the reverse was the case.

Jammed between Willa and Lou in the front seat, Cootie held court about his high school athletic triumphs, how he broke into radio, and how he had met Willa, "the most fortunate event in my life," as he termed it. He prattled on about the R & B scene, politics, boxing, current movies, his beloved Willie Mays and the New York Giants, and life in general.

At twenty-five, Cootie was but two years older than Lou and Blondie. Claiborne Charles Coutrere was the youngest of the six children of Thierry and Felicia Coutrere.

Lou grinned when he learned Cootie and he shared a middle name.

"You're a—Creole—right?" Deuce braved to ask.

If Cootie took any umbrage, he did not show it. "Down in New Orleans, we're called either 'Creole Mulattos' or 'Creoles of Color,'" he replied.

"Is it true yawl don't consider yourselves true Negroes?" Jimmy asked.

"Most folks in New Orleans"—Lou loved the way Cootie pronounced it 'Nawlins'—"black, white, and Colored Creoles consider us a third race. Twilight. Neither, nor. Regardless, we're subject to the same Jim Crow laws as non-Creole Negroes," Cootie explained.

"Do *you* consider yourself a Negro?" Jimmy inquired. Lou, his left thigh pressing against Cootie's right, tensed at the faint challenge in Jimmy's tone.

Cootie laughed. "Man, I graduated from Howard, live in Harlem, and have stomp-down dedicated my life to rhythm-and-blues: now what do *you* think I see myself as?"

"Amen, brother," Blondie piped in from the back seat. Lou pecked into the rear-view mirror and saw Jimmy smiling at Cootie's response.

Cootie next mentioned the thriving funeral parlor owned and operated by Thierry Coutrere and Thierry's three brothers. He told how he became addicted to the various forms of the blues when he was but eight years old—though the closest thing to it his parents allowed on the parlor-room Victrola were records by Duke Ellington's Washingtonians and Noble Sissle's Society Orchestra—which featured a young chanteuse, Miss Lena Horne, on many cuts.

By age twelve, Clai was sneaking off to hear the raucous blues at its Treme district epicenter, a beehive of joints in the Basin Street/Orleans Avenue/North Claiborne area. Too young to go inside, he would—with other youngsters—station himself outside and feast on the overspill of the bouncy, bawdy tunes and lyrics. So that his parents would not wonder where he was, he concocted stories of sleeping over at friends' houses on Friday and Saturday nights. To his knowledge, he never came close to having this ruse revealed.

When Cootie was fifteen, Francesca, his oldest sister, got married. Playing at the wedding was the Seventh Ward Strut Kings. On piano for the Strut Kings was Andre Alexandre—

"Louisiana Fats!" Lou shrieked in utter glee at the mention of the singer's square name. Everyone laughed—and Lou loudest of all—at his little-boy's reaction.

A bond was formed between Fats and Clai that day. Young Clai literally followed the Strut Kings as they made the rounds of jazz and blues clubs, weddings, dances and parties. When Cootie promoted his first dance—during his junior year at Xavier Prep High—he hired the Strut Kings. In response to a question from Deuce, Cootie demurred from having anything to do with Fats' 1951 breakout hit, "The Fat Cat," which charged to the top of the R & B chart and stayed there for three months before Mike Turner and the Monarchs of Rhythm dislodged it with "Highway Rocket," which enjoyed an equally long reign at the top.

Cootie then told how he spotted Little Robert and His Go-Getters at New Orleans' Drop On Inn on New Years' Eve past, had them in a studio two weeks later, and "Hot Lana From Atlanta" on the airwaves and racing up the R & B and pop charts soon afterward. Lou's scalp tingled as he read between the lines: *That could be your story, too…*

Since Cootie had assumed that getting acquainted with the four would be an all-day venture, he had pre-taped this night's—Saturday night's—show. Dusk started to descend, and the huge brunch had long since been digested. Their next stop was in midtown Manhattan. There Willa and Cootie treated the band to dinner at Toots Shor's. After dinner, they returned uptown, to the Apollo Theater, to catch an R & B show.

Once inside the theater, Willa nudged Cootie and smiled as the four gawked at the lobby, the stage, the orchestra seats below them, the balcony behind them, and the box seats that Cootie had finagled at the last minute. They seemed to be soaking up every detail, committing it all to memory. "They look like they're in the most sacred of cathedrals," Willa whispered to Cootie.

He stared at her in disbelief. "They *are*."

The show itself was unremarkable. "Sorry we couldn't have brought you here on a night when somebody *really* fantastic like Claude McPatter & the Wanderers or Hal Dillard & the Moonlighters or Little Johnny Wills or—"

"No, that's fine, Miss Willa. Just seeing the place is thrill enough," Lou said.

By then it was eleven p.m.—usually early on a Saturday night for all involved, but the Jameson Quartet had to hit the highway early tomorrow. The six climbed into the car for the short hop back to Convent Avenue. Once there, they congregated in the living room. The two teams silently, awkwardly sized each other up, like a boy and girl approaching the end of a first date and the obligatory good-night kiss.

Willa spoke first. "Gents, we still have a couple of bits of business to discuss. Would you prefer to do it now, or first thing in the morning?"

The eyes of Lou, Deuce, and Blondie all gravitated toward Jimmy. He read their preferences. "Let's get it out the way right now," he replied.

Cootie, perched next to Willa on a sofa, inched forward and placed his hands on his knees. "Here goes. No two ways about it, we've got big plans for 'Cora Ann.' The Felders *could* rush everything and have it out in two weeks, but…"

"…They'll take their sweet time," Willa continued, "and make sure it's marketed properly, gets in the hands of the most influential jockeys—"

"Excuse me for cuttin you off, Miss Willa," Jimmy darted in, "but what colored jockey's got more clout than Cootie?"

Cootie sat back a little. "Top colored jockey, yeah—but I'm just one cat. No *one* jockey can make a side a smash. Bet the farm on this, though: Roy Rogers never rode Trigger as hard as I'm gonna ride 'Cora Ann.'"

"The Felders will have to—contact—deejays all over the country," Willa said. Her emphasis on "contact" made her subtext clear.

Lou tasted something cold and brackish at the top of his throat. "Can't the jockeys just *hear* how good the song is and realize it *deserves* to be a hit?" he asked, his voice quivering.

Cootie grinned grimly. "Man, *never* give studs who spin platters for a living too much credit for smarts."

"You boys have already done *your* job, in the studio," Willa said in her most assuring tone. "Now it's up to the Felders—with our help—to move that record. And there's no flies on us," she said, brushing imaginary ones off Cootie and herself.

"You're in the best possible hands," Cootie said in a case-closed tone.

Silence, then Deuce spoke. "Cool. We got as much faith in yawl as we dare." The others nodded their agreement.

"You boys shouldn't fret about the song *flopping*. Any record that gets the push we're going to give 'Cora Ann'—and 'Botheration,' afterwards—is a lock for the R & B top five and top-twenty on the pop charts," Willa said.

"Which is not to say our push will be the only—or even main—reason they'll be hits," Cootie amended.

"The question remains: what happens *after* these two sure shots?" Willa continued.

"We dig," Blondie said. "Our popularity, professionalism, how bad we want the limelight..."

"Like, yeah," Cootie said.

Next came the issue of Willa's managing the group. Though this was a foregone conclusion in both camps since the recording session, the formality of the band hiring lawyers to scrutinize her contract loomed. "We'll get on this right away, and get back to you as soon as we can," Jimmy said as he accepted a copy of her contract.

All present knew the chance of the band *not* joining Willa McAshan's fold was the same as a plump turkey greeting the sunrise the Friday after Thanksgiving.

"Like Blondie said, *you-all* will largely determine your own status, and therefore how many gigs I can line up for you," Willa said. "Provided you come aboard..."

"In case you haven't noticed, my lady fair and I have grand plans," Cootie said with a sly smile. "You cats could be—should be—a big cog in our wheel. However..."

"...My standard contract calls for a three-year commitment," Willa took the baton. "If anyone has any pressing issues in terms of family, wives, girlfriends...or jobs...remember that if you sign the contract, you become *professional* performers..."

The musicians batted around a less-than-comfortable look.

"...So you better give this some heavy thought," Cootie said. "Once we put you out on that road, you won't be in Kansas any more."

Blondie made a face. "But we're from Tenne—"

"He was referring to Dorothy in *The Wizard of Oz*," Lou whispered sideways to him.

"Oh."

"I want you boys to think this one through—but *please* don't take too long about it," Willa said.

"Any serious qualms any of you have now can foreshadow future problems, so be honest with yourselves," Cootie said.

"We will be," Jimmy replied.

Silence. Then Cootie rose, stretched, and yawned mightily. "That settled, fellas..."

Willa rose and stood next to Cootie. "We know you've got a long trip ahead of you…"

From the corner of his eye, Lou saw Willa's fingers gently stroke, then encircle Cootie's. He covered her hand with his free one and squeezed. Lou suppressed a smile.

The bluesmen hugged Cootie, gave Willa a goodnight kiss, then enjoyed seven hours of deep sleep. In the morning Willa and Cootie prepared another sumptuous meal, packed them a lunch, and vowed to let them know the exact moment Cootie would give "Cora Ann" its maiden spin. "It'll be four or five Fridays from now," Cootie told them.

"Friday's always the best day to release a record," Willa explained. "It's the start of most people's weekend, so any new record they hear sounds that much more joyful."

Minutes later, the Jimmy Jameson Quartet was headed South.

* * * * *

Drained, physically and emotionally, the four were eerily quiet as they sped down the New Jersey Turnpike.

Behind the wheel, Lou gazed often at Deuce and Jimmy in the rear-view mirror, and Blondie in the passenger seat to his right. All kept nodding off, but never fully, never for long. He knew they would be reluctant—if not too tired—to talk, but he *had* to air some things.

"We can't ask for a better start, can we?" he asked, rhetorically.

"I'm just hopin it's not all too good to be true," Jimmy drawled, half-awake.

Blondie bolted to full alertness. "Don't forget, man, we are brass-assed *talented*! Some people freakin *deserve* success—us among them!"

"Blondie, don't cuss on the Lord's Day—"

"*What*, Lou? All I said was 'freakin!'"

Lou scowled at Blondie and addressed Jimmy and Deuce. "You cats satisfied the folks we're with are on the up-and-up?"

"Like you said, Lou, we couldn't of asked for a better start."

"Gee, Jimmy, don't admit it so reluctantly," Lou replied, unable to squelch a smile.

"I got me one worry," Deuce said. "Just one—but a big, nagging motor-scooter."

"Let's hear it," Blondie said.

"There's a certain balance in this world, in nature, in everything everyone does. In life in general, show business in particular, those

who have it too easy on the front end of their life, their career, usually pay for it later down the road," Deuce said. "I mean—Swampcat
comes to see us—once—makes a call to Cootie, he slides by, signs us
up and presto-change-o: we're on the verge of a hit record! Excuse
me if I think it all happened too—quickly!"

"Hey! We were at the right place at the right time! And it *is* our
time," Blondie said.

"And if it seems like we got—lucky—just remember what Coach
Dusty Lennon always says: 'Luck is what happens when preparation
meets opportunity.' When opportunity knocked, we answered the
door loaded for bear," Lou added.

"And if you think we didn't pay enough dues, then what about
that incident in the summer of '51?" Blondie demanded. "You cats
paid then for all of us now. Account settled."

"And where does it say one has to *suffer* to make it?" Lou continued. "If you're good, you're good, and folks are gonna see it."

"Say what you want," Deuce argued, "if we *do* have as big a hit
as Cootie expects, it was too quick, too easy."

"Deuce, Jimmy, get this through your skulls: we were *meant* to
be stars!" Blondie cried. "The planets aligned just right when we
were born, or our ancestors all got steered to Knoxville, or my ass
survived Korea, or the Good Lord pointed us toward each other, or—
something! But this was mapped out probably before our parents
even met!"

"I believe that to some degree, too, Blondie, but I also see a lotta
truth in what Deuce says," Jimmy offered. "Life, nature, this world
does have a certain balance…"

Nickel-sized raindrops pelted the windshield with frightful sud-
denness: the mildly gray clouds held no hint of such ferocity. Lou
flipped on the wipers, which were slow to respond. "Like Mister
Cootie said, we're not sashaying into any tea party," he said. "I *realize* we got over that first hump pretty easy. I also know that whatever road lies ahead is gonna have its bumps. We've gotta be careful as
all get-out, at all times. That's something we can all agree on, right?"

"No argument here, partner," Deuce said, and the others agreed.

Blondie slouched and pulled his stingy-brim hat over his eyes.
"You cats can philosophize all you want. I'm gonna relax, doze off,
and have me some sweet dreams about bein a rhythm-and-blues star,
don'tcha know."

Lou nodded to him. "Blondie's got the right idea. Our music
should be about *fun*."

"Should be…but life's gotta interfere at times…"

"Jiiiimmeeee…"

"Okay, Lou. Just tryin-a provide the voice of reason, is all."

Blondie's first snore rang out like an electric buzz saw cranking up.

The rain pounded harder, as if someone stood atop the car, dumping buckets of water on the windshield. "Durn," Lou hissed, "if this gets any worse, I'm gonna pull over for a spell…"

"Just go slower, take your time, be extra careful," Deuce said.

The wipers arched valiantly on the windshield. Their rhythm sang to Lou: *Be care. Full of. What you. Wish for. You just. Might get. It be. Care full…*

* * * * *

Part Two

"Summer 1955"

CHAPTER NINE

Friday, May 13, 1955; 12 noon.
Abyssinian Baptist Church, Harlem, New York.

"We're here, and we're all ears. Now convince us to bankroll your high-toned race-music revue," Roscoe "Lumpy" Jackson, Harlem's legendary vice king said as he swiveled his head from Willa at one end of the oblong table to Cootie at the other. His tone was at once challenging and supportive.

Cootie and Willa looked across the table and shared a smile. Of the five prospective backers present, three would be fairly open-minded: Lumpy, who represented the East Coast's Negro sporting-life barons; Reverend Carter Epps, who stood in for a cadre of well-heeled ministers who had no qualms about backing a secular venture; and Doctor Erskine Thalmers, the emissary for several physicians and lifelong friend of Willa's parents. If anything, Willa and Cootie had to be careful not to say anything that would dissuade the three.

The other two would be a much harder sell. Stetson Caldwell had the largest clientele among professional athletes and entertainers of any Negro attorney in the country. As he had warned at the first meeting, it was his duty to be skeptical of all such pitches, nothing personal. Doctor Harvey Manlius, delegated by the group of educators whose backing Cootie and Willa sought, seemed ready to die from boredom barely two minutes into the meeting.

Cootie and Willa noted the awestruck looks Epps, Thalmers, and Manlius kept sneaking at Lumpy. At the height of the Great Depression, in a bloody, deliberate fashion, Lumpy and his army had forced the Irish, Italian, and Jewish mobsters from Harlem. After two decades and several attempts by them to seize it back, Lumpy still ruled. And with his whipcord physique, gravelly voice, and scarred face, Lumpy looked every inch the victor of hard-fought wars…

Willa and Cootie, along with their attorney, Peter Goldfarb, and financial advisor, Chadsdale Worthington, had narrowed the number of those present for this, the second meeting. The goal was to rope in backers for their planned touring rhythm revue. The first talks had been in late January, in Willa's law office on 125th Street. Starting in December 1954, they had distilled a roster of two dozen affluent Negroes from all walks of life who might be receptive to the idea. Surprisingly, all invited attended. The conference was mostly to whet their appetites; Willa and Cootie readily admitted that more concrete plans were still in the works. They and their advisors considered the January meeting a success; many of the invitees were openly enthusiastic, while those with reservations expressed them tactfully.

Over three months later, with new ammunition at hand, Cootie and Willa called a second meeting. This time, though, they broke their list of prospective backers down by profession, and urged all to delegate one person to sit in for the rest. They scheduled the meeting on a workday Friday. "We know you-all are super-busy, and don't want to take you from what made you successful in the first place," Cootie told them all personally.

Of course, the subtext behind this ploy was obvious: the fewer present when they explained their more precise plans, the fewer dissenting comments and sticky questions.

To lend credence to the event, they scheduled it in a room in the basement of the Abyssinian Baptist Church. That alone hinted at the sanction of the beloved congressman and minister, Alan Payton Howell. The sheer grandness of the landmark building underscored the importance of the mission. Furthermore, it planted another seed in the invitees' minds: *If these two were up to anything shaky, they wouldn't try to pull it off in* this *building.*

Also, Cootie and Willa *knew* they had secured the best people for legal and financial advice. Though well-versed in entertainment law, Willa realized her closeness to the project could sully her judgment on some issues. Thus, they hired Peter Goldfarb. His contract with a prestigious Manhattan law firm gave him leeway to do outside work. Forty-two years old, the eldest of five children of semi-literate parents from Austria, Peter had literally fought his way through undergraduate school as an East Coast champion wrestler. Just under six feet tall, he was but five pounds over his collegiate middleweight limit, and still competed in amateur road races when his schedule permitted.

Peter's combative spirit was a prime factor in their hiring him. His pit-bull tenaciousness would be needed in the months—and hopefully years—ahead.

That he knew the front and back of both entertainment and business law made him invaluable. Moreover, he was a social chameleon; two minutes after meeting him, Cootie forgot Peter was white. Yet,

Peter's race was a distinct plus. As Cootie often told him, "You've got the complexion to make the connections that'll ensure us protection."

They brought in Chadsdale Worthington to coordinate the sale of shares in the revue. Thirty-eight years of age, he had been the only Negro in his class at the University of Pennsylvania's Wharton School of Business. For over a decade he had served as the investment advisor to many of the East Coast's wealthiest Negroes—and had many white clients as well. Though medium-height, his wide-shouldered, heavy-boned frame made him appear shorter. His ebony skin covered features that resembled an exquisitely-carved African mask. A high, broad forehead, calmly receding hairline, and black horn-rimmed glasses added to his air of intelligence.

"Let's be clear on your basic premise," Reverend Epps said. "You've figured out an operating budget, and will sell that amount in individual shares, correct?" Cootie and his allies nodded. "Like buying stock from a corporation, on the Wall Street exchange?"

"Exact same set-up, sir," Cootie replied, then nodded toward Chadsdale. "That's Mister Worthington's area of expertise."

Lumpy looked from Willa to Cootie. "And you two will have majority ownership?"

"Yes, sir. Twenty-five-point-five percent each," Willa answered.

Lumpy's eyes narrowed and his face tightened, causing the scar that ran from the outside corner of his left eye down to his jawbone to writhe. "I have to ask you this—but you *don't* have to answer," he began in a manner that strongly encouraged compliance. "You're makin a pitch to the rest of us for the other forty-nine percent. Fine and dandy. But: there's only so many money sources open to—us. And since you can't spend the same dollar twice in the same store..."

"Which means you're wondering where we obtained *our* combined fifty-one percent, right?" Willa said from behind a Mona Lisa smile.

"That's exactly what I'm wonderin." Lumpy made an all-inclusive gesture. "And so are the others, I'm willin to wager." Nodding heads confirmed this.

Willa leaned back in her chair. With a look, she told Cootie to answer the question—or evade it. The others caught the look, and all eyes swiveled to Cootie.

They missed her second silent signal to him.

Cootie laughed nervously. "We *don't* have to divulge it, right?" Lumpy cocked his head and nodded. "Thank you. We'd prefer not to," Cootie continued.

Mild disappointment showed on several faces. Peter stepped in. "Hopefully, you won't hold that against us—"

"Hey! We all got trade secrets we gotta keep," Lumpy interrupted.

Cootie and Willa studied their guests. Lumpy's question seemed to stem from normal curiosity; Caldwell and Manlius appeared to want more details. Reverend Epps looked like he could not have cared less, while Doctor Thalmers already had a strong idea as to the source of Willa and Cootie's seed money.

Cootie and Willa had elected to raise their shares separately. Cootie secured loans from several friends in the business. However, the bulk of his money came from his large extended family in New Orleans. Yet joyful and relieved though he was to have it, the cash from his relatives came at a great cost, and not necessarily in money.

If the show turned a profit, Cootie was to pay the money back, with a nominal interest fee. However, if it failed, Cootie would *not* have to return the money. Rather, he was to forsake show business— for good—and enroll in law school, as his family had planned for him since he was ten years old.

Chadsdale and Peter frowned when he told them of the pact with his relatives. "If, God forbid, the revue *does* go belly up, do you intend to keep your end of this Faustian bargain?" Chadsdale asked.

"It will not fail," was Cootie's cold, quiet reply.

"Nothing is fail-proof," Peter cautioned.

"This *cannot* fail," Cootie's voice throbbed with desperate determination...

As of this, the second meeting, Willa had gathered nearly all her twenty-five and a half percent. Her sources were colleagues from her profession, friends from the chain of exclusive schools she had attended, and lifelong acquaintances from her parents' tight, elite circle of Negroes from all professions. She had patiently strung together numerous small loans. Most were for one-hundred dollars, with an occasional high-roller sporting her to five-hundred or a thousand dollars. The legwork and endless telephone calls had been nerve-wracking. Yet, like Cootie, she derived great pleasure from the hunt itself...

Chadsdale passed around ledger sheets and gave everyone time to study them.

"Is this just a rough estimate of your start-up budget—or one that's as precise as possible at this point?" Caldwell inquired.

"Close as can be, all things considered," Willa replied. The grand estimate was based on the current rates for rentals of venues, travel expenses, insurance fees, advertisements, security, and hotel accommodations. The figures for performers' and musicians' salaries, and discretionary funds to grease the palms of local police chieftains and fire marshals were more hypothetical. Also included was money designed to have judges look past any troublesome company members would invariably stumble into.

"You've covered practically all the bases," Caldwell said. "I'm impressed. Especially your foresight with this look-away money."

"Strange things happen out there. One never knows—do one?" Cootie replied.

Doctor Manlius asked what they had in mind for a board of directors.

"Six people, none who will have any major financial stake in the show," Willa answered. The board members would be from a cross-section of professions. "We'll include at least one white person, and one woman," she wryly added.

"An all-Negro board might smack of reverse segregation, so we'll suffer one token white." Peter Goldfarb said with a straight face. Lumpy was the first to catch the joke, and laughed throatily.

"Conversely, we can't have *too* many whites," Chadsdale said. "That suggests two things: Negroes aren't smart enough to succeed at business and, that Miss McAshan and Mister Coutrere are only fronting for whites."

"Which is the rumor that's gonna fly, irregardless," Lumpy snorted. "And niggers is just as bad as white folks when it comes to thinkin Negroes don't have no business sense." His panning glare at once dared dispute and sought sanction. Most nodded their agreement.

Loudly, Cootie cleared his throat. "Any questions, comments so far?" he asked, carefully.

"Yes." The syllable clattered from Caldwell's mouth like a fist-sized cannonball onto a marble floor. "After the first meeting in January, my clients were quite—enthusiastic. However, the more time we've had to think about it, the more that excitement has…waned."

From the corners of their eyes, Cootie and Willa caught Manlius, Epps—and even Thalmers—making tiny nods of agreement.

"As can be expected," Chadsdale smoothly interjected. "The fizz on the champagne dissipates before long. But—does anyone have any *particular* cause for concern?"

"Yes. The similar shows planned by Adam Freeman, and by Jimmy and Vivian Bradford, using their Jay-Vee recording artists," Caldwell replied. "It's all over the grapevine."

Again, Thalmers, Manlius, and Epps nodded. "That's hardly a secret in the R & B world," Cootie said.

"The R & B world is too *tiny* to have secrets," Willa added.

"They have likewise wooed us for start-up capital," Manlius said.

Cootie felt the room grow warmer. On one hand, the two shows out of Chicago and Cootie's would work together, stagger their itineraries, stay out of each other's way, avoid wearing out welcome in any one area. Still, they *could* cancel each other out, despite that strategy. Nobody had a clue about the potential for live audiences in this new music, and in what regions.

Willa and Cootie, convinced their proposed line-up of talent was superior to Jay-Vee's, were not overly concerned about competition from them. If anything, though, Cootie could see himself coming up short in his friendly but intense rivalry with Adam Freeman. Cootie conceded that Freeman was more influential than he in this fledgling new world. Freeman's show would be integrated—which could prove to be either a breakthrough or a blunder. Moreover, Freeman's seniority—and his race—afforded him a wider, more affluent pool of backers...

Without divulging details, Willa stated how the three shows would work in synch, creating, in essence, a road trilogy, rather than three competing companies.

"All that's well and good," Lumpy declared, "but it's *your* show we're considerin investin in. 'Trilogy' or no, how're we supposed to know yawl can outdraw the other two—and that's not to mention any other shows yawl *don't* know about yet."

Cootie's eyes and voice were cold with assurance. "No matter *how* many shows pop up, one truth remains: we've got the three hottest acts in R & B—Louisiana Fats, Little Robert, and Hal Dillard & the Moonlighters."

"Record-sales figures don't lie," Willa said. "Fats and the Moonlighters have been playing ping-pong with the top two spots on the R & B chart for most of the past two years."

"And here's another feather in our caps: Fats and Roberts' records are taking off with white buyers—by far more than any other R & B artists," Cootie added.

"Getting racially-mixed audiences will be the key," Worthington stated. "Jay-Vee's show should do okay in the Midwest, but their artists' airplay is spotty on the coasts, and they've never shown more than middling appeal to whites."

"Freeman's show should be able to draw the type of integrated crowds we're after," Peter interjected. "But none of his artists, colored or white, have...what's the word I'm looking for?"

"Crossover," Willa said softly.

"Yes, 'crossover'—good word—appeal," Goldfarb concluded.

"There just aren't many—crossover—artists, and we've got the two biggest so far," Cootie shouldered in. "*And* we've got another one chomping at the bit." Several pairs of eyes swung toward Cootie. He placed an acetate copy of "Cora Ann" onto a turntable and hit the switch.

Three minutes later a thick silence greeted the song's fade-out. "Well?" Willa said, more of a dare than a question.

"What the hell was that?" Lumpy blurted. "Country? Boogie-woogie? R & B?"

"Yep, yep, and yep," Cootie replied.

"Shit man, I love it!" Lumpy cried. The others murmured their agreement.

"The artists—colored or white?" asked Reverend Epps.

Willa smiled. "For the record, colored." She put a forefinger to her lips. "But for now that's our secret."

"That could be a song *everyone* buys—city Negroes, country Negroes, hillbilly music fans, white city kids…or…it could connect with *none* of them, because it tries to please everyone," said Doctor Thalmers. Every head in the room bobbed in agreement. Cootie and Willa shared a wincing look; Thalmers had voiced their biggest concern.

"Still, this group, the Jimmy Jameson Quartet, seems like the best bet for—" Cootie was already in love with the word "—'crossover' success." He held the disc aloft. "Gene Autry never rode Champion like I'm gonna ride this bad motor-scooter here."

Caldwell spoke up. "Granted, you're a big man on a big station, but you're *only* one broadcaster. How're you going to get deejays across the country to push this tune?"

Cootie's smile was ironic. "Just about every jock, colored and white, who pushes R & B owes me—big time—for promoting artists *they* have an interest in. If you know what I mean."

"Yep. One hand cain't wash itself. Takes two," Lumpy replied.

Cootie brandished the disc again. "This will bring *those* accounts up to date."

"Who *are* some heavy hitters you've got pushing 'Cora Ann?'" Caldwell's tone was blatantly challenging.

"Clai has the Eastern Seaboard covered, of course," Willa said. "In the Upper Midwest, there's Freeman, and George 'Wild Child' Butler, out of Kansas City—"

Caldwell whistled. "Tough men. Things go according to plan, that's a quarter-million copies sold right there."

"Hopefully. Out west, there's Paranoid Floyd in the Pacific Northwest, and the Fantabulous One himself, who's got California sewed up for us," Cootie crowed.

"I'm impressed that much more," Caldwell said. "Another two hundred grand, maybe quarter-mil in sales."

"Hopefully," Cootie repeated. Lining up the West Coast jocks was easy. Since Cootie's childhood, The Fantabulous Fontaine had been his idol. Now Fontaine was his mentor—and had placed a heavy investment in the revue before Cootie could finish his pitch. The two talked several times a week on the phone; Fontaine gave him pointers and they traded show-business gossip. Moreover, Fontaine was not disturbed that Cootie had equaled, if not surpassed him in popularity and influence. That Fontaine was a millionaire several times over—due to a variety of ventures, not all show-business related—put him above such insecurities.

Fontaine's lofty regard in California was offset by his many enemies among the powerful, made over the years. He owned high-wattage stations in Los Angeles, Oakland, and San Diego. Like Cootie, his playlist heavily informed what other jocks spun. Any record Fontaine pushed *had* to be a hot prospect...

Walter "Paranoid Floyd" Boyd had jumped onto the "Cora Ann" bandwagon behind Fontaine. Of Irish, Jewish, German, and Italian ancestry, Floyd owned a string of stations in the Pacific Northwest and Upper Rocky Mountain states. Like many broadcasters, Floyd's radio voice was the opposite of his physical appearance. As Fontaine described him, Floyd was so square-looking and homely that he was actually cool and attractive. Pushing forty, tall, pale, and stick-thin, his fans had adopted his beatnik's style of dress, and parroted his offbeat catch-phrases.

Upon hearing "Cora Ann" for the first time, Floyd and Fontaine were so charged up that, independently, they demanded co-author's credit for the hard ride they would give it. However, they learned Freeman had beaten them to the punch. They settled on a bonus to be determined by the record's sales figure at the end of the year.

"What about the new gun on the scene? That baby-faced kid down in Philly, with the tee-vee show?" Caldwell asked.

"Rick Claxton. Yep. He's in the club," Willa replied. A murmur rose from those familiar with Claxton's rapid ascent. Starting with a smash radio show, Claxton had expanded with a local television program, *Philadelphia Jukebox*, which ran every day but Sunday. In September his show would go nationwide, though it would be shot in the same North Philadelphia studio. With Claxton's escalating clout, Cootie *had* to have him in their fold. Claxton was well aware of his influence, however, and had charged a steep fee to push "Cora Ann" on his shows...

"One thing concerns me," Reverend Epps interjected. "This favor-for-favor system you jockeys have—is it *legal*?"

"One hundred percent." Cootie's reply was so quick that it raised eyebrows.

"For the *jockeys*, that is," Peter amended. "Station owners can't accept anything."

"And in a few jurisdictions, a jockey could be liable for a bribery misdemeanor charge," Chadsdale added, with some reluctance. "Then again, someone would have to be really stupid not to work his way around that."

The guests nodded grimly. "Stop me if I get out of line," Caldwell began, "but I've *got* to say this." Cootie motioned for him to contin-͗. "I've dealt with Adam Freeman before, and I *know* he's gonna w ͬ his pound of flesh for 'Cora Ann.'"

"ͦ that a question, warning, insinuation, or what?" Willa asked, cooll͓

"A ͏ ͮning, I'd guess."

"Ever͔ ͤ involved knows what Freeman's role is," Cootie said in a case-clo͏ tone. Indeed, with Freeman, Cootie struck a reluctant bargain. Witho͏ ͤlling Lou Cannon, Cootie had maneuvered a co-authorship credit ͨ "Cora Ann" from the Felder brothers. Such an arrangement was c͏ ͮon. The true writer or writers often shared credit with the person ͮ ͳ could do the most to make the record a hit. "Lou will understand," ͏ ͭie told the Felders.

Freeman had flipped ͮ ͤn he heard "Cora Ann." "Best thing since Mike Turner's 'Highwa͓ ͦocket' back in '51," he crooned over the phone. "I thought Turner an͏ ͥs Monarchs of Rhythm would set the standard for the new music with that tune, but 'Cora Ann' will take it where 'Rocket' *should* have!" Freeman gushed. This pleased Willa and Cootie to no end; Freeman, usually stingy with his enthusiasm, had not tried to hide it.

Yet, they soon learned that Freeman's elation would be costly. He got right down to business. "Coot, you know the rules. I give it the big push in the Midwest, I gotta have my name on it as a writer, too."

Cootie knew it would be futile to argue. "Yeah," Cootie replied, "Cannon's already gonna shit a brick when he sees *my* name on his record. What the hell is one more?"

"Can the sarcasm. Just make this kid understand the rules of this trade-off."

"Yeah. He'll have to learn sooner or later," was Cootie's reply...

Doctor Thalmers spoke up. "Looks like all the stations that play Negro records are covered. What about the ones that don't, the pop and country outfits?"

"We were picky with the pop stations, going with only those who *will* play a 'clean' record by a Negro," Willa explained. "But, if—when—'Cora Ann' clicks, others will fall in line."

"And we've got a heavy push on the country & western stations," Chadsdale added. "The irony is they won't even know it's a colored band."

"Until *we* let the cat out of the bag, at the proper time," Willa said.

"Sadly, there's a ton of white folks who'd be crazy about the record, *until* they learned the artists are colored," Peter said.

"Solly Felder at Winchester came up with a brilliant idea," Willa said. "Two different flipsides." She rode out the baffled looks. "On the disc for the R & B stations, the B-side is a blues ballad, Cannon's 'Late, Late at Night.' For the country and pop stations, we're going to have the band cut a stomp-down hillbilly standard by Hank Williams or Bob Wills."

Caldwell smiled, if reluctantly. "You haven't let any grass grown beneath your feet."

Reverend Epps waggled his hand. "Sorry, but I'm *still* concerned about all the money it takes—to make *one* record a hit. The songs that 'crossed over' by Fats and Little Richard—"

"—Robert," Willa politely corrected.

"—*Robert*; did it cost you *this* much to promote them?"

"No...but this record's—unique sound—changes the rules," Willa replied.

"Believe it nor, but this one is not just about the money," Cootie said softly, earnestly. From across the table, Willa's glance cautioned him not to elaborate. Indeed, with the new rock-n-roll taking off, all the elite jockeys would kill to get the credit for discovering the new song, the new sound, the new artist that would propel the music to even wider appeal. All the top-line jockeys who had flipped over "Cora Ann" conceded Cootie had trumped them in that regard—*if* the song became a smash. Yet, rather than try to block their rival from making the magnificent catch, they lined up to help him—at a price, of course.

Astute businessmen all, they realized they would, in the long run, be helping themselves.

"Any questions so far?" Willa asked. "Any glaring omissions on our part?"

"When is this record coming out?" Doctor Thalmers inquired.

"At the best time to release a bouncy tune like this—just as schools let out for the summer," Cootie answered.

"Here's what keeps buggin me," Lumpy said, "the name of the band. The Jimmy Jameson Quartet just don't do it for ol' Lumpy." A loud murmur of agreement followed.

"I'm with you gents," Willa said. "They *definitely* need a moniker with more pizzazz."

"So change it," Lumpy said with quiet authority.

"Is that Jameson on the lead?" Caldwell asked.

"Nope. Jameson's the piano player and founder, but…" Cootie explained how the band skyrocketed, locally, when Lou Cannon joined.

"Decent voice, clever songwriter, excellent guitar picker, that Cannon," Caldwell said. "What's he look like?"

"Tall, lean, brown-skinned," Willa replied. "He gives ol' cute-boy a run for it in the handsome department," she said with a nod toward Cootie.

"Watch yourself, girlie," Cootie snarled playfully.

"He's got all the kitties cream—" she remembered they were in a church "—going ape over him. Natural-born performer; you have to see him to believe him. And you will, soon."

"Cannon?" Lumpy chortled. "I *likes* that name. You can have a blast with it."

Peter angled him a look. "You might be onto something, Mister Jackson."

"Coot, use that name *when* you rename the group."

"That we will, Mister Lumpy."

Lumpy rested the corner of his jawbone on an index finger, peered at Willa, Cootie, Goldfarb, and Worthington, then said: "Tell me if I'm wrong, but yawl seem to be gamblin much of your funds for your road show on 'Cora Ann' flat knockin the music world on its ass, right?"

"I thought about that, too," Manlius whispered to Thalmers, but loud enough for everyone's benefit.

"Let's say this," Cootie began, carefully, "if 'Cora Ann' catches on with both races…and prompts colored and white artists to copy that sound—yeah." He paused before he added, "The song could play a big role in the direction this new R & B/rock-and-roll is headed, and that would be a huuuge feather in our cap."

Silence, then Lumpy spoke: "So yawl know what you gotta do to make these Tennessee boys a sensation, the thing that's gonna separate your show from the pack," he said in a tone that was challenging, but supportive.

"Uh…yeah…that's about the size of it," Cootie said. From the postures and fidgeting of his guests, he knew the meeting did not have much longer to go.

Doctor Manlius spoke up. "Something we touched upon earlier has been nagging me. I would have mentioned it in detail then, but..."

Willa's smile nudged him onward.

"...I see possible trouble down the road. White kids buying Negro records—to any degree large enough to make any type of splash—would that be courting trouble?"

Willa and Cootie made eye contact across the table. They *had* given this some consideration, but their tunneled enthusiasm had blinded them to all but the most obvious downsides.

"How so, sir?" Willa asked, calmly.

"I can't pinpoint any particulars now. But, white kids letting Negroes into their homes—if only on their phonographs and radios...harmless as it seems to us, it's not going to sit well with a lot of the parents..."

Silence.

"Unfortunately, in the world we live in, that *is* an issue," Willa said, "but if it does become a problem, it will be one because of our *success*."

Another silence. Lumpy made a big show of checking his gold, diamond-encrusted wristwatch. "My, my. Time flies when you're talking turkey. Any time you're ready to release us..."

"Any final questions or comments?" Cootie tossed to the room.

Stetson Caldwell cleared his throat and stood. His gaze revolved among the hosts as he spoke. "Allow me to say this much. Everyone here admires—greatly—what you are *trying* to accomplish. You know what you want, and the path to take. You've even identified the— musical breakthrough—that could, should push you over the top..."

Cootie and Willa eyed the others, whose nods and tight faces showed their agreement.

"...I can only speak for me, and for those I'm representing, mind you," Caldwell continued, "but—when you've fully accomplished your self-appointed trial-by-fire, *then* I can encourage my clients to back your play."

"And I can't blame you for taking that approach," Willa said from behind a gracious, but strained smile. "I would too, were I in your shoes." Her gaze spanned the room. "I take it all of you feel that way, to some extent?"

"Yes, ma'am," Lumpy said, softly, empathetically. The rest echoed their agreement.

"As well you should."

Lumpy rose. "No mysteries here. You know what to do." He jerked his head toward the world at large. "So do it."

Cootie smiled thinly. *If only it were that easy...*

Handshakes and hugs all around, then the guests filtered out. "Well...?" Willa sighed, wearily, warily.

"Just because nobody signed on the dotted line today shouldn't get you down—" said Chadsdale.

"Down? Who's down, Chad?"

"Everyone knows we're still a work-in-progress," Peter said. "Overall, I'd say they left with—cautious optimism. And they'd be foolish not to have *some* qualms."

"True. Maybe I *was* expecting too much, too soon," Willa admitted. "The day is still young; we might as well start chipping into all the work that lies ahead," she added, but in more of an aside to herself.

"Yep. I'd better hustle down to the studio. There's a stack of brand-new releases I gotta give a listen to," Cootie said.

"And you better hope you don't come across one that's better than 'Cora Ann,'" Willa said, her spirits perking.

"If I do, I'll *sabotage* that motor-scooter," Cootie cracked. "And I'm not kidding, either."

"I know you're not," Peter said, laughing. A quarter-hour later, only Willa remained in the meeting room. There she plotted out which tasks she would get to, and in what order. That done, she returned to her 125th Street office. She frowned as she considered the long list of chores. Many of the jockeys continued to haggle over what it would take for them to spotlight "Cora Ann" hourly as their "Red-Hot Sure-Shot," "Pick to Click," "The Platters That Matters," or whatever they called their feature-of-the-week.

First thing tomorrow, she would call Phil Samuels of Moon Records and set up the session to record the country & western flipside. *Tell him to bring in a fiddler and a steel guitar player.* She would throw in a little something extra—no, a *big* something—for Samuels to run interference with the country jockeys.

She looked at the ledger that tracked where the promotion money for "Cora Ann" was going. *Great God! We won't turn a profit unless this song sells three-quarter of a million copies,* she thought, alarmed and inspired at the same time.

CHAPTER TEN

Tuesday, May 17, 1955; 4:32 P.M.
State Capitol Building.

After a long day of meetings, Theophilis Briscoe could finally relax in his office in his home state. He had been summoned to head a conference of gross importance. He propped his feet on his desk and poured a Jack Daniel's, neat, from the bottle he kept in the lower right drawer.

It was almost a year to the day since the Supreme Court handed down its landmark ruling on the Brown v. Topeka Board of Education case. The verdict ordered all school districts in the United States to desegregate "at all deliberate speed."

Theo's meetings had been with the supervisors of the state's local school districts; the goal was to make sure the speed of integration would be deliberately slow. The Negro superintendents were also present; Theo warned them that the sooner the schools integrated, the quicker their power would be diminished, or their jobs totally eliminated.

After the Negroes left, the white superintendents mocked them. "Those Knhee-grows sound lhike they whur rayzed in Jahllee Oahld Aing-lund—instead of Coontown, U. S. of A.," mimicked C.M. Whitcomb, the president of the Board of Education in the state capital, as he did an exaggerated imitation of Doctor Valentine Jones, the state's top Negro educator.

"Hey!" shouted Governor Emory Gladieux, a beefy, flush-faced man of fifty. "What do you call a burrhead with a Ph. D.?"

"Tell us, E.G.!" his lieutenant governor hollered back.

"A nigger with a Post Hole Digger!" shrieked Governor Gladieux, and the room roared.

As the laughter waned, Theo raised his hands. "All right, boys, let's settle." His serious look brought quick compliance. He swept the room with a glance. "Backward though nigras are, it's not entirely their fault, and we should strive to help them, by keeping them among themselves, and seeing to it they can take care of themselves as well as possible, without our interference."

"Amen, T.B.," chimed Governor Gladieux. "Long as they got everything to make 'em happy on their side of town, they'll leave us the hell alone."

Theo looked up and lifted his arms akimbo. "Exactly. Segregation in a nutshell. What's so complex—or racist—about that? Stay with your own, do for yourself, keep your ass outta places you're not welcome."

"Segregation, hell—you flat just described human nature its ownself," said the lieutenant governor. Everyone seconded that. Minutes later, Theo adjourned the meeting and thought of what he would do until he met his sister Amanda and her husband for dinner at seven. He noticed several telephone message notes scrawled by Rosa Pearl Atkins, his secretary since he had first served in the state senate nearly thirty years ago. *Shit. Polk Caterfield.*

His former boyhood pal, now the biggest tent-revival evangelist in the lower South, had called several times in the past three days, requesting a brief meeting. *Wonder what he wants? Can't be money; he's doin okay for himself in that category.* He splashed more whiskey into the glass. *I'll just keep dodgin 'im 'til he takes the hint and skedaddles.*

Polk Caterfield. Just goes to show how two lives can fly off in different directions. While Theo's had headed for an ivy-walled college campus, Southeastern Conference gridirons, law school, courtrooms, and board meetings, Polk's had spiraled wildly, sadly.

Polk was twice married and divorced before his twenty-fifth birthday. Six children had to be fed. Averse to the workaday life, Polk fell in with a gang that did burglaries and knocked over small businesses. He spent most of his late twenties and early thirties in and out of jail for penny-ante crimes. If his time among fellow criminals did not teach him how to evade law enforcers, it emboldened him to go beyond small game.

After a three-day bank-robbing spree, Polk was apprehended near Mobile. Later, he considered himself lucky when the judge gave him twenty years of hard labor. His three accomplices were killed in a shoot-out, in which they had slain two bystanders and a police officer. Polk, the would-be getaway driver, had squeezed under the seat of the car they had stolen for the heist.

Like many convicts, Polk found Jesus in prison. He implored his fellow inmates to see the light. Enough mended their ways and thus became less of a problem for the officials that they considered Polk's release after he served a dozen years. Upon Polk's request, Theo wrote a curt, formulaic letter attesting he felt Polk's turnaround was sincere, and that he was worthy of parole.

Once sprung, Polk immediately looked up his old pal. He caught Theo on a visit to their hometown of Athensboro. "I know you're ashamed of me and what I done, don't want nobody to know you *ever* knowed me," he had begun, but Theo cut him off.

"Don't ever think that. You served your time. And who don't know somebody who went astray?" Theo stated. Next, Polk asked Theo to help him find work. The senator got back to Polk three days later with a few leads.

"These is nigger shit jobs, Theo," Polk had scoffed when he cornered Theo in a downtown diner. "I coulda fount these my ownself."

"Best I could do, all things considered, Sunshine."

Polk turned on his heels and, except for crossing paths at a few funerals in Athensboro, they had not spoken at length in the eight years since.

In that time, Polk had become one of the most popular evangelists among the grassroots population in the Deep South. He traded largely on his similar working-class background, and his escape-from-hell angle. He spoke shamelessly—and, Theo figured, embellishingly—of his days as a burglar and stick-up man. "If the Lord could save a man like me, who was on a fast track to Satan's domain, think what he can do for you!" was his standard line, and thousands lapped it up.

Polk Caterfield. Bamboozlin suckers who got no clue as to who they are and what's going on in this world, Theo thought with an acrid smile. *Then again, if not him, someone else would be rookin 'em. Give him credit for the following he* does *have.* Nobody knew better than a career politician how difficult it was to gather a crowd, grab its attention, and keep it long enough to sway opinions in some fashion. *Lord. In a manner of speaking, we both come a long, long way...*

He surveyed his home-state throne room. It was on the fifth floor of the capitol building, which itself resembled a cross between a Roman senate house and a mansion on an ante-bellum plantation. Appropriately, Theo's office was directly over that of the governor. Emory Gladieux, like the two governors before him, was a mere figurehead for the man who really pulled the state's political strings: Theophilis Briscoe.

Theo had taken a page from Huey P. Long, the late former governor and senator of Louisiana. Long had been elected governor in 1928, but relinquished that post when voted to the U.S. senate two years later. Or, he conducted the charade of doing so. In effect, he ran the state from Washington, as Louisiana's *de facto* governor *and* duly-elected senator.

Any observer of the political scene knew that for the past dozen years, Theo Briscoe maintained a similar double grasp on his state's reins.

Continuing his inspection of his newly-remodeled office, Theo marveled at the fresh wood paneling on the walls—the better to keep in the artificially-cooled air. The wall to his right held portraits of President Jefferson Davis of the Confederate States of America and General Robert E. Lee. Opposite them, Generals Thomas "Stonewall" Jackson and Nathan Bedford Forrest stared keen-eyed from their canvases, meticulous in full parade-dress uniforms.

Theo smiled as he gazed at the brand-new carpet, and scuffed his shoes on it. Incredibly soft, it was the same blood-red shade of Ole State's school colors. He admired the grandfather clock that towered in one corner. It was a gift from the estate of Major John Mosby, the Gray Ghost himself. His gaze floated to two framed photographs on his desk: Cassandra, her husband, two girls, and a boy; Theo, Virginia, and their three daughters. He idly toasted the photographs with his half-filled glass of whisky.

Without warning, voices from the outer office roped his attention. Rosie Pearl was speaking to a man with a deep, craggy voice. Tempered heat throbbed in their voices, too muffled behind the thick, wooden doors for Theo to decipher. He checked the snub-nosed .22 in his middle right-hand drawer; he had cleaned it that morning, to occupy himself until the meetings began.

Silence rang for a long moment, then, as Theo expected, the phone cried. He punched the blinking light and picked up the receiver. "Yes, Rosie—"

"Sir, a—gentleman—is here and wishes *desperately* to see you, to use his own words." Theo detected apprehension in Rosie's voice, though she maintained a steady tone. "Polk Caterfield. *The*," she added. "Says he's been trying to reach you for days—"

"Tell him I'd *love* to talk to him—and will—but can't right now. I've got work up to my armpits," Theo said calmly. "Tell him to leave a number, and I *will* get back to him, pronto."

Silence, then Rosie Pearl spoke again. "Sir, he says you've *been* putting him off, and that he's *got* to see you—" she stopped. More muffled conversation crackled on the other side of the door. Then, in half an eye-blink, Polk Caterfield burst into the room and gobbled the fifteen feet from the door to Theo's desk in four strides. Rosie Pearl swept along in his wake, her fear-widened gray eyes further enlarged by her bi-focal spectacles.

"You can't just barge in like this—"

"Dammit, Theo—I hate ta hafta resort to this, but you leave me no other—"

"Senator, sir, I *tried* to stop him, but he—"

"Back the fuck *off* me, woman—!"

Theo bolted to his feet and pounded on his desk with both fists. "Dammit, was there a break-out at the loony-bin?" he thundered. "Calm the hell down—both of you!"

They fell silent for a long moment, then, as if in delayed reaction, caterwauled again:

"Senator, this—maniac—insisted that I—"

"Theo, tell this old biddy to beat it so's we can talk—"

Theo repeated his two-fisted assault on his desk top. "What'd I just say?" he roared. They responded with silence, looking like scolded children. Theo nodded toward the door. "Rosie, step out so me and Polk can—"

"You sure that's awlright?" Rosie asked as she cast a wary glance at the tall, spindly, hawk-faced man.

Theo tried to smile. "Hell, I been handlin this yahoo before dirt got invented. Ain't nothin a coupla old pals cain't hash out..."

Polk set his razor-thin lips into a triumphant sneer at Rosie Pearl.

Rosie peered at Theo, then Polk, and back to Theo. "You *sure* ever'thang's gonna be awlright, senator?"

"Of course," he said, then pushed a more successful smile in Polk's direction.

With her left thumb and index finger, Rosie tweaked the rims of her spectacles. Theo tapped three times with his index finger on his desk top, his fingernail making a clicking sound. He grinned at Rosie. "Now be a good girl and skedaddle."

"Whatever you say," she sighed as she backed out of the room.

Theo motioned for Polk to sit in a chair close to the desk. Their eyes never unlocked as they slid into plush, purple-maroon chairs. Though seated, they resembled two circling cats.

Theo studied Polk as Polk studied him. Though Polk was as thin and stoop-shouldered as ever, Theo had to admit Polk's last few years had been good to him. Everything was the same but the eyes. China-blue and saucer-like, they had once skittered nonstop under his forehead; now they were as clear and calm as ocean water on a windless day.

Before, Theo could easily guess what was going on behind the ice-blue circles; now, Polk had mastered the art of using his eyes as blinds to obscure his thoughts.

Suddenly the realization of what Polk *really* wanted struck Theo like a sucker punch. He wondered if Polk himself realized it...or would admit to it. Regardless, Theo sensed the heat in Polk's eyes, despite the blank expression on the leathered, pinkish-tan face.

Whatever he does want, it's hurting him like hell to have to come here and ask me for it.

They continued to study one another, like a couple on a blind date, each debating the other's pro's and con's. Theo hid a frown as he pondered, *He's obviously in great need of something, coming here like this, after all this time. If I grant him what he wants, he'll be impossible to get rid of, like a dog that keeps showing up on your doorstep, no matter how you try to shoo him.*

He realized he was staring too deeply at Polk, so he lowered the intensity. *Yeah. Gotta let 'im know clearly we'll remain quits with each other. But I can't get him so steamed that he flies outta here half-cocked. After all those years in prison, the bitterness, the way some folks look down on his brand of worship—and some of his followers viewin him as some sort of half-holy man—you never know how he's gonna react, what's real and what's melodrama with him. Guys like him are always just one step away...*

Yet, Theo did not fear that Polk would resort to physical violence. *He's not that crazy; I could always lick that skinny fucker with one arm tied behind my back. He does have a temper, but he knows who to fuck with and who to back off from...and he knows me well enough to know I got to have a roscoe in one-a these-here drawers...*

Theo reached into the top left-hand drawer and pulled out a box of cigars, a gift from one of Cuba's tobacco magnates. "Have one?" he said as he nudged the box toward Polk.

"Don't mind if I do," said Polk as he rose and reached into the box. "Thank ya much."

Theo smiled lightly. "Hell, boy, take a few for the road. G'on, don't be shy."

Polk hesitated, looked at Theo, then pulled out but one more. "Thanks. This'll do me just dandy," he said as he slid back into the chair. Both lit up and continued their wordless inspections.

Polk's sheepish smile did not fit well as he nodded toward the family pictures on the desk. "Right purty gals you got you there. All four of 'em. Cute granbabies, too," he said, clumsily.

"Thank you," Theo replied tonelessly.

Polk picked up his cue that it was time to begin the discussion proper. "Theo, I'm sorry I had to barge in on you like I did, but it seemed the *only* way I could—"

Theo deflected the rest with a wave of his hand. "I understand. The fault's partly mine. I should've got back to you in some fashion." This appeared to relax Polk.

"But—before we begin: let's lay down a few ground rules," Theo stated, and Polk twitched at the well-timed, sudden sternness. "First of all, this is a fine howdy-do, after all these years." He paused for even a mild protest from Polk, but there was none. Theo propped his heels on the edge of his desk, folded his hands across his midsection and swiveled his head around his handsomely-dressed office. He smiled contentedly.

"*You* came to see me, surely to ask for some favor. And, if this sounds like I'm pullin rank, talkin down, then that's how you interpret it. But remember where you are and who you're dealin with. There's more than a forty-odd year difference between then and now." Theo repeated his proud, panning gaze of his office and its trappings. "Let's keep this thing civil."

"Yes, sir...Senator. Man to man," Polk said with a smile most would have read as genuine.

Theo laughed inwardly. *Any preacher who packs 'em in like he does is automatically a good actor.* Aloud, he said "Sunshine, I know you didn't drop by to shoot the shit from long-ago days..."

Polk chuckled. "No, Theo, 'course I didn't..."

Theo eyed the whisky bottle and poured a quarter of a glass. "Want a snort?"

Polk pursed his thin lips. "Thank ya, no."

Theo responded with a scoffing smile.

"Hell, I ain't gone temp'rince or nothin like that, Theo. I got long work to do on a short day. Gotta be over to Lee City by six, all set up and ready to roll for nightfall."

"Well, hell, Sunshine—state your case, and we'll see what we can do you for," Theo said with a pleasant smile. *Don't bet on it, Bible-thumper.*

Polk leaned forward and placed a typed list before Theo. It contained the names of about two dozen of the larger cities in the lower South. In a column next to that was a list of parks and public spaces. Theo noticed at least half the words were misspelled, even many simple ones. Polk allowed Theo time to scan the sheet, then sucked in a deep breath and began.

"Long story short. These're burgs I'm due to preach in durin the comin weeks, and I flat-simple gotta pull some strangs to get me these here prime venues."

Theo picked up the list and feigned interest in it. "These are the biggest parks in their cities, Sunshine," he said noncommittally.

"Yup. Central-located, ev'r one. Draw me some big crowds...if I can get them spaces..." Polk looked hopefully at Theo. His brow furrowed at Theo's blank stare at the paper. "Theo," Polk continued, his voice quavering faintly, "your arm reaches as far as anyone's in Dixie. Mayhap you can get on the horn, put in some good words for your old bud...?"

Theo stared hard into Polk's disk-like blue eyes. On the surface they had a look not unlike a hound dog with his tongue hanging out, shamelessly asking his human to throw him a bone...but beneath that surface, Theo detected the years of resentment. He decided not to challenge that attitude, however concealed, just yet...

"Have you already tried to get the permits for these places?" Theo stalled.

Polk wagged his head up and down. "Yup. Stomp-down got denied." He braked himself. "Well, truth told, not by all. Some did grant me some spaces, but they was all third-rate, on the fringes of town."

So—what'd you expect? Theo thought. He flushed when Polk's flint-eyed look implied he had read that thought.

"Look: I know if I was Billy Sunday or Billy Graham astin for them venues, I'd of got 'em quicker'n soon," Polk groused.

"Not true, Sunshine," replied Theo. His furry baritone dropped two octaves. "Know this: I got a shitload of pull on the national scene, but that local stuff is a whole 'nuther shootin match."

Polk's eyes widened in disbelief, but his voice remained even. "Nationwide, statewide, local—Theo, what Dixiecrat's got more say-so on *any* matter than you?"

Theo smiled to himself. *He's gonna lose it before he leaves.* With a wave of his hand, he pushed the remark to the side. "My friend, I wish I were *half* as powerful as I'm made out to be." He paused to sip his bourbon. "And I'm a politician, remember? That means nearly half the folks I'd hafta talk to would be my foes, or foes of my allies."

Polk's only response was a tightening of his facial muscles.

G'on—say what you're really thinkin, gator-bait, Theo gloated internally. *Just give me the excuse I need to send you packin for all time.*

"Theo, we're still talkin, man-to-man?" Polk ponderously resumed the discussion.

Theo nodded, smiled mirthlessly, and cautioned with his eyes: *Careful, buster...*

Polk read the message, swallowing hard as his Adam's apple bobbed in his reed-thin neck. "Theo. I know the *real* reason them officials denied me permits for the best spots. They're confusin me with them minstrel ministers who got folks babblin in tongues, the snake handlers, the faith healers, them charlatans. The only thing I got in common with them is my travelin ministry, that I pitch tents and sometimes fire up flambeaux to draw a crowd. That's it. The only dif'rence in how me and 'respectable' preachers conduct business is my church is wherever I can set up shop…and that I appeal to the poor whites and niggers who them high-falutin ministers has forgot is Gawd's chidruns, too."

Theo took a casual sip of his drink. "*That's* why you get lumped with those who steal in the name of the Lord. The niggers and the poor-assed crackers. The spirit hits 'em, they don't react any different for you than they do for the faith healers and snake wavers."

"Thank you, my friend, for that honest assessment," Polk responded, his eyes unblinking and his voice without color.

"And don't take this wrong, Sunshine," Theo continued, carefully, "but there *is* that matter of those twelve years in the Alabama state—"

"I served my time! Ev'rbody knows that! I don't make no secret about it—"

Theo signaled for Polk to stop. "I know. But you know how some folks can't look past somethin like that."

"Tell me about it, brother."

Theo sighed internally. He did not want to insult Polk gratuitously, yet he had to keep him at a distance—and eventually make a permanent cut of ties. "Hell, Sunshine, don't think for a minute I look down on what you do, or how you go about doin it. A preacher's gotta deliver the Lord's Word in the best way his audience understands it," Theo said. He realized that might have sounded condescending, so he added: "Many a time when we was boys we'd sneak off and hear some fire-and-brimstone evangelists…"

Polk smiled thinly. "Yup…and I'd of *never* reckoned I'd one day be part of that world."

Theo nodded. "That's part of where I come from, and you can rest assured I'll *never* forget my roots, 'cause a man who don't acknowledge from whence he started is gonna end up never knowin who he is." Theo paused. "And nobody knows himself better than I know me."

"Likewise applies to this boy, bud," Polk said as he tapped himself above his heart. He then jerked as the grandfather clock pealed five times.

Theo gave the clock a long look, then slid his gaze to Polk. "You said you had to be over to Lee City and set up by nightfall?"

"That's what I said," Polk replied, having caught the hint.

"Forty-mile drive."

"Always has been."

Theo exhaled mammothly. "I'm sorry, Polk," he said as he tapped the list with his index finger. "I cain't help you in none-a these places."

Polk's pinkish-tan skin flushed crimson. He swallowed hard, then spoke. "I came to you, man-to-man. One old chum to another. What I requested should *not* be that difficult for you."

Theo smiled before he realized it. He had never heard Polk enunciate so precisely. Yet, Theo tightened his eyelids and repeated the earlier message: *Careful*...

Polk's anger retreated. "I cain't say any more than this, Theo: I *desperately* need you to run interference for me..."

Theo was silent. Polk continued: "But I cain't beg. Not sayin you'd want me to—and I know *you* wouldn't respect no man who would. But. I. Do. Need. Your. Help."

Theo looked and listened hard, disappointed that, despite all, Polk had not let slip enough anger to earn a permanent exile. *If the mountain won't come to Mohammed.* He said, quietly, evenly, "I told you from the giddy-up to watch your tone with me, boy."

Polk's eyes bulged in pained amazement. "Theo, I *been* monitorin my tone! I *cain't* be no more civil! You *know* that. You know me, my pride, and my temper."

Theo knew Polk's whining tone was an act, that it was killing Polk to play this role. It was time to force Polk's hand once and for all.

"Don't try to shit me, boy. That dammed-up resentment is jumpin off you like a heat from an iron stove," Theo snarled calmly.

Silence. Theo pictured the wheels spinning in Polk's head, and knew his former friend was debating whether to continue to take abuse or to fire back, the venues be damned.

Finally, Polk spoke, slowly, flatly. "If I resent ennythang, it's this mill you're runnin me through, right here, right now."

"I'm sorry you see it that way..."

Polk tendered no response, verbal or otherwise.

"Back to the issue that brought you here: these 'better venues' you're tryin to secure...they mean bigger collection plates, right?" Theo asked, returning to a civil manner.

Polk's eyes jittered as he tried to filter the question's true meaning. "Of course—though I don't measure success by the money we collect," he answered, tentatively.

Never taking his eyes from Polk's, Theo reached into the top center drawer of his desk and pulled out a leather-encased checkbook. He fondled a ball-point pen, opened the checkbook, and stared at Polk. "Money you need? How much? Name your figure—within reason, of course. And this is not a loan; consider this a contribution to your ministry."

Polk flushed crimson again. "Money, Theo? Hell, if I'd-a wanted to hit you up for some moolah, I'd-a slunk in here like a coon on welfare hand-out day. You can keep your money, my friend," he said, spitting out the last two words as he would tobacco slime.

They eyed each other, like boxers awaiting the next punch. *Polk's gettin a perverse kick outta all this, or else he'd of been long gone, the way I'm shootin him through the grease. Still, it's time to put a stopper on this dick-wavin contest,* Theo thought. He smiled meanly, then tapped the list again. "These here spots ain't why you dropped by, are they?" he said in a seductive voice.

"Kill the sy-kowlogy okey-dokey and talk straight, Theo."

"It's really about me acknowlidgin our friendship, as it were. If I made those calls for you, it'd give you a measure of respect...and some sort of—absolution—for your past misdeeds..."

Polk stared at Theo and said in a clear, cold voice: "You got *all* the answers, don'tcha? Then again, that's why you're the great, Honorable Senator Theophilis Briscoe, and I'm just a li'l ol' squirrel tryin-a get a nut." He added, backpedaling nimbly: "And I mean that in the most admirin fashion. Swear to Gawd I do."

"Thanks," Theo replied, "but am I right? Theo Briscoe 'acknowledges' Polk Caterfield, and presto-change-o, he jumps from the ranks of the tongues-speakers and serpent-diddlers to up close to Billy Sunday and Billy Graham. Am I right, or what, Sunshine?"

Polk's eyes avoided Theo's. "Sure ya right if you say ya right," he sing-song-ed.

Theo swallowed a remark about Polk and nigger catch-phrases. Instead, he picked up the list and pretended to study it again. After a minute, he looked pointedly at the list, then the phone, and finally, at Polk. For effect, he repeated the sequence.

Polk hunched forward and eyed Theo, the list, and the phone in a way that reminded Theo of a hound drooling over a blood-drenched, off-limits beefsteak.

"Am I right?" Theo repeated. "Respect? Absolution?"

Silence; Theo knew Polk's deep pride dangled between telling him what he wanted to hear, and telling him to go fuck a duck. He read Polk's flinty-eyed look: *You're gonna flat* make *me say it, ain'tcha?*

Theo's grin was icy. "Read all the classical tragedies. *Pride*. It's what laid low all those great heroes. Simple, everyday pride," he murmured.

Polk sucked in a deep breath, as if about to sprint through a gas chamber. "Yeah...there's more'n a few folks who'd look more favorably at me if you'd just..."

Theo feigned heavy consideration, then said, "On second thought, no can do. That would violate a basic American principal: the separation of church and state."

Polk cocked his head toward Theo. "Excuse me?"

"As an elected official, I can't use my influence to decide on church-related matters—"

"'Church-related?'" Polk sputtered. "I ain't got no friggin church!" He braked himself. He looked as if he had been pole-axed between the eyes. The pained, dazed, look dissolved into a chagrined frown, then he laughed sadly, softly.

"Fuck me—just fuck ol' Polk Caterfield, straight up the hoo-hoo. And don't bother with no Vaseline," he cackled.

"Nice language for a—man of God."

"I shoulda seen that one a-comin," Polk snarled. "Shoulda knowed you'd pull somethin like that. No, you couldn't tell me to fuck off from the git-go. Had to strang me along. Had to show me the candy from your side of the display case, let me press my nose to the glass, then sneak up behind me and mash my face against it. Fuck. I deserve what you just done to me. Fuck me. And you did—royally." Polk punctuated this with angry, staccato laughter.

"Dammit! You make out like I'm gettin some big thrill from not grantin your request!"

"Well, ain't you?"

Theo stole a glance at the clock. *What's keeping ol' Hez?* He rose from his desk, grabbed the edge with both hands, leaned forward and glowered at Polk. "Never once contacted me after you got out the hoosegow—"

"Did too! To ast you to help me find a decent job, place to stay—"

"Well—I *did* try to find you a job, gave you several leads—"

"*Nigger* work."

"Beggars and choosers, bud." *Where the fuck is Hez? He's usually Johnny-on-the-spot! Gotta get this peckerwood outta here. I'm startin to smell danger...*

Theo rubbed the bridge of his nose with his thumb and forefinger. He slathered his tone with a case-closed weariness. "Polk. One could say we're at the top of our professions. We were friends once. We still are in...in a manner of speaking. Let's keep it like that."

"Like *what*? We ain't 'friends' if you gonna play me like a cheap-ass gee-tar—!"

"Do not interrupt me. We'll let bygones be bygones. Maybe we can get back on more cordial terms. I pray to God we can. But I cannot grant your request. Understand that, walk out of here before one of us *really* says the wrong thing…okay, bub…?"

Polk rose slowly and took three backing steps toward the door. His grin had all the warmth of a coiled rattlesnake. "Okay, Theo. You win. Again."

"Polk, Polk, Polk. It's not about winnin or losin—"

"But we *do* share a secret, don't we?" Polk braved a step toward Theo. "Right?"

Theo reacted with a small, crooked smile. "Careful, boy," he growled. He remembered that his office might be bugged. He caught Polk's delight in his new discomfort. He pasted on a carefree expression. "Polk," he began softly, "I been in politics for over thirty years. If you think you're the first yahoo to half-ass threaten me, guess again. I'm hardly an unprotected babe wandering the woods…if you know what I mean…"

He and Polk traded twin glares.

"And you *know* what I mean, bubbachuck…"

What in holy hell is takin Hezekiah so fucking long?

Polk snorted a laugh. "You're *threat'nin* me? Like two cain't play this game?" He whisked a casual but pointed look at the photographs of Theo and his loved ones.

A bomb burst in Theo's temple, but he remained outwardly calm. "Such wicked thoughts for a man of God," he murmured, hotly.

"Got a problem that needs fixing?" a soft voice asked from beyond the cocoon Polk and Theo had spun around themselves. Polk turned toward the door, and flinched at the sight of the sturdily-constructed man.

Theo, from behind Polk's diverted attention, sighed with relief before he spoke. "Naw, Hez…an old chum paid me a drop-by…but now he's leaving." Silently, Theo scolded Hezekiah: *Boy, it took you long enough…*

Hezekiah smiled pleasantly. "Reverend Caterfield…" He gestured toward the door.

Polk picked up his hat. He looked at Hezekiah, who stood frozen in his gesture, then at Theo. Polk's voice was clear, even, and theatrically wounded. "I came in peace. Truly I did. To ast an ol' bud for a favor. But you…you just had to…remind me who was who and what was what…"

Theo's grin was vulpine.

Polk squeezed the brim of his hat as he backed toward the door in measured steps. He ignored Hezekiah and never took his eyes off Theo. "You're gonna rue this day, Theophilis Briscoe. As Gawd

Almighty is my witness, you'll pay for this." He swiveled to catch Hezekiah midway through a cat-like, carpet-muffled step, stopping the all-purpose man with a glare. He turned for one last look at Theo, then slowly, his spine a ramrod, marched out of the room.

Hezekiah waited until they heard Polk exit the outer office. "Sorry it took me so long, Boss. I was lifting weights—"

Theo waved away the apology. "No matter. It was your time off. Every man needs a few hours to himself."

"I'm on your clock twenty-four hours a day, Boss. Three-hundred sixty-five days a year."

"And I appreciate it." *And pay you damn well, my friend,* Theo thought, even if he had no idea what Hezekiah did with his salary. All Theo knew—wanted, *needed* to know—about Hezekiah was that he was thirty-seven years old, had elderly parents in Frankfurt, Kentucky, had survived a grenade explosion in World War Two, and was as loyal an all-purpose man as money could buy. It was the latter two facts that convinced Theo to hire Hezekiah five years ago, after he received several ominous letters. Prank mail or not, Theo would be prepared for anything.

"Did he make any threats, Boss? Outright or subtle?" Hezekiah asked, his tiny, gun-metal gray eyes glistening behind the black, horn-rimmed, thick-lensed glasses.

Theo gave it a long moment's thought. "Not really. Just a half-batty bible-thumper blowin smoke, is all."

"You sure he was just blowing smoke, Boss? Never can tell with those Jesus junkies."

"True." Theo further pondered the matter. "Nah...he had a notion to barge in here and let off steam he's been withholdin a goodly while. I know that peckerwood. He's all dirt, no crop."

"You—knew—Reverend Caterfield before today?" Hezekiah asked carefully. Theo briefly related their boyhood together.

"Just to be safe, though, we'll tape-record his services every now and again. Stay up on what he's saying, make sure he's not tellin tales out of school...if you know what I mean," Theo said. He noticed that Polk, in his haste, had left his itinerary list. He motioned for Hezekiah to survey it with him. "He's gonna be in Gulf City, sundown tomorrow. Can you make it?"

"Need you even ask, sir?"

"Good. And make sure he sees you."

"Done."

"Good man." Theo swatted Hezekiah on the shoulder. *Mercy, feels like he's iron plated.* He knew Hezekiah put in three hours each day in a gymnasium: lifting weights, swimming, boxing, practicing judo, and doing a smorgasbord of endurance exercises. Theo had seen Hezekiah run around tracks, swim laps in pools, and ride stationary bikes for lengths of time that belied his five-foot, eight-inch, two-hundred-plus pound frame and that he was at the threshold of middle age. Only Hezekiah's prematurely graying hair—styled in a severe crew-cut—gave indication of his true age. And though Hezekiah had never said so, Theo knew he could easily kill a man—and larger mammals—with his bare hands.

"Boss," Hezekiah said in a voice that was distinctly Southern, but neutral as to a particular locale, "I could touch him up a bit, send him a message…"

Theo chuckled. "Thanks, but that shouldn't be necessary. This time tomorrow he'll of either apologized, or forgotten it," he said, unconvincingly.

Hezekiah smiled grimly and shook his head. "I don't know, Boss. My gut tells me he's gonna be trouble. Somewhere down the road, a *big* problem."

Theo stared into Hezekiah's thick glasses. "If that day comes, we'll just have to take care of him, won't we?"

Hezekiah nodded. "All due respect, sir, but we could prevent any trouble if I—"

Theo stopped him. "Blowin smoke, is all. I *know* that pecker-wood." *Do you—really?* he asked himself. *Nah, drunk on Jesus or not, Polk's too smart to jeopardize what he's accomplished over some piddlin envy.*

Theo gave Hezekiah a smile of dismissal. With a grimace, the man-of-all-work padded out the room noiselessly.

Theo returned to his desk. He half-filled a water glass with bourbon and tossed it down in four gulps. Yet, rather than push back the encroaching image, the alcohol etched the picture that much sharper onto his mind's eye…

…he had to give it to Peggy she was clever she never settled into a pattern for seeing her nigger so the next time she begged out of a date with Theo he followed her again to the nigger's shack then following just closely enough to the negro's automobile not to be spotted, but staying within sight, he trailed them to an obscure hard-to-get-to spot on Lake Como and Theo watched the car from afar as he saw the rocking and heard the moaning and Theo thanked his god that his blood was as cold as the night was hot despite all so he rounded up Polk Caterfield and Clifton Clowers and Smack Releford and Smack's younger brother and a cousin and had them at the ready the next time Peggy tip-toed off with the nigger though he never told the boys exact-ly what was up so the next time she had a rendezvous with her black stud Theo and the boys followed them again stay-ing just far enough behind to see them without being seen and Theo parked a half-mile from the lake and had his boys hoof the rest of the distance lest they be discovered...

...but Theo never told them exactly what the mission was about except for there was a nigger who needed to be taught a lesson and they crept up on the rocking bucking Model-T (how could a nigger who sang the blues and lived in a shack afford an automobile?) and Theo's boys were sur-prised to see Peggy was the bitch to the black boy's dog in the back seat but the boys were nowhere near as shocked as Peggy and her black Injun she began screaming in a series of high-pitched yips while the nigger's thing was long hard and thick as a steel rod as he pulled it from Peggy but in nothing flat it shrunk to human size and things got really crazy when Theo pulled out a Peacemaker Colt .45 and pressed it to the nigger's temple and Peggy and the boys filled the air with screams and Polk and Clifton especially were pleading with Theo to let the darkie go he'd already had enough of a scare thrown into him and the nigger first pleaded for his life then suddenly seemed to accept his fate and began to speak in tongues to his god but Theo wasn't going to let him off that easily he flicked his gun barrel against the nigger's weapon and told him to get it up or get it shot off and the boys hollered at Theo that *nobody* could get it up under such a cir-cumstance but Theo told the nigger he might as well die in a white girl's poon 'cause he was gonna die anyway...

...then the strangest light clicked on in the nigger's eyes and he stared at Theo then motioned for Peggy to position herself so he could have at her from the back and then he stared at his peter as if to will it up and sure enough it went from a limp purple worm to a black kingsnake and he rammed it up Peggy causing her to scream her loudest of the night then never taking his eyes off Theo and his boys he rocked and rocked and rolled and rolled and soon Peggy seemed to forget the situation and moaned her pleasure and after what seemed like hours (though for whatever his reason Polk noticed the time which was only two minutes) the nigger achieved the height of his pleasure and as precisely close to that moment as Theo could gauge it he pulled the trigger and the nigger's brains spewed from his head and Theo's boys cried and screamed and hollered for nearly five minutes straight and when things finally calmed down Theo made them vow on the threat of death that nobody was to know who was in on this to let people think it was the Klan...

...and they left Peggy there and Theo offered to sport his boys to a brand-new whorehouse just over the county line but they glumly declined so Theo went by himself and had him his first genuinely black black whore not like the three or four light-bright-damn-near-white ones he had visited before...

He made them vow never to mention that night again among themselves, let alone anyone else. His action had made clear of what he was capable. Besides, they would be incriminating themselves—and even most fools know there is no statute of limitations on murder.

No, Polk neither hated him that much or was that crazy.

Since that night the event returned in his dreams, sometimes as often as two or three times a week. Shortly before he married Virginia, he visited a hypnotist. Without going into detail, of course, he told the hypnotist of a traumatic experience in his youth he wanted to forget, had to forget. Theo realized beforehand that the memory was probably too horrific to erase entirely. Yet, the mesmerist was successful in a sense: the event was largely blocked from his conscious mind...but since that night of the run-in with the young Negro outside Chattanooga—no, *Knoxville*—that hot summer 1917 night was creeping back into his dreams, once every week or two now.

And then came Polk with his shit...

Theo briefly considered another trip to a hypnotist, but vetoed it. *That memory ain't never gonna fully die.* He gave more thought to Hezekiah's suggestion to lean on Polk, but again deemed it unnecessary. *Nah...Polk is crazy, but like a fox. He wouldn't jeopardize all he's accomplished just like that...*

His nerves still jangled from the encounter. He took a long swill of the whisky, this time straight from the bottle, to calm them down.

CHAPTER ELEVEN

Tuesday, May 17, 1955; 7:20 p.m. Knoxville.

Lou and Blondie had just joined Jimmy and Deuce for their Tuesday brush-up when Jewelle, Jimmy's wife, entered the garage. "That radio guy—Cootie—is on the phone and wants to speak to you-all," she announced.

Stunned, the four stared at each other, then bolted from the garage and into the kitchen. Jimmy grabbed the receiver and Deuce wedged his ear as close as possible. Jewelle pointed for Lou and Blondie to pick up the extension in the living bedroom.

"Mister Rhythm-and-blues. What's the latest?" Jimmy struggled to sound calm.

Cootie filled them in on the marketing strategy he, Willa, and the Felders were crafting. Lou noticed how hedgingly Cootie spoke, editing his words, omitting certain details.

"Coupla things you cats may not be crazy about hearing, though," Cootie tiptoed.

"Oh?"

"First, you guys have gotta lay low. Don't worry, I'll explain later—and you *will* be compensated for the dates you *won't* be playing."

"Cootie, we're *musicians*! Boxers have to fight, musicians have to—"

"Slow down, Lou. You studs can continue to play at the Full Moon—and anywhere else you're already known—within, uh, two-hundred miles of Knoxville. Trust me, this plan is gonna pay off bigger in the end."

"Whoa! 'Plan'? What's this 'plan,' man?" Deuce demanded.

"If I could explain it now, I would," Cootie bristled. "You gonna trust us, or what?"

All sighed. "We trust you-all," Jimmy murmured. *We got no other choice.*

"What's the second stipulation?" Blondie asked.

"I've set up a recording date for you-all. Saturday, at noon. Moon Records in Nashville."

"What for?"

Cootie explained the tactic for the country & western market. "So we keep it on the hush-hush that we're colored?" Lou asked, rhetorically.

"Like, yeah. Sell more records that way. At least on this release, 'til *we* let the cat out the bag. That's why I don't want you-all performing where you're not already known."

"You're the boss, Boss," Jimmy said.

"I *know* this sounds a bit roundabout to you studs—"

"You're the boss, Boss," Jimmy repeated. Cootie gave them the particulars of the session, told them to have fun, to rip it up, then bade them good-bye.

"'Move it on Over.' That oughtta be a gas. I *love* me some Hank Williams," said Lou as they discussed the choice for the alternate flipside.

"But *we* don't know that song," Blondie squawked.

"We'll have it in a coupla hours," Jimmy said. "We'll just follow Lou's lead."

"Well, heck—let's get to rockin," Lou said, and minutes later they were doing just that.

CHAPTER TWELVE

Saturday, May 21, 1955; 6:02 p.m. Nashville.

"And while I was in the bathroom section, I saw the cutest li'l ol' vanity set that had your mama's name *all* over it, Philip. Right down to the gold embroidering, it was *her*, you hear me? But I only brought enough cash to get what was on my list, and since we done already run up such a big big big bill in that place, I decided to wait until her birthday. Which is easy for me to remember, of course, 'cause it comes three days on the heels of *my* mama's birthday. Philip Samuels, you haven't heard one word I just said!"

Phil Samuels looked across the table at his wife, Cindy Fae. They were in a beer-and-hamburger joint on Broadway, Phil's downtown haunt. Here he could have a quick snack, listen to the juke, and hold court with his admirers as they paid homage to him. Whether they came to express their love for the records he produced, or to try to finagle an audition, the bear-like young entrepreneur was as approachable as anyone in his position could be. In fact, he had met his wife in this very place, six years ago, when she sidled up to him and solicited an audition for the fledging Moon Records. She proved to be a better prospect for matrimony than a country & western chanteuse.

"Sorry, dawhrlin," he drawled as he gazed into her huge, copperpenny eyes that chopped five years from her actual twenty-six. They were in the middle of their Saturday ritual: he had a short day at the studio; she had spent the afternoon shopping; they would have a quick meal before the early show at the Grand Ole Opry, a few blocks away at the Ryman Auditorium.

"Long day," he said in continuation of his faint apology. "Strange, too, I guess."

"How so, honey?"

Phil told her of the Negro quartet that blew in and recorded Hank Williams' "Move it on Over" in five takes—though Phil thought the second try was a winner. "And unless you was lookin right at 'em, you'd of sworn they was white boys. Had that country thang down pat, and the lead singer sounded more like ol' Hank than Hank himself, God rest his soul."

"Why for a bunch-a colored boys wanna come in your studio and sound all country?"

"Beats me." Phil remembered his promise to Cootie Coutrere, the slick New York deejay who arranged the session. "You didn't just hear me tell you they was spades. And when their record comes out, you keep it under your hat, y' hear?"

"Sure, Philip—but why would I give a hoot about who's colored and who's white on some record?"

"Good." Coutrere had wired him a nice bit of cash a few days ago, for the studio, a steel guitar player, and a fiddler. Coutrere had overpaid slightly, and added some keep-quiet money. "Hell, it don't make me—and my boys who'll be playin in the session—no never mind 'bout no race thang," Phil told Coutrere when the jockey broached the issue of silence—but he took the hush money nonetheless.

Though he had never met Coutrere in person, Phil liked him, based on a few long-distance dealings. Coutrere had leaned on a few Moon releases. Of course, Phil had taken care of him, and now the jockey needed a favor.

Phil thought the Jameson Quartet's session was—intriguing. Anyone with a finely-tuned ear knew the chasm between country and the blues was not that wide, save for a few superficial differences. A solid blues outfit could usually bang out an authentic-sounding country song, and vice-versa...but seldom on a consistent basis. This quartet, however, straddled the lines in a way that appealed to Phil's personal tastes, and his notion of what was commercial.

He had convinced Coutrere to let him hear a raw tape of the A-side of the record that Coutrere was so riled up about. Coutrere complied with reluctance. He was so concerned that the song might get into the wrong hands before its release that he dispatched a teenaged cousin to Nashville with a reel-to-reel tape. Coutrere's cousin, after making Phil vow he had no machines running with which to *copy* the tape, allowed Phil to hear "Cora Ann." Only twice. The cousin, who barely said ten words, took the tape off the machine, packed it into his bag, and was off to Union Station to catch the next train back to New Orleans.

The more Phil thought about the band's cross-bred sound, the more he admired how they pulled it off. He had a few Negro artists under contract whose music resided in the half-world between down-home blues and the hipper, younger, big-city R & B. Similarly, most of his younger country artists straddled the fence that divided stomp-down hillbilly music and the slicker sound that was really white Southern cats shouting Negro R & B. Based on the collage of styles that constantly entangled in his studios, Phil *knew* that the sound of the Jameson Quartet would hit the music world like a torch in a kerosene tank.

I probably got as much faith in that song creatin a shit-storm as Coutrere does, he mused as he bit into a forkful of French fries.

Now...all I need me is a pretty white boy who can duplicate that Negro sound—and feel. One that at the same time makes all the li'l gals wet their underwears, yet is acceptable enough to their parents—if any such person exists.

He stifled a notion to be angry at himself for not even *listening* to the Cannon kid when he had called a few weeks back. *How could I of known he and his boys would be this hot...same chance as gettin struck by lightnin...*

Phil had half expected Cannon to gloat when he and his mates rolled into the studio—forty minutes *early*. Yet, Cannon was cordial, polite in that courtly but non-deferring manner of well-raised Southern Negroes who did not hold white folks in awe. Phil's first impression was that the lad surely had the *look* of a star. *Given the right push, this kid could go a loooong way,* Phil thought as he furtively studied Cannon, and knew that Coutrere's army would pull no punches in promoting this youngster and his group.

No sooner than he's a star, I'm gonna find me a whiteboy version of Lou Cannon. And in the good ol' U.S. of A., guess who wins that shootin match?

He knew he had but two things to do on the matter: wait for this new sound to detonate...

And find that pretty white boy who could sing like a Negro—or closely enough to palm off on white teens.

Yes, he would do everything he could to see that *Cannon's* song broke big on the country stations. That would open doors for his artists...and one in particular, though still undiscovered...

"Finish your meal, honey. That Opry ain't gonna wait for us."

Cindy Fae's words brought Phil back to the diner. "Uh. Yeah." He called the waitress over for the check.

"Heard ennythang worthwhile lately in that-there studio of yours?" asked the waitress, a part-time back-up singer in sessions all around town. Her oversized front teeth waged a merciless attack on a giant wad of gum.

"Same old honkers and shouters, pickers and fiddlers," Phil replied with a watery smile.

CHAPTER THIRTEEN

Wednesday, June 8; 8:07 p.m. Knoxville.

Ruth was washing the dishes and Sarah drying when the phone bawled. Ruth answered. "Good evening. Cannon's residence. Ruth speaking."

"Good evening, dawhlin." The voice at the other end was like warm syrup sliding down a pile of steaming buttered pancakes. "May I speak with Louis Cannon, Jr.?"

"He's not in at the moment. May I take a message?"

"Yes. Please tell him Cootie the—"

Ruth clomped her hand over the receiver and wailed: "IT'S—HIM!"

"Who?"

"*HIM!*" When Sarah realized who "Him!" was she let out an even louder whoop.

On the other end, Cootie chuckled.

When the girls composed themselves, Cootie said, "Tell Lou I'm going to lead off my Friday night show with 'Cora Ann.' Got that? I'm going to play it for the first time Friday, at seven sharp. Seven. Sharp!"

"Okay! We'll tell him, like right now!" Ruth bubbled. She dropped the phone and grabbed Sarah. They whirled about the kitchen, screaming.

On the other end, Cootie laughed and hung up.

Ten minutes later, the girls charged into the Austin High gym. Lou, Blondie, and Deuce were in the middle of a basketball game. Their reaction was more of an "it's-about-time" grumble of relief than surprised joy. They left a message for Jimmy when he got back from fishing. Lou invited the two dozen people in the gym to a near-by greasy spoon for chili dogs and Coca Colas.

* * * * *

Thursday, June 9; 11:55 p.m. New York City.

"Hey, cats and kitties in the towns and cities, it's time to pack the shellac, smack the track, hit the grit and make a night of it. Gotta turn things over to the wee-hour rover, Captain Midnight, who's gonna set things right until the hour of the dawnin, so stop your yawnin. Never forget, pet, that Cootie loves you, you, and little sister, too. The next sound you'll hear, dear, is me shiftin into gone gear. Oo-papa-dow, it's ciao for now!"

Signed off, Cootie mulled over the feedback from deejays on "Cora Ann." Many jockeys—black and white—in the non-Southern states saw it as a can't-miss prospect. Not knowing the artists were colored, the platter pushers on the country stations raved about it. Oddly, many white jocks in the North Central states predicted it would be a smash for the exact reason a few colored deejays feared it might flop: the vocalist sounded like a Negro trying to pass for white, or a hillbilly trying to sing black boogie-woogie.

Regardless, Cootie knew they had done all they could to saturate the airwaves with the song. Now it was up to the record-buying public to respond.

* * * * *

Friday, June 10, 1955; 6:58 p.m. Armstrong's Lookout.

The Lookout was aswarm with Lou's family and friends. Since only a dozen cars could fit safely on the hill, a pecking order, based on kinship to the band members, was established. Reverend Cannon presided, and his decisions were not to be disputed. Those who could not park on the hill crowded around the car radios of those who did.

The atmosphere in the gloaming was festive. The heat of the late-spring day was giving way to the cool of the evening. A handful of gigantic cotton-ball clouds wafted lazily overhead. Picnic baskets made the rounds. Since the event was a self-styled ritual, no music would be played until the magic moment.

At 6:59 Lou leapt atop the hood of his car. "Ladies and gentle-men—turn on your radios!" They obeyed, and the final chorus of "Hot Lana From Atlanta" greeted them.

Something's wrong, Lou thought. The jock before Cootie should be signing off, and they should be hearing Cootie's opening theme.

Oh, well, he reasoned, *they can't always time those change-overs down to the minute...*

"Hot Lana" ended. "Hey, Daddyoes and Mommyoes, it's eight-oh-one in the Big Apple—"

A collective groan drowned out Cootie's voice. Tommy Lovelace was the first to realize what was amiss. "Oh, shit!" he cried. "Nobody remembered we're on *Central* time, an hour behind New York!"

"Cootie-maniacs, I played this one to lead off the show and your calls have been driving us kuh-raaaay-zee ever since! Here's some Tennessee cats who knooooow where it's at, the new rhythm masters, Lou Cannon & the Blasters, with 'Cora Ann!'"

Joyful howls rocked the hill. Radio dials went as high as they could. Even those who could not dance did their best. Lou hugged Alba so hard she shrieked involuntarily; he was in turn smothered with hugs by his sisters and others. Out of the corner of his eye he saw people exchange embraces and handshakes with his parents.

His knees buckled as the realization blind-sided him: *That's us! That's really us! On the—radio!* Yet, as he listened to his voice and the band blaring from a dozen dashboards, he could hear all the hard work they had put in, and the wild responses from the Full Moon audiences...

Yeah! Why not *us?*

The scene reminded Lou of the aftermath of the big Joe Louis victories from his early childhood. People floated among him and his mates, congratulating them ... but was it his imagination, or were his mates slipping him fish-eyed looks?

"Guess I'll have to find me a new employee," said Tommy.

"Whoa! Let's not be premature," cautioned Lou.

When the hubbub finally ebbed, Jimmy, Deuce, and Blondie confronted Lou. "We gotta talk," Jimmy said somberly. They excused themselves and went off to a patch of pine trees.

"What's this 'Lou Cannon & the Blasters' jazz?" Deuce huffed.

"It's as new to me as it is to you—"

"Bull! What kinda deal you and Cootie got goin?" demanded Jimmy.

"I swear on every sermon my daddy ever preached I had no idea about a name change!" Their anger subsided; they *had* to believe that. "It must be one of those last-minute decisions no one bothers to tell the artists about," Lou added.

"Mmm-hmmm," Deuce growled, folded his arms, and glared at Lou.

"I'll call Cootie and find out what that was all about," promised Lou.

"Yeah, you do that," sniffed Jimmy.

"I *swear* I didn't have a thing to do with—"

"Yeah, yeah," Deuce cut Lou off.

"Well, shit—this should be the happiest day of our lives, and here we are, arguin like some crabs-in-the-barrel-assed niggers," Blondie interjected. "We can straighten this out later. Me, I'm goin back to soak up the affection of our adoring public!" He dashed back to the party.

Lou could tell Deuce and Jimmy were still angry. "Honest to God, fellas—"

"We'll see what Cootie and company have to say," interrupted Deuce. He and Jimmy glowered at Lou, then walked away.

Lou breathed deeply, then rejoined the celebration.

Alba picked up on his forced smile. "What's wrong, baby?"

Lou's face was half-grin, half-grimace. "Honey, I've only been an R & B star for five minutes, and already it's tough work."

Alba smiled wanly, squeezed his hand, and hugged him.

* * * * *

Wednesday, June 29, 1955. New York City.

As Cootie had so precisely contrived, 'Cora Ann' exploded like an atomic bomb. It was hot with urban black fans and white teens across the nation. The song became an anthem for the country crowd in the South and West. Surprisingly, it scored well with the Pat Crockett/Perry Martin/Frank Maggio pop-music disciples. Cootie spun the record hourly. Because of his reputation for sniffing out a hit, numerous dee-jays followed his lead—and with ungreased palms. If Cootie's hip New York cult was jumping on the tune, then to prove they were just as hip, other jocks *had* to play it and their listeners *had* to buy it.

One disk jockey in Buffalo, Plucky Chucky, was so gone on the song that he locked himself in his booth and played it twenty times in a row. The station's owner called a squadron of firemen to batter down the door and escort Chucky out. Cootie howled when he heard the news; Plucky Chucky was *not* among the jocks paid handsomely to ride the record.

In its second week, it roared onto *Cashboard* magazine's "Hotshot Hundred" chart at sixty-eight with a bullet. A week later it jumped to thirty-six. The music world was in a tizzy. WHO *ARE* LOU CANNON & THE BLASTERS? was the question that remained coyly unanswered.

One could not travel fifteen minutes in a populated area without hearing the song. It blared from jukeboxes in northern inner-city corner bars where C.C. Prince, Gutbucket McDaniel, and Moody Rivers were near-deity. Countless copies wore out needles in southern road-houses where the late Hank Williams was a step below Jesus. It made even the wallflowers hit the dance floor in schools named after Booker T. Washington and Jefferson Davis; Frederick Douglass and Robert E. Lee; George Washington Carver and Thomas "Stonewall" Jackson.

At a Veterans of Foreign Wars hall in a sleepy, dusty, Delta town, a strange thing happened because of "Cora Ann": as was the custom at the Friday Night Record Hop, colored and white teens danced on opposite sides of the thick rope that bisected the hall. After a few strains of "Cora Ann" someone—or several someone's—removed the rope. The unthinkable resulted: colored and white kids danced togeth-er. The chaperons, Negro and white, immediately telephoned the law. When the cops arrived, all they saw was a hurricane of salt and pep-per gyrating madly to the witty wailings of some outfit called Lou Cannon & the Blasters.

Though the expected violence showed no signs of erupting, the officers replaced the rope and ordered the races to their proper sides. "Hmmmmph!" sniffed the white chaperon. "Music that sounds white and Negro at the same time and makes white and colored kids wanna dance together—*we cain't have that*!" she cried.

"It strictly ain't American," clucked her colored counterpart.

To the north and east of Knoxville, "Cora Ann" was growing on Theophilis Briscoe. The jocks on his favorite country station could not play it enough. *That's the cutest ditty since ol' Hank Williams bought the farm*, he thought. Yet, he heard it when his ears picked up the over-spill from R & B stations. He thought it odd that a country tune would appear on Negro stations, but knew it *did* happen, if rarely.

He tried to recall a song that white and black, young and old, were all so crazy about.

He could not.

In Nashville, a handsome nineteen-year-old blond lad almost wrecked the truck he was driving the first time he heard the song. *That's* my *type of music, the kind I wanna become a star sangin*, Pervis Elmsley told himself. By the third time he heard it, he had all the vocal inflections down to perfection.

At precisely the same moment Pervis nearly rammed the Humes Plumbing Supplies truck into a wall, the board of directors of Moon Records convened a few blocks away. The members discussed "Cora Ann" and wondered just who the hell were Lou Cannon & the Blasters.

Phil Samuels told them.

"They're *nigras*?" screeched a member over a general caterwaul of disbelief.

"Yep." Phil refrained from telling how Cannon had called in April for an audition, or how the band had recorded the disc's flipside in the Moon studios. He knew he would never hear the end of it about the one that got away.

"Boy, I'd give my right nut to have them niggers under contract. They sound like they gonna be around for a spell," said C. V. McCluskey, Phil's second-in-command. Everyone seconded that.

"Hell, they're good—no doubt about it. The public's eatin 'em up. But remember: good as they are, they can only go but so far—they're still Negroes. Unfair as it is, that's the way it goes." Phil let that sink in, then continued. "Sheeeyit, I got me a search out for a good-lookin white boy with a solid Negro sound. Once I reel him in, I'll be richer'n an ocean of Pet Milk."

A few blocks away, Pervis had parked the truck and was unloading it. His twelve-year-old cousin, Priscilla, and three of her friends passed him and waved. He almost didn't notice them; he was studying the latest song by the Five Fevers, a Chicago doo-wop group. He listened intently to get the proper inflections.

"Your cousin is sooooo cute," a friend told Priscilla, "but he is soooooo weird. Always sangin them R & B songs, tryin-a sound like the nigras." Priscilla assured them despite that quirk, Pervis was as nice as he was cute.

* * * * *

"Cora Ann" continued to barrel up the pop, R & B, and country charts. And—though not to Cootie's surprise—"Move it on Over," the country-market flipside, was climbing that list.

Meanwhile, in Knoxville, the first three weeks of the song's debut were bittersweet for the band. The thrill of their wild popularity was blunted by not being able to enjoy it in the spotlight—at least not yet. Willa did have a stack of engagements set for them, however, once they could divulge who Lou Cannon & the Blasters actually were.

As promised, the New York team paid them handsomely for lying low. At the Full Moon, and clubs in East Tennessee from Bristol to Chattanooga where they *could* perform, they drew integrated, squirming-room-only crowds. Their original fans affected an I-knew-they-were-great-before-everybody-else haughtiness.

Much to Lou's surprise, Jimmy and Deuce were largely silent about the name change. Lou called Willa and Cootie the day after their record made its debut, and their mentors explained the reasons behind the change. That seemed to be enough for Jimmy and Deuce.

Still, Lou knew it had to be a blow to Jimmy's pride to *some* degree. Yet, he decided to let the matter rest if Jimmy remained mum.

Moreover, the issue of Jimmy and Deuce and their workaday jobs was squashed with the success of "Cora Ann" and the scheduled gigs. And to allay further qualms, Reverend Cannon assured them that he and other ministers would speak in their behalf if they needed to return to their jobs (which they had yet to leave). If that did not work, the ministers would help them find new well-paying jobs.

The song's success wreaked havoc with Alba and Lou's wedding plans. Though they had never set a date, Lou leaned strongly toward mid-October. However, Willa told the band to keep everything from the last of August to the end of the year open—though she could not offer details. Thus, Alba and Lou looked toward early August; neither could wait until the new year.

On the fifth of July, Willa and Cootie summoned the Blasters to a meeting in New York to be held three days later.

* * * * *

"It takes money to make money," Chadsdale Worthington had told Willa and Cootie at the outset of their rhythm revue proposal. "And while we're kicking around clichés, success breeds success," he added. Now, with "Cora Ann" on its way to the top of *Cashboard*'s three major charts, most doubts about the road show were laid to rest. Moreover, Cootie and Willa were quick to point to the R & B and pop charts, where the other artists on their planned roster were faring well, on one, if not both.

The success of "Cora Ann" inspired the revue's backers to ante up half again the necessary start-up funds. The extra capital would go mainly to advertising—and, of course, to deejays to give that extra push for any records by the artists in the show.

Four weeks after its release, "Cora Ann" weighed in at numbers ten, three, and five, respectively, on *Cashboard's* pop, R & B, and country charts. Willa greeted the group with that news at the top of their July 8th meeting in her office. The musicians sat across a mahogany table from Willa, Cootie, Goldfarb, and Worthington. The New Yorkers informed the Blasters about the rhythm revue, which was but a few signatures from a reality. The Labor Day week would mark its debut. The Blasters, of course, would be a cornerstone act.

"Get ready for the wildest, most unforgettable months you'll ever experience," Cootie said, half-cautiously, half-seductively.

"Bring 'em on!" Blondie crowed, "good and bad, we're ready like Freddy!"

Willa made a face before she spoke. "I've got to commend you gents for not getting too done in about the surprise name change...or, at least *we* haven't heard of any dissension." She explained again how the original name had not grabbed the targeted backers. "Which told us it would also fall flat to jockeys and record buyers."

"As for sticking Lou's name out front," Peter said, "it's usually better to have one person's name with whom the public can identify, than that of just a—group—which can seem faceless, impersonal, and with interchangeable members."

"Lou's the songwriter, lead vocalist, the one closest to the audience, who'll get the most camera close-ups," Chadsdale said.

"On top of that," Willa continued, "Lou's got just the right look to lead a Negro group—not too light, not too dark; handsome, but not too—pretty; in other words, the boy next door."

"Yeah—if you live in a middle-class colored neighborhood," Blondie cracked.

Cootie waited out the laughter. "Any lingering problems with the name change?" Despite his smile, his tone was challenging.

"If it meant that much, me and Deuce would be long gone," Jimmy replied.

"Long as the pay's on time and correct, I could care less what you call us," Deuce said.

Cootie then told them who else would be in the show: Louisiana Fats, Little Robert, Hal Dillard & the Moonlighters, Moanin' Lisa, and the Philadelphia Belles.

"The Belles. Ooo-la-la," Blondie leered.

"Be nice," Willa said.

The Blasters stayed until Sunday morning, again at the Convent Avenue brownstone. During a whirlwind Saturday, they met Sugar Ray Robinson at his club on Seventh Avenue, watched the Giants trounce the Dodgers 10-2 before a large Ladies' Day crowd at the Polo Grounds, and caught an R & B show at the Apollo. The headliners were Claude McPatter & the Wanderers, who had four number-one R & B hits in the past two years. After the show, Cootie and Willa took the band backstage to meet McPatter and his group. The Blasters expressed their admiration of McPatter, widely considered the best pure singer in R & B, and the Wanderers, the kings of group harmony. Claude and the Wanderers were equally praiseful of "Cora Ann."

The next morning, Cootie and Willa saw the Blasters off and made plans for them to return in three weeks. "We'll have a sharper picture of the kinks we'll have to iron out before we hit the road," Cootie said.

On Monday morning all four were back on their regular jobs.

CHAPTER FOURTEEN

Reverend Cannon was enormously proud of his son. He let him know in subtle ways, without mushy pronouncements. Yet, like nearly everyone who had *any* sort of stake in the new music fad, Reverend Cannon had doubts about its longevity. Filtering all pessimism from his tone, he cautioned his son to make money and enjoy the fun times while they lasted. However, Junior agreed that *nobody* should put all his eggs in rock-n-roll's basket.

The reverend saw the withholding of the group's identity as a blessing in disguise. It would give them more time to get over the shock of their flash fame—even if most of America did not yet know who they were.

Junior had returned yesterday evening, Sunday, from his second trip to New York. He was ecstatic about a road show that was practically a done deal, according to Coutrere. Reverend Cannon restated his warning about hopes getting too high—but *this* time the caution seemed to miss Lou's ears.

Now, late on Monday afternoon, at his home, as Reverend Cannon went over the collection plate figures for the last three Sunday morning services, he had to chuckle. Attendance, which had grown steadily in the first months of Junior's rise as a local blues star, had exploded to mirror the hit record's climb. A fire marshal came around every Sunday morning, to make sure no more than seven hundred or so were squeezing into the six hundred-seat church. Though Coutrere was keeping the rest of the world in the dark about Lou Cannon & the Blasters, every blues fan in the eastern third of Tennessee knew who they were.

Even *more* young women were attending the Sunday morning services. Many sported dresses more suitable for a juke joint than a church. Moreover, white people—mostly about Junior's age or younger—were showing up by the dozens. Long-time members who had been lax in their attendance resurfaced.

Yet, the offerings at the Brighter Day's Sunday evening services—which he had always delegated to one of his assistant pastors, and where Junior *never* sang in the choir—were lighter as of late. It was time to read the riot act to the bandwagon hoppers.

Just yesterday, upon Junior's *not* marching out with the men's choir, a buzz rose from the gathering. Reverend Cannon then announced that Louis, Jr., was out of town. A loud groan thrummed. Testily, the reverend reminded all that the church was in the business of serving the Lord, and not tendering peeks at people they now heard on the radio. He suggested that anyone there only to "gawk at the 'Cora Ann' man" should leave. His subtext was blatant: *And if you go now, stay gone.*

Though many surely had a notion, none took him up on that.

His perusal of the weekly ledgers finished, the reverend turned his attention to a note about two defective air conditioners in the church. From the kitchen, "Cora Ann" wailed from a radio whose volume had been raised for his behalf. He smiled Florence, while she prepared dinner on weekdays, usually listened to a country station. *That Coutrere fellow is the goods,* Reverend Cannon mused, *he covered* all *the bases promoting that song.*

Since Coutrere's visit over two months ago, the reverend had several phone conversations with him. Reverend Cannon was impressed by how a man so young had so many irons in the fire, but all within his control, and tied in some way to the others. He was especially intrigued by Coutrere's planned road revue. Understandably, Coutrere was evasive on the finer details. However, upon Reverend Cannon's request, Coutrere had Chadsdale Worthington draft a letter that explained how to set up a co-operative business venture.

The reverend realized that Junior and his group could make a quick killing in this rock-n-roll—with two or three more hit records, he figured. For the short term, anyway, they could rake in more money than they *needed* for their day-to-day expenses. The reverend would try to convince them to lend whatever they could, to be used as seed money for local Negro businessmen. Since it was virtually impossible for a Negro to get a business loan from a local bank, this money would be a godsend. He would emphasize that this was the precise way Coutrere had raised money for *his* revue.

The reverend had plans for what types of businesses he and his colleagues could set up, and had already chosen who would manage them. Then he reminded himself he was tuning the engine before he had a car; the Blasters had yet to prove they could reap such a windfall.

Furthermore, they still had not been paid for their hit. Coutrere told them royalty checks were issued after quarterly audits—and their first would not be until mid-October. To his credit, however, Coutrere had mentioned a possible "good faith" advance before then...

The Reverend offered up a quick prayer that rock-n-roll would be more than just a fast-flaming, fast-fading ember, then answered his wife's call to dinner.

* * * * *

For Alba, the popularity of "Cora Ann" turned out to be a mixed blessing.

Lou would call when he got off from work that evening. Until then, she would make a list of what they needed for their first home together. She gazed about her bedroom and thought of how—child-ish—the furnishings and her possessions seemed.

Of course, she was proud of Lou's success, and boundlessly happy for him. As far back as she could remember, her intuition told her that Louis Cannon, Jr., would make a name for himself in *some* fashion. It pained her, though, to see how frustrated he and the others were over the imposed "secret," but she knew the day was near when they could answer all the "Who *Are* Lou Cannon & the Blasters?" questions. They had heard, however, that in the music world the truth about the band was seeping out, like air from a punctured tire.

By far, the biggest change the hit record had wrought was with their wedding plans. Rather than wait until Lou returned from the road tour, Alba, Lou, and Reverend Cannon decided that a simple, near-private ceremony would be best. They set it for the first Saturday in August. They would exchange rings before a score of relatives and friends at the Brighter Day. After a brief reception, she and Lou would hit the highway for New Orleans. Then they would return home, as the band made final preparations for Cootie the Cutie's All-Star Rhythm Revue and Road Show.

When Lou returned in January, *then* they could have the grand ceremony and reception. The Brighter Day congregation would be invited, along with a hundred or so other guests. To help defray the monumental cost, Reverend Cannon assured the father of the bride that the Cannon clan and the church members would absorb part of the wedding's bill.

The early, bare-bones ceremony was largely Reverend Cannon's idea. Alba was equally in favor of a pre-tour wedding. She told Lou, frankly, "I don't want you to be out there, amidst all that temptation, without..." —she blushed and squeezed his hand— "...you know...you and me *not* already having..."

"You're right," he came to her rescue, "if I have a long, looong, drink of water before I cross the desert, I won't be thirsty along the way." She punched him, playfully but hard, on his shoulder blade.

Moreover, the Reverend, in his graceful, tactful way, had tiptoed around the same issue.

Though it would be another six weeks before he left, Alba missed Lou already. Even in his presence she had to prepare for his absence. He still had his old habit of being far away mentally at times, but she knew that was one of his artist's quirks and he would always be that way.

Her fear that Lou would succumb to the endless temptations was starting to wane. He hardly glanced at the attractive, smartly-clad, perfume-drenched women who flocked to the Sunday morning services. (And Alba knew that Lou—and the reverend—were the only healthy adult males *not* constantly sneaking peeks at the Jezebels.)

"Alba. Phone." Sam ended her reverie. She dashed down the stairs to the vestibule.

She already knew who it was. "Hey, Big Time. What's doin?"

"Let's go out and get some chili dogs," Lou replied.

"None for me. Just had dinner. A girl's gotta watch her figure, you know."

"That's cool. You watch me eat, and I'll watch *your* figure."

"Just honk, and I'll be there with wings on my feet."

"I'm on the way." They hung up.

Yes, I miss him already, she thought as she pondered the long weeks from Labor Day to the end of the year.

* * * * *

In late July, as "Cora Ann" continued up the charts, the Blasters made their second trip to New York. Willa filled them in on the latest developments.

The Rhythm Revue would kick off the Friday before Labor Day, on the second of September. The show would play a week at the Apollo, then hit the major venues in the Northeast: the Howard Theatre in Washington; the Uptown in Philadelphia; the Back Bay in Boston; and the Century in Buffalo. Next, the Upper Midwest: a swing along the Great Lakes basin, then across to Saint Louis and Kansas City. After that, stops in the Great Plains and Rocky Mountain regions, to the Pacific Northwest. The tour would end in mid-December in Los Angeles; the company would have the week before Christmas off, but not the holiday week itself: they would return to the Apollo for six days of Cootie the Cutie's Holiday Week Rhythm Extravaganza.

Willa and Cootie promised the Blasters they could go public in mid-August, just three weeks away. As a warm-up for the tour, Willa booked them in Pittsburgh, Erie, Buffalo, Rochester, Syracuse, and Albany. They would appear on local televisions and radio shows, at record hops, and in a few clubs not unlike the Full Moon.

The four howled when Willa told them they would appear on *The Ned Mulligan Show,* the day before Labor Day. "Us? On *Ned Mulligan?*" Lou shrieked.

"Only the biggest wheels get to go on *Ned Mulligan!*" Deuce thundered.

"Who has show-biz more abuzz than you cats?" Cootie asked.

"You're right about that," Blondie replied.

While in New York, Willa had them fitted for a variety of stage costumes. All were the standard entertainer's suits: chiffon-green, candy-red, canary-yellow, hot-pink and sky-blue silk jackets, all bordered with black piping; black silk pants with a stripe down the side of the leg to match the jacket.

The issue of hair surfaced. Most Negro entertainers straightened their hair with chemicals, but Lou and Blondie, both with naturally wavy-curly hair, decided against the "conk." Rather, they chose to keep their hair short, heavily pomaded, and brushed hard to make it lie flat. Jimmy and Deuce elected not to get their hair "fried, dyed, and laid to the side," as Cootie described a well-done barbershop conk.

"If the Good Lord wanted me to have straight hair, He'd of given it to me at birth, and not after thirty years and a hit record," Jimmy declared, and received an "amen" from Deuce.

"Suit yourselves," Cootie responded.

"Besides, Cootie—you got enough process for *everybody* in this group," Lou cracked.

"Yeah, buddy," Deuce chimed in, "if that conk don't kill you, you'll never die!"

Cootie laughed louder than anyone at that.

In the late afternoon on the second of two crowded days, the Blasters wound up in a photographer's studio in Greenwich Village. Sporting a prototype of their stage outfits, they posed as a jittery, reed-thin, beret-clad man called the shots with an indecipherable

French accent. Afterwards, Willa took them to a beatnik-filled diner near Sheridan Square. When they finished the meal, Willa announced, "Now you boys are *really* in for a treat!"

They exchanged hopeful looks. "What you got in mind?" Blondie asked.

Willa looked at Cootie, who nodded toward the door. "And awaaay we go!"

A half-hour later they nestled into box seats overhanging the balcony at the Apollo Theatre. "Wow!" Lou burbled. "Amateur Night! This oughtta be a gas!"

"We'll see," Willa replied, with a smirking smile.

The first performer was a rotund, not-so-young man trying his hand at stand-up comedy. The crowd booed lustily thirty seconds into his act. Despite the catcalls, he was reluctant to leave. The cavalry charge sounded; out rode "Sandman" Simms on a hobby horse, brandishing a huge broom to sweep the comic off the stage.

Next was a doo-wop quintet. "Not bad—but not good, either," judged Cootie. "Decent presence, good energy, they sing well, but nothing to write home about; no real hook." Nonetheless, the demanding Amateur Night crowd gave them respectful applause.

After them came a short, frail girl. Before she got one note out, the crowd hooted her down. "Girl, take off them Coke-bottle glasses!" someone yelled. "Child, you *homely*—which means you need to keep yo' ugly li'l narrer-behind *at home*!" shouted a hard-looking chick from the second row. Others hollered similar comments. The girl flew offstage, bawling.

"This crowd's got their dicks hard *tonight*, boy!" Cootie chuckled.

"Nice language, Coutrere," Willa sniffed in mock indignation.

A blues chanteuse followed. Her singing talent did not match her comely looks. Judging her on her voice, the women tried to hoot her off. Judging her on her curves and face, the men cheered her on. "Work yo' show, gurlie!" Cootie shouted. Willa gave him a hard elbow to the ribs.

Next was a bunch of faces familiar to Cootie—one of the groups that sang at the intersection of 145th Street and Saint Nicholas. The Lexingtons, five handsome, clean-cut lads in their mid-teens, spilled onstage. They wore matching white V-neck sweaters with a big green "L" on the chest. As they took the stage, a gaggle of girls in the front row screamed wildly.

"Clai—aren't those the kids who've been pestering you to see them perform?" Willa asked.

"That's them. Now's their chance to show what they got."

"The smallest, youngest one—isn't he just too cute to look at?" gushed Willa.

"He's a killer-diller, all right," Cootie agreed. The Lexingtons launched into "Lost Love, Last Love," an uptempo ballad. "Don't know this tune—but it's a good one," remarked Cootie. "*Must* be an original."

The lead singer, a caramel-skinned, straight-haired, shortish lad, barreled into the first verse. The others backed him with tight harmonies and choreography that was basic but crisp. The chicks went wild, and the guys in the audience also voiced their approval.

Cootie's face glowed as he watched them.

They were halfway through the song when the wheels came off. Instead of the crowd's approval bolstering the lead singer's confidence, it warped his concentration. He blew half the second verse, and the words he remembered stumbled out off key.

Down came the boos.

"They'll have to get 'em next time," Cootie said, in tight-lipped disappointment.

If he could have, the lead singer, Sammy Rios, would have crawled into a crack in the stage. Three of the Lexingtons stared at each other, confused, just going through the motions, waiting to be swept off. The microphone sank slowly into the stage as the catcalls rained.

The tiniest kid was the only one to keep his head.

Thirteen-year-old Lydell Franklin pushed Sammy aside, flopped to his knees, and wailed desperately into the descending mike. His haunting soprano rang out like a church bell on a crisp, still Sunday morning. Hundreds of jeers switched to cheers in mid-throat. Revived by the crowd, the others got back on track. The microphone returned to its original height. The audience screamed. Lydell caressed the mike and made love to the lyrics as if this were the last song he would ever sing.

As if sprung from a catapult, Cootie was out of his seat and down the stairs.

When the song was over, the Lexingtons had to bulldoze their way through a wall of fans. When they were safely off-stage, Cootie materialized from the shadows. He pulled them to the side and began the negotiations.

In the box seats, Willa stared at the now-abandoned stage.

"Hey, Willa—think these kids're worth your time?" Jimmy asked.

She snapped out of her trance. "Are you kidding? By this time tomorrow, I'll have their parents' names on contracts."

Actually, it took her two days to get all the necessary signatures. By then the Blasters were back home, hoping yet another weekend of shows at the Full Moon could tide them over until they entered the next phase of their careers.

* * * * *

Between the retainer from New York and the weekend gigs, Lou did not want for money. Thus, out of a sense of loyalty to his cousin, Lou continued to assist Tommy as the Blasters awaited the go-ahead signal. He saw nothing strange in toiling under a hot sun while his own voice shouted from a nearby radio. Still, he had wanted to take Friday, July 22nd off—the day "Cora Ann" would hit the top spot on the R & B chart. However, Tommy was shorthanded, so Lou grabbed his lunch pail and trudged to the work site.

During his lunch break, Lou drove downtown to Gay Street, where he purchased a copy of *Cashboard* at the city's most complete newsstand. He opened it to the charts, and indeed, "Cora Ann" was number-one on the R & B, third on the C & W, and fourth with a bullet on the pop chart. The manager, cashiers, and several customers congratulated Lou; the manager told him Jimmy and Deuce had already bought five copies each. "Only five," the manager said, "had to save some for you and the bright-skinned boy."

Lou called Blondie's house, but nobody answered. He looked at his watch; he had overstayed his lunch break; he would call his family and Alba after he got back to work. When he got there, he showed the paper to Tommy and his co-workers.

"G'on, take the rest of the day off," Tommy ordered. Before Lou could protest, Tommy said, "How many times are you gonna have your first number-one record?"

"Just this once, I guess."

"So, beat it!" Tommy commanded, and Lou complied.

As he pulled up to his house, he was surprised to see his parents, sisters, Alba, and Mother Cannon clustered on the front porch, aglow with excitement. He got out of his car and started toward them, waving the *Cashboard* issue. "Hey, did you all—?"

"Checks! *Royalty* checks!" Sarah cried, sprinting toward him, waving two long envelopes. "From the record company!"

"Is that a fact?" Lou took the envelopes. Yes, they were from Winchester Records. He eyed his relatives suspiciously. "How'd you-all know they're *royalty* checks?"

"We held them up to a light," Ruth admitted. Lou arched an eyebrow at her. "But we didn't look to see the dollar amount, didn't even *try* to," she added, without apology.

"After all, it's *your* money," Alba said, less for Lou's benefit than his relatives.

The six surrounded Lou. "Well, Junior, aren't you going to open them?" Florence said, half-request, half-command.

"Eventually," Lou sighed.

"Kill the melo-drammer and open the consarned thangs!" Mother Cannon snapped.

Lou's second sigh was grander than the first. "Yes, ma'am." Sarah and Ruth pressed closer. "Back off, pipsqueaks; a man needs his oxygen," Lou said in his best W.C. Fields voice.

"Junior! You heard your grandmother!" Florence barked.

"Yep." Everyone moved a step closer. "Anyone got a letter opener?" he asked, daintily.

"BOY!"

"Yes, Grandmama." Lou slowly pried open the first envelope. He began to pull the check out at a glacial rate.

"Daaah-deeee!" Ruth wailed. "Make Junior stop teasing us!"

"Yes!" Sarah chimed in. "*You* take the check, Daddy—"

"No, dear. It's Junior's. And maybe he'll pull it out while he's still young."

Lou sighed yet again, then jerked the check from the envelope, like a magician yanking a rabbit from a top hat. "Ta-da!" he said as he looked at the amount, then clutched it to his bosom.

Nobody noticed the glassy look that flashed in his eyes, or that his knees slightly buckled.

"Well?" Ruth demanded.

Lou caught Alba's eye. *Wow!* She responded with a tiny wink. He painted on a serious look, then turned to his father. "Daddy, is it not ex*tremely* impolite to inquire as to the income of another person?" he asked, biting off each syllable.

"Normally, yes. But this time, no. What's the early return on a hit record?"

Lou passed the check slowly before everyone's eyes. "Five. Big. Ones."

"Five grand?" Sarah squealed. "And the record isn't even halfway through its run!"

"I declare! Five thousand dollars! That's a decent wage! For a whole *year*! Off one blues record? Sweet Baby Jesus!" Mother Cannon exalted.

"Too bad we're *already* middle-class," Reverend Cannon intoned. "This would make one of those great 'Negroes-up-from-poverty' stories white folks love so much!"

Alba looked closely at the check. "'Performer's royalty.' Does that mean the other guys got the same amount?" Lou nodded positively. "Then what's the second check for?"

"Only one way to find out." Lou tore into the second envelope. The check was for the same amount as the first.

Alba took it and read the tiny, hand-written notation on the bottom. "'Co-writer's royalty.'" She looked up and frowned. "With whom did you 'co-write' this? We all know you wrote every word and note of 'Cora Ann' by yourself."

Lou thought for a moment. "Maybe they're referring to the flip-side with the Hank Williams tune."

"And maybe not," the Reverend said. "I'd call this Coutrere fellow, like right now. Perhaps this is his way of collecting his pound of flesh."

Lou bolted into the house, with Alba trailing. They picked up a copy of "Cora Ann" and saw three names beneath the title in parentheses: L. Cannon, C. Coutrere, and A. Freeman.

"Are *these* supposed to be the songwriters?" Alba demanded.

"I—uh—guess."

"You 'guess?' You didn't notice those names before?"

"No. Never had a reason to," Lou lied. He had seen the other names, but assumed they were there as producers' credits or something similar.

"And who the heck is this 'A. Freeman' person?"

"Adam Freeman, I suppose. He's been riding 'Cora Ann' just as hard as Cootie."

"And now we know why." Alba pointed to the telephone.

Neither Cootie nor Willa was at the Hamilton Heights brownstone, so Lou tried the radio station. "Mister Coutrere is not here, but he will be in less than an hour," a secretary trilled. "I'll have him give you a call when he arrives, Mister Cannon."

"Yes. Please. Do that."

Florence entered the living room. "Ten grand. In one afternoon. Lord ha'mercy!" She hugged Lou and Alba. "And it came just in time. That Mister Cootie is *so* thoughtful!"

Lou had to smile. "That he is. Perfect timing." *You wash my car; I'll mow your lawn.*

"You call Jimmy and Deuce to see if they got theirs?" Florence asked. "I *know* Blondie did. He came tearing out his house about noon, screaming, jumped in his car and off he flew."

"Most likely to the nearest Cadillac dealership," Lou laughed. He phoned Deuce and Jimmy; they had received their checks, and were overjoyed.

Lou then asked his mother if she could postpone dinner until after Cootie returned his call. "Sure, if he's not too long about it," she replied.

Lou sat next to Alba in the living room and waited. Mercifully, within five minutes, the phone brayed. He sucked in a breath to slow his racing heart. He picked up the phone and screened any anxiety from his voice. "Cannon's residence—"

"Oo-papa-doo! My main man, Lou! What's cookin, Daddy-o?"

"Got the checks, man. Both of them—"

"You boys weren't scheduled to get paid for a couple more months, but we decided to whip a good-faith advance on you —"

"Thanks; we appreciate—"

"Plush, weren't they?" Cootie crowed. "But I *distinctly* remember telling you on Day One that you studs were the cat's meow!"

"Yeah, yeah, right. Cootie—about the royalty check—"

"Yeah, we've projected that the record'll sell a million and a half copies by the end of the year. Since the writers get two cents per single, that tabs out to ten grand for you—"

"Slow down, Cootie. That's not the issue. What I'm wondering is why you—and Adam Freeman—are listed as co-writers?"

"Louis, Louis, Louis. Remember the many times during the session I bopped out the booth, stopped you studs, made a chord change here, a lyric change there—"

"Of *course* I remember—"

"That was to make the songs more *commercial*. And it obviously helped. Have you seen today's issue of *Cashboard*? Number-one, Lou. *Numero-uno!*"

"Yes, I saw it, I understand what you did, and I appreciate it. But does that merit imposing your name as—"

"Louis. I am trying not to be appalled. Standard procedure, my friend. Three guys usually get writer's credit on *any* record: the cat who actually wrote the song; the lead singer of the group; and the producer of the session," Cootie explained.

"That accounts for you and me. How did Freeman horn his way into the picture?"

"Lou. We couldn't've *raised* enough dough for Freeman to pimp 'Cora Ann' like he's doing. So we gave him a writer's credit, too. We'll all be collecting off that song for years—decades. Besides, you'll be making hits 'til the last horse spits the bit, I guarantee it.

Long term, Big Picture. What's a few grand here or there? A teaspoon out of a barrel." Cootie paused, then continued. "Now, Lou: does all that make sense?"

"Yes," Lou reluctantly agreed. "So... how long is this—royalties arrangement—supposed to last?"

"'Botheration' will be your next release after 'Cora Ann,' and if memory serves—"

"Yeah. You made some changes on that, too."

"Let's not get snarky, Lou. I promise that after 'Botheration,' only you'll get credit for anything you wrote alone. Dig?"

"Gee, golly willikers, Mister Coutrere! Thanks a zillion!"

"Again, kill the sarcasm. I told you on Day One that you wash my car—"

"—And I'll mow your lawn. Yep, that you did."

"Oh...by the way, Lou," Cootie cooed, "have you and your girl decided where you're going on your honeymoon?"

Lou knew that Cootie knew. "Your hometown. The Voodoo City."

"I like it like that! Well, guess what? You're gonna spend your first days of connubial bliss on me, Willa, and the Felders."

"We are?"

"Five days and nights at the Palmetto Inn. Swankiest colored hotel in Louisiana. Everything's taken care of."

Lou read the subtext: *Now don't you feel ashamed for challenging me on the royalties?*

"Gee...thanks...what more can I say?" Lou fumbled.

"Hell, just enjoy yourself. I'll call some hotshots and let 'em know you'll be slidin on through. Hey, cat—gotta cut. See you on August fifteenth. Later, skater; I'll catch you when your hair gets straighter."

"After while, crocodile." Lou hung up and recounted the gist of the conversation to his family, honeymoon gift and all.

"That boy's a caution," Reverend Cannon said. "Not to mention a wheel."

"Cootie taketh away and Cootie giveth back. Blessed be the name of Cootie," Alba said. A chorus of "amen's" greeted that.

Not one person was being sarcastic.

CHAPTER FIFTEEN

The first thing to register on Lou's slowly awakening mind was the ceiling fan whirling directly above him.

He sat upright in the bed. Alba slept beside him; her plush, bow-shaped lips and dimpled smile lent her the look of a contented baby. Sunlight strained through the curtains. Lou looked at the clock on the bedside table. It was just after nine a.m.

He struggled to recall what day it was. *Monday.* They had arrived at the Palmetto Inn shortly after Saturday night gave way to Sunday morning. From the time they checked in and followed a grinning bell-hop to the honeymoon suite, they had not left the room.

Lou's gaze took in the room's gold-and-white color scheme. Despite Cootie's praise of the inn, it was classier than Lou had imagined.

As he unfurled himself from the bed, invisible pincers lanced his temples. *The champagne.* Lou smiled. *Since it was part of the package...*

Lou's thoughts drifted back to the exchange of vows on Saturday. At precisely one p.m., Reverend Cannon began to steer Alba and Lou through the "I do's." Since they would reaffirm their vows in January before hundreds, the fifty people present Saturday was a tiny gathering—but four times too many for Lou. His immediate family, Alba's parents, and his groupmates would have been just fine. Yet, the reverend and Florence had a list of people they just *had* to invite, for reasons Lou did not bother to ask about.

After the abridged ceremony, all repaired to the church's community room for a reception. Remaining as long as protocol dictated, Alba and Lou then hopped into his brand-new car, a souped-up, cherry-red '53 Chevy, and sailed south on Highway 75.

The trip to New Orleans became a ten-hour blur to Lou. He drove the first and last thirds, while Alba handled the middle. Both maintained a strict focus on the highway; they passed little more than polite conversation.

They realized the quicker they reached New Orleans, the sooner they could finally have at each other.

Careful though they were about the speed limit, patrolmen pulled them over three times: in northwest Georgia; on the outskirts of Birmingham; and while approaching Slidell, Louisiana, forty miles from their destination.

Each time Lou politely explained their situation. Whatever the officers may have thought about Negroes in general, they quickly empathized with the newlyweds. The Alabama trooper tore up the ticket, eyed Alba up and down, and said, "Yeah, boy, if'n I was goin to git with that, I'd have a heavy foot on my pedal, too."

Lou smiled brightly, said, "Yes, sir, I am one truly lucky man," thanked the officer and drove away.

In Slidell, the officer, Johnny Joe Romaine, leered at Alba and said, "Boy, must be nice, just married to Miss Lena Horne's baby sister."

Lou smiled brightly, said, "Yes, sir, I am one truly lucky man," thanked the officer and drove away.

Forty-five minutes later they cheered as they entered the New Orleans city limits. Lou found Carrollton Avenue and followed it to Palmetto Avenue, where he made a left. A few blocks later, across from the Xavier College campus, sat the Palmetto Inn. From the outside, it scarcely looked like the place Cootie had raved about. However, once inside the check-in cottage, they found it to be impeccably clean. A small but energetic crew of attendants bolted to attention when the newlyweds rolled in.

"We've been waiting for you-all," said a pretty lemon-colored girl with a beguiling gap between her perfectly straight, perfectly white teeth.

"Any guest of Clai Coutrere is a V.I.P. around here," said the night manager, a dark-skinned, wavy-haired man of about thirty. He snapped his fingers and a bellhop materialized. Handsome, brown-skinned, and at the midpoint between six and seven feet in height, he was a basketball star at Xavier named Ivan, Lou soon learned.

The Palmetto was actually a *motel*, consisting of two main, one-story buildings that resembled army barracks. Painted eggshell white, wood-framed, both buildings housed a dozen rooms. In separate cottages were the check-in area and the honeymoon suite. Ivan deftly piled the luggage—two medium-sized suitcases for Lou, four large ones for Alba—onto a cart and led them toward the suite, all the while grinning wildly as his gaze bounced from Alba to Lou.

The suite was spotless. A lemony fragrance filled the cooled air; someone had already turned on the air conditioner. A dozen roses lay primly across the drawn-back bed sheets. An ice bucket stocked with two fifths of Dom Perignon sat on a coffee table.

Lou tipped the ever-grinning Ivan two dollars. "If you need anything, just ring," the lad said as he thanked the couple and wished them a good night.

After Ivan left, Alba switched off the air conditioner and flicked on the overhead ceiling fan. Its monstrous blades resembled junior helicopter propellers. "You know what that fake air does to my sinuses...and we don't want Alba to get sick on her wedding night, do we?" she said in a husky voice.

"Oooohh, nooooo!" Lou replied, unconsciously aping the refrain from "Botheration," the band's next release. He offered up a silent prayer of thanks. He had feared the long trip would cause Alba to postpone the final part of their marriage rite until after a good night's sleep. However, the twinkle in her eye and the jingle in her tone told Lou she was as anxious as he.

"I'm, going to...uh...take a bath, then...you know...slip into something more comfortable," Alba said, giving the line her most seductive Marilyn Monroe delivery.

"I'm not going anywhere," Lou replied. Alba winked heavily, then closed the bathroom door behind her.

Lou lay back on the bed and tried vainly to be patient. On sheer reflex action, he started to disrobe as he heard Alba run water in the bathtub. He lay back again, this time with a divining rod aimed at the overhead fan.

He continued to battle impatience. He turned on a bedside radio, fished along the dial, and hooked a station with a colored-sounding, butter-voiced jockey. "This is Sweet Willie Walker, the smooth talker, the fox stalker, playin those cherished Midnight Melodies. So cuddle up with the one ya love and get cozy like a hand in a glove. Here's Claude McPatter & the Wanderers with 'Do Whatcha Wanna'..."

Yeah, perfect station, he thought, as McPatter's voice oozed from the shoebox-sized radio. Five minutes passed, then ten. "You okay in there?" he shouted. "Didn't fall in, did you?"

"Mmm-mmm..."

"I take that to mean you're okay..."

Alba responded with a laugh. "Patience...patience..."

"I've *been* patient ever since I've known you." A plan formed in Lou's head. *She can only tell me to go back out and wait...*

He rose, donned a bathrobe, and padded into the steam-filled bathroom. Half-expecting her to squeal at him to get out, he grinned broadly when she gave him a shy, yet come-hither smile. He kneeled beside the tub and splashed water on her glistening, grapefruit-sized breasts.

"Mind if I join you?" he asked, innocently.

She fluttered her wedding band hand across his face. "Why not?"

Lou let the robe drop to the floor. She made room for him in the tub; he climbed in and fitted himself so that he, Alba, the hot water, suds, and tub were one. They rubbed each other with washcloths and Ivory soap in slow, nerve-tingling motions. She rose from the tub and he followed. They languidly patted each other dry with fluffy towels. It was then Lou decided Alba's second pair of dimpled cheeks was even prettier than the set he had admired for years.

They walked hand in hand to the bed. As Alba primly sat on the edge, "Louisiana Moon" by Louisiana Fats purred from the radio. "Dang!" Alba blurted. "Did Mister Cootie set *that* up, too?"

Lou laughed. "He's got a lot of clout, but I think The Big Guy Upstairs put that one on the turntable," he said with an upward glance.

Their gazes brushed, then locked. Suddenly, they heard neither the music nor any other sound. Instinct took over; they melted together and molded...

...And made up for all the frustrating moments on Armstrong's Lookout and other places until well past dawn. At one point they took a breather. Lou looked at his watch; it was a quarter to five; he could barely tell if he was dead or alive. After what seemed like minutes later it was a quarter past seven; Lou wondered if he had died and gone to Heaven. The next time he looked at his watch it was nearly nine; Lou groaned, "Baby, looks like we're at the end of *this* line."

Soon both were fast into the deepest sleep of their lives.

Lou woke up shortly after four p.m. The adamant sub-tropical sun hurt his eyes, even though the thick, floor-to-ceiling curtains held back most of it. Alba was already awake, staring at him. "Heeeey," she growled, melodically.

"Heeeey," he mimicked. "You hungry?"

"For food, no. For you, yes."

"Bad girl. Where's that champagne?" She nodded toward the refrigerator. He trotted to the box and retrieved the last bottle. Never taking his eyes off her, he worked the cork until it popped, jetting toward the spinning blades of the ceiling fan, spilling some of the bubbly liquid over the bottle's neck.

"Ooooo," she cooed. "What's *that* remind you of?"

Lou handed her the bottle. "Girl, you're a mess," he said as she took a long swig.

"Whhheee...!" she sang.

"The Plot: to get you drunk and seduce you," Lou intoned.

"*Une fait accompli,*" she said as she dusted off her high school French.

They went at it for another set of rounds. By eight p.m., they were too sore and tired to continue. They ordered a room-service meal of steak, French fries, cornbread, and turnip greens. The waiter—Ivan again—brought them two more bottles of Dom Perignon.

"We figured yawl'd be—thirsty," Ivan said with a naughty-little-boy's grin.

"We're that and more," Alba said as she tipped him a dollar. "Now shoo."

"Yes, ma'am." He grinned, genuflected, and left.

The meal put them to sleep. Now it was Monday morning, and as Lou stared at the ceiling fan, he reflected on the nearly day-and-a-half they had spent in New Orleans—without seeing any of New Orleans.

He turned to see that Alba was awake and drinking him in with eyes filled with sleep and love. He planted a sloppy kiss on her forehead. The phone shrieked. "One guess," said Lou. He picked it up. "Hey, Cootie, what's doing?" Lou greeted.

A loud laugh registered from thirteen hundred miles away. "Yeah, who else could this be but li'l ol' me? What's up, hotshot? Oops—poor choice of words."

Lou shook his head and chuckled. "From anyone else that would've been corny as all get-out...but from The World's Hippest Human..."

"Yeah, yeah, yeah. Hey, Big Time, look under the door, why don'tcha."

From where he sat, Lou saw a small, rectangular booklet. "Looks like the *Jet*-book, or something," he said.

"Or something. Go get it, check it out."

Lou sprang from the bed, picked up the magazine, and was greeted by his own smiling face, surrounded by Deuce, Blondie, and Jimmy. Above was the caption: "Tennessee Bluesmen Reach Top With 'Cora Ann.'"

Lou hollered on sheer reflex.

"What?" Alba cried hopefully. Lou flung the magazine across the room and she made a nifty, one-handed catch. "Gracious me!" she squealed.

Lou picked up the phone again. "Wow, man!" was all he could say.

"You're with the gold-medal team now, poppa-stoppa. We don't bullshit. Now put the little lady on the horn."

"Hi, Mister Cootie!" Alba trilled into the phone before Lou had secured it in her hand. "Thanks for *everything!*"

"You behaving yourself in my hometown, girl?" Cootie demanded, his tone familiar, though he had never met Alba in person.

"Oh, no, sir—I'm *not*. And neither is Lou."

"Good for you-all. That's what honeymoons are for. Acting buck-
wild with the one you love. Create all the disturbance you want. Now
put your brand-new hubby back on the line, why don'tcha, honey."

She returned the phone to Lou. "Hey, Cootie," he boomed softly.

"Tuesday afternoon, Louisiana Fats and his band have a recording date. The next evening, Little Robert and his Go-Getters are
gonna cut some tunes."

"And…?"

"Told 'em both you'd sit in, and for them to have you a guitar ready."

"Look out!" Lou cried. "Details! Where? When?" Lou wrote
down the times and addresses as Cootie gave them.

"Now will you two finally *leave* that room and see my wonderful city?" Cootie said.

"Soon as we get off this line."

"If you-all want to spend a few extra days…"

"Thanks, but no thanks. Remember: somebody's got to get back
to New York and prepare for some new-fangled rock-n-roll show…"

"Good answer, Lou." He then gave Lou a list of places to visit
and people to meet, his parents included. "And you better enjoy yourself while you can," Cootie added, "because the rest of this year is
gonna be like living in a tornado. Now lemme speak to that sweetie-
peach one more time." Lou returned the phone to Alba, and she
exchanged good-byes with Cootie.

"See you in two weeks, Lou," Cootie closed.

"'Til then, Coot." Lou hung up and began to pore over the *Jet*
story with Alba.

"It's too brief—and shallow," Alba groused after they read the
article. "Tells nothing about you except you're from Knoxville, and
have the number-one hit."

Lou chuckled. "The reporter got how we were 'discovered'
entirely wrong." According to the article, Cootie had chanced upon
the group as he made a random stop on a motor trip. He signed them
on the spot, in the dressing room at the Blue Moon Club.

"Full, Blue—what does it matter what kind of moon it is?" Alba
cracked. Her face suddenly clouded. "The article doesn't have *any*
facts about any of you! Not even your ages." She tightened her
mouth. "Or that any of you guys are married."

Lou explained how publicists manipulated "facts" about their
artists to create—or squash—certain images. Still, Lou was relieved

that Cootie had lifted the veil of secrecy. However, he realized Cootie had timed the article for a precise purpose.

"He talks more about his new road show than about you guys," Alba continued to complain. "It's just one big plug—"

"Of *course* it is. What's wrong with that? And you can bet Cootie made a trade-off deal with the *Jet* publishers."

Alba's frown was indelible. "*Still...*I mean, all the other acts in the show have their pictures in *your* write-up—and who are these kids?" she asked as she tapped a picture of five tawny, handsome teenagers in white V-necked sweaters.

"The Lexingtons." Lou recounted the wild Amateur Night scene. "Besides," he continued, "the main purpose of the article is to hawk the revue." He nestled closer. "You don't want America knowing *too* much about me, do you?" he whispered.

"Noooo, Lou," she drawled.

He patted Alba on her curved, unclad thigh. "Let's get a bite to eat, then see what lies beyond these four walls."

They dined in a restaurant on South Claiborne, touted by Cootie as the best breakfast spot in the city. After a meal of eggs, grits, broiled catfish, biscuits and honey, juice and coffee, they were ready to tackle New Orleans.

They drove downtown and parked in a lot. They immersed themselves into the river of humanity that flowed along Canal Street, and the narrow streets of the French Quarter. They could not walk ten minutes without "Cora Ann" blaring from a radio or jukebox. Lou figured the *Jet* cover story would ignite recognition of him, and he braced for it. Then he remembered that Cootie had sent him an *advance* copy; the issue would not be out for another two or three days.

That he would not have his vacation constantly interrupted by autograph seekers and well-wishers both relieved and disappointed him.

After three hours, Alba's feet started to ache. Lou left her at an outdoor café in the French Market and promised to return in three hours. He would branch out on foot beyond the downtown/French Quarter area, while she watched the sideshow of human traffic, sipped *café au lait*, nibbled on beignets, and resumed sightseeing on her own, if her feet recovered.

He walked up Orleans Avenue and surveyed what had been Congo Square, the Sunday afternoon meeting place for slaves and free people of color, so Cootie had informed him. He continued up Orleans to the beehive of blues clubs where Basin Street, Orleans, and North Claiborne converged. He did not go in any; he knew he would stay too long if he did. He realized he would *have* to tell the people in the clubs he was the "Cora Ann" man; surely someone would hand him a guitar and have him prove it.

I'll come back when I don't *have to tell 'em who I am*, he promised himself.

He walked further up Orleans, turned right on North Broad, and followed it to Esplanade. He made another right for his return to the French Quarter. He was starting to adjust to the heat. Knoxville was hot enough at the height of summer, but the extreme heat and humidity of Louisiana in August defied his imagination. Moreover, his feet had started to pulsate, but the last thing he needed was to hear his number-one record from the back of a Jim Crow streetcar, so he continued his stroll.

As he sponged in the city, Lou saw firsthand that its reputation as the nation's race-mixing capital was well-deserved. With the combinations of olive skin, wavy hair, and degrees of fullness of lips and noses, Lou wondered how anyone could discern light-skinned Negroes from naturally-swarthy Mediterranean whites. He also thought it strange that in one of the deepest outposts of the segregated South, whites and Negroes often interacted with ease. He was surprised to see colored and white eating and drinking together in some neighborhood, working-class saloons in and around the French Quarter, off the beaten tourists' paths.

He delighted in separating the individual sounds of the city from their cacophonous whole: overheated motors gasping to keep running; the sing-song pitches of street vendors; the snoring riverboat horns; clanging streetcar bells; the symphony of car horns when the pace of traffic became too slow, even by New Orleans's standards.

Lou marveled at how these sounds—and casual, everyday phrases—had found their way into the recordings of New Orleans-based hitmakers like Louisiana Fats, Little Robert, Floyd Rice, and others. He had to give them credit: New Orleans moved to the rhythms of its own composite beat, and the artists had captured and spun them into vinyl gold.

Thinking of Fats and Little Robert caused Lou's guitar-picking fingers to tingle. He hoped the singers were as eager to meet him as he was to see them. He looked at his watch; it was twenty minutes past the time he was to meet Alba. Ten minutes of brisk walking got him to their appointed spot. He expected her to be miffed over his tardiness, or to have caught a taxi back to the inn. Instead, she greeted him brightly; a pile of souvenirs surrounded her.

"My feet recuperated, honey," she smiled.

"Obviously. I'll go get the car, then try not to get a hernia while I'm loading all this." He playfully, lightly stepped on her foot.

"Ow! That *hurt!*"

"Guess they need a massage. When we get back to the hotel, I'll start with the feetsies, then slooowly work my way up..."

"Careful, buster. Don't make promises you can't keep..."

"We're wastin time talking 'bout it."

"Well, heck—let's motorvate!" Alba laughed. Lou kissed her and went to get the car.

* * * * *

They spent Tuesday morning with more sightseeing and shopping. That afternoon, while Alba visited some distant relatives, Lou embarked for the Cosmo's Studios on Treme Street, where Andre "Louisiana Fats" Alexandre and his band would be recording four new songs.

The moment they saw each other, Fats and Lou fell into a hug, expressed their mutual admiration, and briefly talked R & B. When it was time to record, Fats nodded to a guitar on a bench and said, "Let's cut some blues."

"You know it, brother," Lou replied, and they went to work. Five hours later, Fats was so pleased with the session that he phoned a Cadillac dealership on Loyola Avenue and ordered a gold '56 Seville. He then telephoned his wife, to tell her they would have guests for dinner.

Fats' wife, Rosetta, looked not unlike him, with her round, brown baby face. She was not as chubby as him, though. Though only in their late twenties, Fats and Rosetta already had six sprightly, stocky children. "And we're only halfway to where we're gonna wind up," said Fats, as he patted Number Seven inside Rosetta's tummy.

"Four's going to be our limit—if that many," Alba responded.

"Amen to that," Lou chimed in.

The couples sat around listening to music; Lou and Fats learned they adored—and were influenced by—many of the same artists: Gutbucket McDaniel, Moody Rivers, Big Joe Turner, C.C. Prince, Gene Autry, Leadbelly, Hank Williams, Louis Armstrong, Louis Jordan, Louis Prima, Bob Wills, Larry Darnell, Lionel Hampton, Cab Calloway, and Duke Ellington. They expressed how they especially loved the flawless phrasing of Nat "King" Cole, Frank Maggio, and Perry Martin—and admired their tastes in choosing material. Before anyone realized it, midnight was two hours behind them. "Man, we've *got* to go—we're having brunch with Cootie's parents at noon."

"Don't yawl *dare* eat nothin before you go," Fats said with a laugh. "The way them Coutreres feed you, by the time you roll outta there, they'll be callin *you* 'Tennessee Fats.'" The couples then reluctantly parted company.

The next day, at noon on the dot, Alba and Lou were on the porch of a magnificent, white-brick, two-story house on Saint Bernard Avenue. A stunning couple at the midpoint of middle age slowly opened the door. The Coutreres, Thierry and Felicia, gave the Cannons courtly nods, then led them into the house.

"Mister Cootie's the spitting image of his mother," Alba whispered as they followed the Coutreres. "And his daddy looks just like that classy British actor, Rex Harrison, but with a gorgeous suntan." Thierry turned and smiled, to let her know he had heard and appreciated the remark. He and his wife then took them into a high-ceilinged parlor, pristinely clean and stocked with what were obviously priceless antiques. Obligatory, introductory small talk followed, then the Coutreres opened a bulky family album, and proudly displayed their ancestors and living relatives. Some of the pictures were made in the infancy of photography itself. Lou was amazed that several of Cootie's relatives were darker than he and many of *his* relatives.

They then repaired to the backyard patio, where platter sized leaves of live oak trees kept the August sun at bay. The Coutreres told the Cannons *their* version of how Cootie got into the broadcasting business; Lou filled them in on his young career, and how Cootie had engineered the band's big break. After twenty minutes on the cool patio, a Negro maid announced—first in French, then English—that brunch was ready.

Thierry and Felicia led them into a bright, airy dining room. The maid, Odette, then served the meal. For the appetizer, she placed gumbo and hot, freshly-baked bread before them. Rice, squash, fried red snapper, crab cakes, and spinach followed and soon disappeared, washed down by endless glasses of iced tea.

As Lou started on second helpings, he remembered he was to sit in with Little Robert and His Go-Getters that evening; he did not want to be sluggish. When Odette brought the dessert, he passed on the small mountain of homemade peach ice cream, but devoured a healthy chunk of German chocolate cake. The couples then reluctantly parted company, and Lou and Alba drove to the nearby French Quarter. Miraculously, they found a parking space on Royal Street. It was minutes past six o'clock; the session was to begin "anywhere between seven and eleven, whenever Robert decides he's ready to roll," Cootie had told Lou.

"Your feet up to walking off some of that meal?" Lou asked.

"I'll let you know when my dawgs start barking."

"Let's ambulate."

They strolled through the French Quarter and darted inside a drug store on Dumaine Street when a flash thunderstorm attacked. For five minutes, the rain thudded in watery staves; then the torrent ended as abruptly as it had begun, and they resumed their stroll. The rain had lowered the temperature by at least five degrees.

At a quarter after eight, they entered the Unique Records studio on Frenchmen Street, just off the French Quarter proper. The musicians and technicians greeted Lou and Alba as if they were visiting royalty. Yet, Little Robert himself had not arrived.

The hitmaker ripped in at nine-thirty, leading the fanfare of his one-man parade. "The Kang is here! Let's peel the paint off these walls, chilluns!" he cried. Lou sauntered over to Robert and introduced himself. Little Robert, thin, medium height, barely twenty, his complexion indiscernible because of the thick pancake make-up, painted-on rosy cheeks, mascara, plucked eyebrows, purple lip gloss, pompadoured hair stacked nearly a foot high and all, gawked at Lou for a lengthy moment.

"You's a *Negro*! The 'Cora Ann' man is one of us, chilluns!" he shrieked.

"Been that way all my life," Lou said with a smile.

"I knew it! I just knew it! Hunny, I bet me some *good* money you was cullud, you hear me, chile?" Robert hollered to the room: "All you persons that bet me Lou Cannon was a white hillbilly boy—pay up! JUST PAY UP! Have my moolah on this here pee-anno 'fore we leave here tonight, I'm here to tell you!"

Robert calmed down long enough for the session to begin. Lou, sitting in on rhythm guitar, helped the Go-Getters lay down three raucous tracks. Even Alba got in on the act, singing background, hand-clapping, and playing the tambourine on two of the songs.

Although the session lasted until a quarter to three, nobody was tired when they filed out of the studio. In parting, Little Robert wailed, "You, me, Fats, that Hal Dillard person, them cute li'l ol' Philly gals—we gon' SHAKE UP AMURICA! This country's got three more weeks of PEACE, then WE gon' ex-ploooode, like a nuclular bum! You hear me, chillun? Gon' turn the joint OUT, from coast to coast! Now what I just say?"

"Yeah, we're going to make history," Lou said, more out of self-defense than agreement. They reluctantly parted company. As soon as Alba and Lou returned to the Palmetto Inn, sheer fatigue overtook them like an unexpected storm.

Still, Lou was up and about at ten that morning. He had a full day in front of him with the city's top disk jockeys, colored and white. He toured a half dozen radio stations. The jockeys interviewed him but briefly, all asking roughly the same cotton-candy questions—that Cootie had scripted and sent them.

Before they realized it, Friday tiptoed up, and it was time to return to Knoxville. They made "thank you" calls from their hotel to Fats and Rosetta, the Coutreres, Little Robert, and the deejays. When Lou tried to tip the staff at the Palmetto, the manager smiled, shook his head, and said that Cootie had long since taken care of that, too.

"Of course," Alba said.

Before they hit the highway, they telephoned Cootie. "Thanks again for everything—"

"All the thanks I need is sitting atop *Cashboard*'s pop chart."

Lou was dumbfounded.

"I take it you haven't picked up an issue yet," Cootie continued.

"No, I haven't," Lou admitted. His last few days were so hectic he had forgotten 'Cora Ann' would probably head the pop listing, also.

"And next week, we'll make it a trifecta; we'll be top dawg on the country chart, too," Cootie crowed, "even if I have to grease the last few reluctant, squeaking wheels."

Lou laughed loudly. "Whatever you mean by that—I *don't* want to know."

"You know exactly what I mean. And while you-all won't be the first to make that triple play, you will be the first *colored* studs to pull it off!"

"I like it like that!" Lou cried. Alba hooked his attention and rolled her eyes in the general direction of the highway. "Later, Coot— gotta motorvate. Call you when we get home."

At that same time, twenty-four hours later, Alba and Lou were in the Cannons' living room, regaling their friends and relatives with tales of the Voodoo City.

"Wow, man—life as R & B stars is gonna be one nonstop blast!" Blondie wailed when Lou recounted the Little Robert session.

"Yeah—but let's hope we don't get burnt when the bomb goes off," Lou retorted.

Everyone chuckled. Lou felt Alba squeeze his hand; he cut his eyes to catch his father gazing at him, oddly concerned.

* * * * *

Part Three

"Rhythm Revue"

CHAPTER SIXTEEN

Tuesday, August 23, 1955; 2:46 p.m.
Newport News, Virginia.

In a rare moment away from his two capitals—his nation and his state's—Senator Theophilis Briscoe enjoyed a week of something akin to relaxation.

He was sprawled in a lounge chair on the porch of the family's getaway cottage. Congress would not resume for three weeks; nothing in his home state demanded his presence. Virginia and the girls were careening about Europe on one of those whirlwind tours. He missed the girls, but cherished the moments of solitude.

From the ocean a quarter-mile away, a rush of salty, cooling breeze caressed him, as pleasant as a surprise kiss from a comely woman. He sipped from the tall, thin glass of Jack Daniel's on the rocks. From inside the wood-frame cottage he heard his colored maid, Esther, making noise with the dinner pots and pans. Esther's husband—and Theo's valet—Abner, was behind the cottage, tending to his vegetable garden. Theo heard faint strains of the local Negro station from Abner's tinny-toned, fist-sized transistor radio.

Today is what—Tuesday? Theo looked at the knee-high stack of Sunday editions of the nation's major newspapers. To stay on top of current events, he got into the habit years ago of browsing through them to get the local perspectives. While Congress was in session, Theo stole moments throughout Sunday and Monday to read the most pertinent articles; he would read the rest by Tuesday. Now, on vacation, he could read them in a more leisurely fashion, then move on to the Negro press.

Every Tuesday morning Esther handed him what she called "the colored papers": the *Pittsburgh Courier, Chicago Defender, Baltimore Afro-American, Los Angeles Sentinel, Louisiana Weekly, New York Amsterdam News,* the latest issues of *Ebony, Jet* and *Negro Digest.* Theo kept a tight eye on the shifting tides in Negro America, keeping current on which leaders were compliant, which were too militant, which could be negotiated with, which had to be silenced in one manner or another...

As always, Theo began his study of the Negro press by thumbing through *Jet* magazine; he liked to take a gander at the bronze bathing beauty in the center leafs. He fished the magazine from the pile. The cover photograph startled him. *Who'd-a thunk it? The boys who made "Cora Ann" are Negroes!* He held the magazine closer to get a better look at the lead singer.

Mercy! Looks like that boy I almost ran into outside of...uh...Knoxville a while back.

He studied the photo yet more closely. *Nah...the world cain't be that small...*

Still, the caption said the band *was* from Tennessee. He opened the book to the cover story. Yes, the Blasters were from—Knoxville. *It could be him—but not likely. Probably someone who looks like him. Towns like that, half the folks are kin, anyway,* he reasoned.

Besides, I didn't get that *good a look at him,* Theo told himself. *Nah...just coincidence.*

Yet, he could not stop his eyes from returning to the lead singer. Does *sorta favor Peggy's black Indian. Sharp, high cheekbones and thinnish lips for so dark a nigger.* He tried to deny the resemblance as quickly as he acknowledged it. *Nah...that's a fairly common look with nigras mixed with Indian...*

He read the brief article, which was not so much about the Blasters, but a plug for the rhythm revue in which they would perform in the near future. He studied the picture of the disk jockey promoting the revue—and, according to the article—had discovered the Blasters. He remembered Coutrere from an *Ebony* cover story just months ago. From the name and features, Theo placed him as a New Orleans Creole Mulatto. *Slick bunch, them. Got to watch 'em. All that white blood went straight to their brains. Smartest, most industrious Negroes there are—that is, if you want to lump them with the Negroes.*

Then, there was the music, and the sensation it was becoming.

The news, and especially the Negro press, was full of the reactions of teenagers—white and black—to tunes like "Cora Ann." Records by Negro artists were more routinely showing up on white charts, and the reverse was also true. Just yesterday, Theo forced himself to listen for an hour to a station that played the new-fangled rock-n-roll. On about a third of the records, he could not guess which singers were white or colored. Many of the lyrics he considered inane, others downright smutty, though often in a clever way—that is, if he could understand the words at all.

The music, and the teens' reaction to it, reminded Theo of a slow gas leak in a large room: early on, it was harmless, but could have disastrous results if it went unchecked.

Though it was vacation time, he felt compelled to make a handful of phone calls.

* * * * *

Two afternoons later, Theo met with Chance Elam, his personal attorney for the past ten years, and Reece Stracker, a member of the House of Representatives from Theo's home state. Both were vacationing in nearby cottages. He gave Esther and Abner the day off; he would be saying things he did not want them to hear—and they were experts at "overhearing" private conversations. The attorney and the congressman met with Theo in his air-conditioned den; he deflected them from their planned fishing trip with the pretext of a high-stakes poker game, followed by the latest in stag movies.

When he told them the true reason for the meeting, Reece turned crimson. Lantern-jawed, six-foot-five and a still rock-like two hundred fifty pounds, Reece, like Theo, was a man of humble origins whose ticket through Ole State had been punched with a helmet and shoulder pads. Unlike Theo, who had been a reliable but unspectacular performer, Reece had been All-Southeastern Conference as a two-way end. He played nearly three years of pro ball with the New York Giants until his knee was pulverized on a frozen Polo Grounds field against the Chicago Bears. When Theo *finally* retired from his senate seat, forty-year-old Reece was the odds-on favorite to be elected his successor.

"Theo!" Reece thundered, his pale gray eyes wide in outrage. The veins popped in his trunk-like, sun-burnished neck. "This sounds too damn close to official business to me, bub!" he said when Theo introduced the topic of their discussion. Reece wrapped his paddle-like hands around a quart bottle of J & B scotch, poured a quarter of a water glass and knocked it back, all in a single, fluid movement.

"Hell, yeah—Reece is right! We're on *vacation*, by God!" Chance Elam groused. A pale, graying, balding, unathletic man in his late forties, Chance was regarded as having one of the shrewdest legal minds on Capitol Hill. Thus, Theo kept him on a healthy retainer. Though Theo had great confidence in his own knowledge of the law, he believed in the adage that anyone who serves as his own attorney has a fool for a client. Chance's expertise was invaluable for Theo when he needed to know and sidestep fuzzy legal areas.

Moreover, Theo often tried out his ideas on Chance, knowing that Chance would play the Devil's Advocate. With Chance's input, and sometimes Reece's, Theo saw the flaws in his more offbeat notions— or the cockeyed logic. Afraid he could be reading too big a threat into the new rock-n-roll, Theo would see where his two friends stood on the matter.

"You're gonna keep us cooped up, gassin about *that* cater-waulin?" Reece squalled in disbelief. "Hell, we're on vaca—"

"I know we're on holiday—but that's why we vacation near each other when we can, so we can stay on top of things like this," Theo said, patiently.

Chance scowled. "Niggers and hillbillies blending their music so it's hard to tell who's who on a record. Will you *please* tell us why that's so all-fired important?"

"Just look at the Big Picture. You boys are aware of how rock-n-roll has become the most popular music with teenagers overnight, right?"

"Of *course*, Theo," Reece replied, testily.

"Sure, we've heard the rumblings about the 'voodoo music' and the encoded lyrics about sex and race mingling," Chance said.

"I'll tell you what this rock-n-roll is *really* about," Reece snort-ed. "The record folks have rinsed off that same race music—"

"They call it rhythm-and-blues now," Theo interrupted.

"—that white parents wouldn't let their kids buy and bring in the house, made it 'acceptable' under its new name. The old bait-and-switch, is all it is," Reece completed.

"Yep, you're right," Theo seconded. "The parents know what cooks with all them gruntin baritone saxophones answered by them high-pitched horns. They know the score on all them leer-ics about sixty-minute men and drippin honey and big pistols and twelve-inch rulers and cherry pies and long, slow rides through the tunnel of love and whatnot."

"Me, I don't see what all the ruckus is about," Reece declared. "White kids listenin to nigger music for a sliver of a moment. Big fuckin deal. Just tryin-a be—rebellious. A new way to get under their parents' skin, is all."

"Yeah, buddy. That fad'll last about as long as a fart in a hurri-cane," Chance scoffed.

"Twenty years from now, those kids are gonna wonder what the hell possessed 'em to plunk down their allowances for that crap. And they'll be dead set against *their* kids bringin similar mess into the house," Reece predicted.

"What harm's gonna come from white kids listening to a few half-smutty records over a short haul? No different than buying fuck-books, sneaking off to ogle them, then yanking their doodles," Chance added.

Theo looked at them, carefully aghast. "Yawl don't get it. Most adult white Americans don't, either. This music is gonna be around for more than a minute—and it's gonna have more impact than you can imagine, judgin from your nonchalance toward it."

"Okay, Theo, let's hear it. What makes you think it's gonna stick—and be so influential?" Reece asked, and settled back in his chair.

"White kids started noticin that R & B in '52. Adam Freeman—"

"That Jew boy Chicago disk jockey?"

"That's him, Reece, but don't interrupt me. Freeman started promotin record hops and live shows. Since Chicago's got no official Jim Crow laws, his audiences were always mixed."

"But that was three years ago. Why's the music just taking off *now*?" Chance asked.

The three nodded to Hezekiah Hester as he slipped into the room, carrying two large manila envelopes.

"Three reasons. Until recently, most R & B songs sounded too much alike—like most music within the same genre does. Sure, there were a coupla groups who cut decent tunes—by *those* standards..." Theo paused to fish for the names.

"Hal Dillard & the Moonlighters, and Claude McPatter & the Wanderers," Hezekiah softly replied.

"Yeah, them. White kids liked them, too, but they weren't—aren't—*crazy* about them," Theo continued.

"So who—or what—got white kids goin bat-shit over this music?" Reece asked.

Hezekiah opened an envelope and placed four eight-by-ten photographs on the table.

"I know him," Chance said as he pointed to one. "The little round nigra from New Orleans. Hell, I *like* some of his records," he added, without shame or irony.

Reece pointed to another photo. "Ain't this the girlie-boy who screams on his records?"

"He's only had two hits," Theo said disdainfully, "that white folks bought, anyway."

Reece pointed to a third picture and laughed. "And this is the Johnny-come-lately who had white folks thinkin he was the second comin of Hank Williams."

"Yep. Cannon fooled even me," Theo admitted.

"This quadroon," Chance tapped the fourth picture. "Who's he?"

Theo explained how Coutrere engineered the breakout hits of the three artists, using his syndicate of jockeys, white and colored, across the country. "And, in a roundabout way, he's the manager of all three-a them, too," Theo added.

"Is that legal?" Reece asked, looking at Chance, then Theo.

"Yep. And I bet it's pretty common in that world. We just started lookin into that," Theo replied as he clapped Hezekiah on his hard, round shoulder.

"Theo. Don't tell me you're gonna spend precious time and money snooping into rock-n-roll folks's lives," Chance said, carefully. Theo nodded affirmatively. "It bears repeating: you might be aiming atom bombs at anthills," Chance said.

"Boys," Theo began, as if addressing stubborn toddlers. "You know how in the ancient myths there's a musician who seduces women by his songs alone—"

"Theee-oooow," Reece groaned.

"Don't interrupt. Listen. The Pied Piper. Then there's the real-life equivalents. Frank Maggio, in the early forties—had all the bobby-soxers goin ape."

"What's *any* of that got to do with rock-n-roll—and these niggers?" Reece growled as he pointed to the photographs.

"Listen and learn, bubbachuck. All adds up to one thing: women, throughout history, have lost their senses—among other things—to any good-lookin musician who strikes their fancy. Rock-n-roll keeps expandin, there's gonna be an epidemic of young white gals creamin their panties over nigra singers. And," Theo held up Lou Cannon's picture, "a shitload of white gals are gonna think he's handsome as all get-out."

"He *is*, Theo, but so what? You make out like all any white gal's gotta do is hear one-a them spades sing, and next she's yankin on some nigger's big black pipe."

"Reece is right. I hope you see the future mothers of our race in a better light than that," Chance said, scoldingly.

Theo threw up his right hand, palm outward. "Okay, maybe I overstated the case…a bit. But: some race mixin is *inevitable* if this music continues. And any at all is too much."

"You're right, Theo—you *are* overstating the case—"

"He may have something, Chance," Reece interrupted. "These things *do* snowball…and with the colored folks startin to get off their asses and demandin integration…"

"*Now* you're beginnin to see what cooks. Black boys dancin with white gals at record hops and live shows, white gals moonin over colored singers: that's where it starts. Where it winds up, only God knows," Theo said.

Chance eyed Theo sideways. "So this is about some pre-emptive strike?"

"Bingo."

"So…what's the early game plan?" Chance asked, warily, weari-ly. Theo pulled out an eight-by-ten photograph from the second enve-lope, of a white man in his mid-thirties. He was blandly handsome, with oversized, oddly attractive Basset-hound eyes. "Adam Freeman?" Chance guessed.

"You betcha. Coutrere's starting an all-Negro revue out of New York around Labor Day; Freeman's got an integrated show that hits the road from Chicago two weeks later. The Jew and the Creole are rivals, but good friends; they team up behind a record and it's a smash; they look out for each other, and stay out the other's way."

"They probably mapped their shows' schedules with that in mind," Chance speculated.

"You know it, bubbachuck. Hez and a few other boys are gonna shadow 'em, keep tabs on what happens in the audiences, try to dredge up the skinny from behind the scenes. Nobody lives wilder and looser than a pack of nigra musicians. After a week, Hez'll have enough dirt to fill the Grand Canyon, I'll wager," Theo said.

Hezekiah met his boss's words with a glimmer of a grin.

Theo shared with Chance and Reece what Hezekiah had netted in the last forty-eight hours. He supplied the names of Rick Claxton, The Fantabulous Fontaine, Paranoid Floyd Boyd, and seven others whom, along with Coutrere and Freeman, were the dozen biggest jockeys in the new teen-targeting music.

Several rounds of drinks later, the sun began its descent. Reece and Chance rose to go. As he left, Chance turned to Theo and asked: "Do you *really* think this Negro music fad is something we'll have to line up our battleships for?"

Theo smiled. "It better be. My adrenaline's already pumpin to beat the band. Can't let it go to waste on a false alarm."

"Like the Negro problem isn't getting ugly enough, with that mess in Mississippi over that kid from Chicago," Chance moaned. "And don't even mention last year's Supreme Court ruling that says we've got to integrate the schools…"

"Like I said: Big Picture. It all ties together," Theo replied.

"Yeah…maybe it does," Chance said in hedging half-agreement.

Reece eyed the near-empty bottle of whisky. "One for the road, boys," he said as he poured himself one.

"Just a splash for me," Chance said. Theo declined; he had already exceeded his limit.

"Mark my words: you boys'll be glad we had this little sit-down, when that nigra music whitens out and begins to infiltrate regular white society," Theo said. "Movies, commercials, television, whatnot..."

"If it does, we'll be ready for it," Reece replied, more than a little boozily.

"*Now* you're talkin like the Ole State Rebel you are!" Theo crowed as he slapped Reece on his shoulder blade. Chance and Reece departed; Theo nodded to the bottle. "Kill it, Hez."

Hezekiah went into the kitchen and returned with a half glass of milk. He poured the remainder of the scotch in and stirred it with his forefinger.

"Isn't there a Greek myth, sir, where a musician comes to town, seduces all the women, gets them to leave their husbands?" Hezekiah asked.

"Yep. But only temporary. The spell wears off, the hubbies ketch that fucker."

"Yeah," Hezekiah chuckled as he sipped his drink. "The music man didn't fare too well."

"Nope," said Theo, softly. "Not at all." He started to tell Hezekiah of a dream he had three times in as many weeks. Negro and white couples exited a rock-n-roll show from an enormous arena. Actually, they came out of a cavern in a mountainside. The music still throbbed from within. Each couple brandished a coffee-colored, sandy-haired, cat-eyed infant in swaddling clothes. The babies stared at Theo, daring him to comment.

Front and center were Dion Eason and Peggy, thrusting their issue inches from his face.

"Sir...?" he heard Hezekiah say. He looked up to see a quizzical, faintly pained look on Hezekiah's face.

"Yeah, Hez?"

"You mumbled something about never downplaying the effect nigger music had on white gals, sir," Hezekiah replied, cautiously.

"I did? That's 'cause it's true," Theo said with a chuckle and a shrug. He looked directly into Hezekiah's eyes. "Thanks for everything. That's all I need for now."

"Sure, boss. I understand."

Soon Theo heard Hezekiah start his car and drive off. He opened a fresh bottle and poured a drink. As the fiery liquid snaked down his throat, he eased into his favorite chair and his memory winged to the summer of 1917, like a homing pigeon guided by pure instinct...

He blocked the image before it formed completely. And though he never liked to use alcohol as a crutch, he downed two quick shots, to help keep *that* memory at bay...

CHAPTER SEVENTEEN

Cootie and Willa spent the two weeks before the Rhythm Revue's opening night in a hurricane of preparation.

They finalized dates, venues, hotel accommodations, and contracts. Vocal and band arrangements were smoothed, teeth fixed, hair straightened, costumes tailored, chaperones lined up. In two cases, they made deals with probation officers. Moreover, all seven of the acts in the revue would be showcasing new singles, so they took care of the important jockeys.

They began pushing the Lexington's debut release, "Lost Love, Last Love," the smooth ditty that wowed the Amateur Night crowd. Two weeks after its release, the song, a bouncy lament of teen love gone awry, was streaking toward the top ten on the pop chart. If it did not hit number one on the R & B, it would surely land in the top three. The composer was Marquette Walch, who taught English at George Washington High in upper Manhattan, where three of the Lexingtons attended. Willa and Cootie met Walch, listened to his other compositions, and had the Felders sign him as a staff writer at .30/.30. Next, Willa took him under her managerial wing.

"This kid is going places," said Willa of the twenty-three-year-old, baby-faced, scholarly-looking tunesmith.

Willa established the Philadelphia Belles as the "sister group" to the Lexingtons. Both were comprised of fresh-faced, clean-cut teenagers. Willa scheduled them together at record hops and on radio and television shows. She felt this was a low-risk way to give them the experience and exposure they needed.

"We may need some extra security men to keep the guys—our guys—away from Shirley Williams," Willa said of the tall, vivacious, eighteen-year-old lead singer of the Belles. "That girl's got an hourglass figure that could give Marilyn Monroe a run for it."

"Don'tcha just know it," Cootie said, a wolf-whistle in his tone.

Willa elbowed him hard in the ribs. "Don't be so quick to agree," she said, laughing.

On Tuesday, the day before they began two days of marathon rehearsals, Cootie and Willa took a rare holiday. They motored out to Montauk Beach on Long Island and held down beach blankets until sunset. They savored the respite; they knew it would be their last day of leisure until the first week of the next year.

* * * * *

The two weeks between Lou's return from his honeymoon and the revue's opening passed in a jumble of appearances in the Northeast: television dates in Buffalo, Philadelphia, Pittsburgh, and Syracuse; gigs in the better colored nightclubs; too many radio interviews to count. Many of their appearances were payments to certain jockeys for riding "Cora Ann." The four were relieved when it was time to return to New York for the show's rehearsals; at least they would not have to try to remember what city they were in.

Their whirlwind ride *did* have its share of joyful moments. On a Saturday night in Buffalo, just hours after their appearance on *Buffalo Jukebox*, the band went to see the legendary bluesman, McKinley "Gutbucket" McDaniel, perform at the Pine Grill. A shade under six feet, lean as a bean, a good guess of Gutbucket's age was between thirty-five and seventy-five.

When Gutbucket took a beer break, the Blasters cornered him and introduced themselves. "'Cora Ann'—sounds more'n a bit like Leadbelly and Blind Lemon's 'Silver City Bound,'" Gutbucket mentioned, without accusation.

Lou smiled; Cootie was the only other person to make that connection. "Then you must *really* like the flipside, 'Late, Late at Night'—"

"Yep. Changed a few notes of my 'It's Dawn and You're Gone.' Nineteen-hunnerd and fo'ty-four. Cain't for the life of me recollect who *I* stole that damn tune from," Gutbucket said with a dry laugh.

Cutting short his beer break, Gutbucket announced to the packed Pine Grill crowd, "Them 'Cora Ann' fellas is in the house." Before they had time to think about it, the Blasters borrowed instruments from the house band and wailed away on three numbers. Afterwards, Gutbucket told them, "You boys might do okay after all. I'll keep my eye out for you." The Blasters fell over themselves thanking him, then jumped into Jimmy's Cadillac and headed for Pittsburgh.

Lou told only Blondie that Alba would join him in New York for the Apollo kick-off. He felt it was no one's business, nor of any importance in the overall scheme of things.

* * * * *

As promised, Willa and Cootie devoted the two days before opening night to run-through and technical rehearsals. They drilled their charges from noon to nearly midnight on both days. They practiced until every entrance, fanfare, lighting cue, dance step, musical and vocal note was seamless. The tiniest mistake called for a repeat. Though exhausted, by quitting time Thursday night, all forty-five members of the cast and crew *knew* the show was as exact as possible.

Cootie began Wednesday morning by introducing everyone. First were the Philadelphia Belles, who signed with .30/30 Records one week after graduating from Overbrook High in June 1954. The men in the company tried not to leer at the four cute teenagers, especially Shirley Williams. Shirley's unmarried paternal aunt, Miss Wynona Williams, stood up, faced the company, and glared balefully when Willa introduced her as the Belle's chaperone.

Next were the Lexingtons, whom everyone already knew. The five lads had taken it upon themselves to meet everyone weeks in advance. Big fans of all the established acts, they had waited outside stage doors, staked out hotel lobbies, and slipped into dressing rooms to meet the hitmakers. Since the boys were so charming and polite, nobody regarded them as pests. "You're good kids—now stay that way. Don't let your hit go to your heads," Hal cautioned.

Because they ranged in age from thirteen to sixteen, the Lexingtons would require a tutor on the road. Gloria Franklin, Lydell's mother, would chaperone the boys during the first few weeks. She would then return to Washington Heights and Lydell's four younger brothers."Mark my words," Cootie confided to Willa. "The Lexington's are gonna do their share of cutting up—but that Little Lydell's gonna be a *pistol*, you hear me! He's got that twinkle in his eye."

"If he's going to be a pistol, he'd better be a *good* pistol," Willa replied. "*I* wouldn't find anything—cute—about bailing him out of trouble in some town whose name he can't even spell," she said, and left it at that.

After the Lexingtons, Willa introduced Moanin' Lisa, whose real name was Othellia Brayley. Little Robert's description of her was the consensus: "That chile so ugly 'til she cute." Short, muscular, hard-looking, she hailed from Cincinnati. She was one of those artists whose records sold well in the R & B market, but was considered too "colored" to connect with general audiences. Thanks largely to Cootie, her recent "Twelve-Inch Ruler" had become a cult classic. Cootie cleaned up her original lyrics so the song could get *some* airplay, albeit only late at night, and on shows like his own. Willa and he harbored no delusions that Lisa was crossover material, but felt she added diversity to the lineup—and she did have a decent following among Negroes.

Cootie then had Hal Dillard and his Moonlighters stand up. They needed no introduction. In the two years since Hal had escaped the assembly line at Buffalo's Chevrolet plant, half their eight releases had topped the R & B chart, their weakest-selling faring no worse than sixth. Their reputation as R & B's reigning bad boys, comically risqué lyrics and all, prevented all but the most daring white deejays from playing their records. Regardless, their tunes were simply irresistible; the surest way to revive a dying party was to spin a Moonlighters disc.

Lou recoiled with surprise when he saw Hal in person for the first time that Wednesday morning. The shortish, downright skinny lad hardly looked like the owner of the gritty baritone that wailed the raucous rhymes. Lou was startled further when he learned Hal was three months shy of his twentieth birthday. Lou liked him instantly; he could look into Hal's eyes and tell there was a permanent party going on inside.

Lastly, Cootie and Willa introduced Little Robert, Fats, and the Blasters, in that order.

The rehearsals slogged on. Wisecracks, intentional flubs, card and dice games, and gossip on the latest in the R & B world helped relieve the boredom. Willa and Cootie pretended not to notice as privileged performers smoked reefers, snorted a bit of cocaine, or took long pulls on half-pint liquor bottles in secluded areas. They knew these artists would not let their vices interfere with their work. As the hours snailed by, Cootie and Willa played the father, mother, favorite uncle, big sister, confidante, and referee to their charges—donning the appropriate mask for the situation.

Before Lou reported to the rehearsal Thursday morning, he picked up Alba at Pennsylvania Station. He had told Willa and Cootie she would be there for the opening; they had replied, with uncharacteristic abruptness, that rehearsals were off-limits to *everyone* but the cast and crew. They were, however, cordial to Alba when he introduced her during a dinner break that evening. Lou almost forgot his bride had never met them when Willa hugged Alba and purred, "It *seems* like we've known each other for a while," and Alba agreed.

Finally, shortly after ten on Thursday night, Willa and Cootie gathered the company in the front rows. Both admitted the show could still use a nip here and a tuck there, but a full night's rest would be of greater benefit to everyone.

Cootie thanked them for their hard work. He reminded them of the show's format at the Apollo and that, on Fridays and Saturdays in the bigger cities on the road, they would perform three or four shows. The Belles would lead off, followed by the Lexingtons. The teen groups would sing two songs each. Next would be Moanin' Lisa with "Twelve-Inch Ruler" and two earlier hits.

"That's the easy-to-figure part. The rest is trickier," he soft-shoed. The four remaining acts knew the issue at stake: who would close the show, and the order of the other three.

"Meritocracy," Willa said. Blank stares greeted this. "Plain and simple, we go by the last posted *Cashboard* chart. Whoever has the highest record closes the show, and that also determines the order of the remaining three."

"We usin the R & B or the white chart?" Hal Dillard asked.

Cootie smiled. He knew someone would ask that, and figured it would be Hal. "Pop chart." He threw up his hand to stem a wave of groans. "Aside from the biggest Negro houses, most of our ticket-buyers will be white," he explained.

"Especially once we're west of Chicago," Willa added.

Cootie gave his company a panning look. "Anybody got a problem with any of that?" he asked, measuring the right amount of vinegar into his voice.

"It's your highway, Coot; the rest of us is just hitchhikin," Hal replied.

"Long as we don't hafta go to Mi'sippi, where those crackers can do to us what they did to that poor Emmet Till boy," Moanin' Lisa said and touched off a chorus of agreement.

"I wouldn't subject you-all to nothing like that—"

"We know that. That's not what she meant," Lou intervened.

"Like, yeah," Cootie replied. He paused, then: "Now listen closely to what I say, and *understand* it." The troupers leaned to the edges of their seats. "The foreplay is over; now it's time to put the biscuit in the basket," Cootie began. "Let's walk through the ground rules one last time. I know none of you are *gross* foul-ups. I wouldn't've hired you if you were. Still, there's no lateness in this camp. Regardless of where you appear in the lineup, *everyone* will make the call for the show. Once you are in the building, you will not *leave* the building until that performance is over. On the days we do multiple shows, plan on remaining in the building. We'll send out for anything you need. You-all with me so far?"

"Preach, brother!" Blondie shouted.

"I have no use for anyone who hits my stage drunk or high on drugs." Cootie stopped as he saw this made some people squirm. "It's one thing to have a few pops or tokes *after* the show, to wind down; that's the nature of this business. But if you get tore up *before* you go on, and mess up on *my* stage, you just bought yourself a bus ticket home. No cocaine, no heroin, under *any* circumstance, while you're on *this* payroll."

Cootie knew that, despite what he had just dictated, he would look the other way for the Moonlighters, Moanin' Lisa, and many of the Rhythm Revue Orchestra members. They did their *best* work after snorting, smoking, or a few drinks. For them, Cootie had an alternate set of rules: they would not use drugs in front of anyone *not* in that small circle; they would neither buy nor sell drugs while at a performing venue; and they were never to try to encourage anyone to use drugs. Moreover, most of the veteran performers who abstained knew of this double standard, but understood its necessity.

"You will be prudent about your grooming and behavior on and off stage. I'm not telling you to tiptoe around like sanctimonious sissies, but you better not be running around tore up, pointing your pipes at anything that moves. Behind closed doors, with a willing partner *of legal age*, you can do any freaking thing you want, but in public, fellas: keep your zippers up; girls: keep your dresses down."

He peered into the audience. "Mrs. Franklin, Miss Williams, Belles, please excuse me—"

"Oh, hunny—we know you ain't squirin no Angelic Choir," Gloria Franklin interrupted. Miss Wynona Williams fidgeted and scrolled her eyes in the general direction of Heaven.

"One more thing," Willa added, "now that white kids have—discovered—our music, and are even trying to perform it—"

"And done re-named it rock-n-roll, chilluns," Little Robert cut in.

"We may have a rock or two—no pun intended—strewn in our paths," Willa continued after she cut Robert a don't-interrupt-me-again look. "This trip will not be all peaches and cream."

"At the risk of sounding paranoid," Cootie interjected, "there's talk that a backlash against rock-n-roll, R & B, race music—whatever you want to call it—is inevitable." He let this sink in. "In a sense, being the first big show to hit the road, we're the advance guard, the test case, venturing into uncharted land. We'll have to expect *everything:* pickets, boycotts, folks trying to interrupt our performances—the whole nine yards."

He saw worried looks sweep over many faces, especially the younger ones. "Not to say that *will* happen to any great degree," he backpedaled, "but we have to be ready for it."

"*That's* why you've got to be on your best behavior on and off stage," Willa took over. "Whoever our enemies may prove to be, let's not hand them the guns to shoot us with. Do you read me?" A murmur rose to the affirmative.

Cootie passed out sheets of paper to his crew. "I know you'll try your best to do right, but here's a list of infractions and fines, anyway." After giving them time to browse over the rules, he said, "Go home, get some rest, and come in ready to wail like you've never wailed in your lives. Sleep well. Cootie loves you all."

The cast and crew mumbled their love in return, then Little Robert leaped up, did a Jackie Gleason shuffle, and cried, "And away we go!"

Cootie looked at Robert, then Willa, then the company at large. "Yes," he chuckled softly. "And away we go."

* * * * *

And away they went. For weeks, the main topic of conversation across Negro America was Cootie the Cutie's Rhythm Revue, particularly its opening night.

The company performed two warm-up shows that Friday afternoon. Then came the official Opening Night, with its celebrity-packed audience.

The Philadelphia Belles, visibly nervous when they began, settled down enough to satisfy the tough Apollo crowd. The Lexingtons had no problems with stage fright; Little Lydell took the microphone and acted as if he had been born beneath a spotlight. Legend states that two-dozen pubescent girls were so overcome as Lydell warbled "Lost Love, Last Love" that they needed medical attention. Five, however, was the more accurate number.

Moanin' Lisa's bluesy, more subdued songs allowed the audience to catch its breath before Cootie loosed his chart-busting final four acts. The walls of the Apollo shook as Little Robert danced, pranced, mugged, and shouted his way through "Hot Lana From Atlanta" and "Good Night Kiss," his latest. Hal Dillard & the Moonlighters, resplendent in scarlet silk suits, kept the frenzy alive with a medley of their eight smashes. Louisiana Fats, as energetic on stage as he was reserved away from it, created the perfect musical bridge between the Moonlighters and that week's headliners: Lou Cannon & the Blasters.

Yet, as people discussed that opening night in barber shops, beauty parlors and pool rooms, over games of checkers, chess, dominoes, and poker in colored communities throughout America, much of the talk focused on its opening and closing moments.

Anyone who was anyone among New York City's Negroes attended. Searchlights in front of the theatre slashed across the late-summer night sky. Traffic logjammed on 125th Street from Lexington Avenue all the way to Broadway. A human tidal wave covered the block on which the Apollo sat. After a great struggle, the battalion of ushers jammed the guests into their proper seats. Finally, all was quiet in the fourteen-hundred-seat house and the house lights faded to black.

The Rhythm Revue Orchestra swung into "Cootie's Theme," then a Cockney voice announced: "Ladies and Laddies, an 'istorical event is about to unfold. Sit back, relax, and experience Cootie the Cutie's All-Star Rhythm Revue and Road Show! Look sharp now— 'ere's the dear lad—the World's 'ippest Yuman, Mister Rhythm-and-Blues 'imself—"

The audience, familiar with the radio-show incantation, drowned him out: "Cooootie the Cuh-yuuuuuutie!" A spotlight thudded on the back center aisle of the main floor. The crowd shrieked with outrage, disbelief, and sheer joy as a tuxedo-clad Cootie sat bareback astride a milk-white Arabian stallion. Two pretty bronze lasses, their hard but feminine muscles bulging in the scandalous two-piece swimsuits they barely wore, guided the steed down the aisle. Cootie waved and smiled, seemingly oblivious to the horse's uncertain gait, and the pandemonium around him.

When they reached the foot of the stage, Cootie dismounted gracefully. He then slid into a sedan chair, which four new brown musclegirls hoisted to shoulder height. The roar from the Apollo resounded for blocks as the strongwomen carried Cootie up the stairs, to downstage center, and deposited him before the microphone.

Never mind that his patter was well known to nearly everyone in the house. Each guest greeted each couplet as if hearing it for the first time.

When Cootie vanished into the wings after introducing the Belles, his tuxedo was plastered to his body with sweat. As rehearsed, Willa and a valet helped him change into a fresh one. He swilled down a pint of honey-laced lemon tea just in time to rush back on, lead the Belles off, and send the Lexingtons into the world of professional music.

Nearly two hours later, Cootie, realizing the ending had to top the beginning, dragged out his introduction of the topline act. Suddenly, the lights bumped up on a corner of the stage to reveal three musicians clad in sparkling, powder-blue, black-bordered tuxedos. Then the audience screamed as a special spotlight blossomed on Lou. The band ripped into "Cigarette Blues," the flipside of their brand-new release. The chicks—and cats—went wild. Next came the new release itself. As Willa and Cootie predicted when they first heard it, the "ooooh, noooo!" refrain in "Botheration" was an instant winner. The crowd picked up on it the second time the Blasters wailed it, and chanted along when it re-appeared.

The Blasters slowed the pace with the languid, tantalizing "Late, Late at Night."

Then came the song for which the fourteen hundred-plus awaited.

The band got through the first verse and chorus before a hurricane of screaming women engulfed Lou. He was aware that Cootie's security men and a goodly number of uniformed city officers struggled to keep even more bodies from landing on him. As suddenly as he was rushed, he was led offstage by Cootie and Willa. Jimmy, Blondie, and Deuce received similar escorts. As Lou collapsed against a brick backstage wall, the last thing he heard was the voice of Congressman Alan Payton Howell pleading for order.

When Lou came to ten minutes later, he was stretched on a downstairs dressing-room table. The first thing he saw were the concerned faces of his bandmates. Willa brought him up to date. The crowd had had to be dispersed, but did so peacefully. Alba rushed in, wild-eyed, her hair matted with sweat.

"You okay, Lou?" she gasped, surprised he was still alive.

"I'm fine, baby. Just wasn't expecting—that!"

"See, honey, I told you there was nothing to worry about," Willa said. She nudged Alba toward the door. "Now be a doll and leave us alone for a second."

Alba never took her eyes from Lou. "You *sure* you're—"

"I'm fine. G'on, now, do as Miss Willa says," Lou replied and Alba left.

"Mercy," Cootie exhaled, "your girl almost lost it."

"Man, *I* almost lost it. My life." A thought hammered Lou. "Cootie, did you *pay* those chicks to swamp the stage?"

Cootie hooted. "Only the first thirty. The next three or four hundred flew down on their own accord."

"You could've gotten me killed," Lou said, laughing but half-serious.

"Shit, Lou—that's all colored folks're gonna talk about for a while," Blondie said.

And he was absolutely correct.

* * * * *

Two nights later, Sunday, a limousine whisked the Blasters down to The Ned Mulligan Theatre at Fifty-fourth and Broadway, where they performed "Botheration" and "Cora Ann." In Knoxville, Reverend Cannon cancelled the Sunday evening worship at Brighter Day so his parishioners could catch his son on *The Ned Mulligan Show.* Along Bethel Avenue—and many streets in Knoxville's Black Belt—people placed their televisions on front porches, to catch the late-summer breezes and to accommodate those who did not own a set. Cheers arose whenever the camera moved in for a close shot of Lou and mates.

Across the country, millions got their first look at the exciting new band. Based on the avalanche of letters to CBS, most liked what they saw.

Others, of course, did not. Their appearance sparked another blizzard of complaints that Mulligan, the squarest of white men, was pandering to vulgar tastes with another rhythm-and-blues act. "Allen Stevens on NBC would *never* stoop to such depravity!" a New York society matron expressed on the *New York Times* editorial page.

In Newport News, Virginia, days before his return to Capitol Hill, Theo Briscoe missed the Blasters' performance. He simply did not know they were on; as usual, he watched the rival *Allen Stevens Show.*

In Nashville, Phil Samuels raised a glass of Miller's High Life in toast to the television, and wished more power to Lou Cannon & the Blasters and Cootie Coutrere and everyone connected with them.

A few miles away, in a less affluent neighborhood, Pervis Elmsley, the young truck driver, stared at the tiny screen in his parent's parlor. Sprawled on the floor, at the feet of his parents seated on the couch, he soaked in all of Lou Cannon's inflections and movements. He noted the shrieks from the girls in the studio audience. He knew that was nothing compared to the reaction Cannon had caused two nights ago at the Apollo—Pervis had heard about it yesterday in a colored barbershop, while delivering plumbing supplies.

"There's enough out there for us all, buddy," Pervis murmured as Lou Cannon sailed through "Cora Ann."

"You say somethin, Pervis, dawrhlin?" his mother, Grace, asked as she stroked the back of his neck.

"No, ma'am. Just thinkin out loud."

* * * * *

Two weeks after Cootie's show embarked in the Northeast, Adam Freeman's show, dubbed The Rock-n-Roll Road Party, started in Chicago and fanned throughout the Midwest. As Cootie's revue rolled westward along the Great Lakes basin, Freeman's show trekked east, as far from Cootie's caravan as possible. The Rock-n-Roll Road Party hugged the Ohio River Valley, with Louisville, Kentucky, its only stop in the unofficial South. If one looked at a map of their itineraries, the shows appeared to be moving in a loop.

Jimmy and Vivian Bradford, of Jay-Vee Records, postponed their Cavalcade of Stars until the spring of 1956. Much of their financing fell through because many of their artists refused to play the Southern dates, in light of the recent lynching of fourteen-year-old Emmet Till in Sunflower County, Mississippi. The Jay-Vee artists felt a special sadness over the child's murder; like most of them, the boy had called Chicago his hometown.

Largely because of the novelty of the music, the crowds on the first go-round were large, curious, and enthusiastic. Willa surveyed each venue in advance to gauge the seating capacity, dressing rooms, nearby hotels and eateries, and to take note of any extra security precautions they might need.

One of the first things Cootie had done was hire a dozen permanent security men. All were gargantuan former boxers or football players and possessed speed and quickness that belied their bulk. In addition to "Coutrere's Gorillas," as they became known, the civic officials always supplied a phalanx of uniformed officers. Freeman took similar precautions.

The naysayers against rock-n-roll—and their numbers swelled as its popularity widened—were both right and wrong in their predictions that violence would break out because of the traveling shows. They were correct in that isolated fistfights and minor donnybrooks erupted at roughly one-third of the performances. Cootie and Freeman explained away the brouhaha as inevitable when teenagers gathered, clanging hormones and all. "There's surely more violence at school football and basketball games than at our shows," Cootie told an interviewer from *Jet*.

Still, any misbehavior from the mostly teenaged crowds was fodder for the anti-rock-n-roll factions. Never mind that Cootie and Freeman's security armies were adept at spotting problems early and rousting the instigators. Yet, even the quickest, toughest regulators could not be everywhere, or stop every fight in time. The few instances in which any real damage was done were overplayed in the mainstream press.

All the anti-Negro groups jumped full force onto the "kill rock-n-roll" bandwagon. The president of the White Americans' Council declared during a *Face America* interview that, "We've set up a twenty-man committee to do away with this vulgar, animalistic nigger bop." The spokesman for another group, the Nathan Bedford Forrest Memorial Society, spewed from a newsreel that ran in virtually every American movie house: "The obscenity and vulgarity of the rock-n-roll music is obviously a means by which the white man and his children can be driven to the level of the nigger. It is obviously nigra music."

"I'm laughing, but it's not funny," Cootie told his charges, as they watched the reel as it was played as part of the pre-show entertainment at Chicago's Regal Theatre. "They're showing how sick and silly those yahoos are—but not everyone's gonna see them that way."

Days later, as the Revue's vehicles streaked westward on an Iowa highway, the message on a billboard caused Cootie to halt the caravan. Beneath the image of a Ku Klux Klansman in full dress, pointing an authoritative finger, were the words:

> Notice: Stop! Help save the youth of America! Don't buy negro records! If you do not want to serve negroes in your place of business, then do not have negro records on your juke box or listen to negro records on the radio. The screaming idiot words and savage music of the records are undermining the morals of the white youth of America. Call the advertisers of the radio stations that play this type of music and complain to them. Don't let your children buy or listen to these negro records!

Cootie, Willa, and most of the troupers posed for pictures beneath the sign. They learned the next day that the Klan had flooded places of business all over the country with mimeographed flyers that bore the same message.

Meanwhile, the Washington grapevine whispered that the President of the United States greatly loathed the new music. Yet, his advisors warned him to keep mum about this. Though millions shared his opinion, to air it would make him appear to disdain Negroes and young people. Despite his official silence, his views on rock-n-roll were well-known off the record.

To Lou and his mates, the autumn of 1955 bled into one city after another: Boston, Springfield, Hartford, Albany, Syracuse, Rochester, Buffalo, Erie, Pennsylvania, then into America's heartland. The high school auditoriums melted into poorly-ventilated civic arenas, which dissolved into musty hockey arenas, which faded into ballrooms the size of airplane hangars. Seldom did the performers get to see much of the cities. Each day featured but a few hours between rising and having to be at the show's venue.

Lou passed the time as did most: playing endless card games for low or no stakes. Most of the performers were as cordial as necessary, but knew better than to become too familiar with too many people. He chummed around to some degree with everyone in the show, but stayed closest to his three bandmates.

He got to know Louisiana Fats fairly well. Fats, a clean liver and somewhat of a loner, pined for his large family back in New Orleans. He and Lou had lengthy discussions on the Bible—Fats was a devout Catholic—and the joys and drawbacks of being part of a huge, close, extended family.

Lou kept pictures of Alba in his wallet, and often pulled them out and displayed them. He and Alba ached with a mutual loneliness, so when the Revue played in Cincinnati, its closest stop to Knoxville, Alba made the seven-hour drive. Many in the company were aghast—wives and girlfriends had to remain outside *this* universe. Never mind that Alba and Lou were newly wed. Nobody said anything to Lou during the two days she spent with him, but nearly all the men remarked on it after she returned home.

Before Alba left, Willa pulled her aside. Based on the silent treatment and leathery looks from his roadmates, and Willa's metallic politeness toward Alba during her stay, Lou had a strong idea of what his manager had told his wife.

Regardless, the rockers rolled on. A bang-up four-day run at the Regal Theatre in Chicago preceded a Sunday off in the Windy City. The Lord's Day was automatically an off-day; thus, Cootie and Willa used that day to fly performers, when requested, to appear on *The Ned Mulligan Show.* By early November, all except the Moonlighters and Moanin' Lisa had appeared on the program, singing their hits live to America. Mulligan—and nearly all mainstream producers—still considered these two acts too "colored."

Two Sundays before Thanksgiving, the Blasters made their second appearance on *The Ned Mulligan Show.* With ten weeks on the road under their belts, they were much more relaxed as they belted out "Botheration" and, before that, their rendition of "Don't Get

Around Much Any More." Ned Mulligan presented them with a gold record for "Cora Ann." Lou noticed how much more enthusiastic the audience was—and not just the dozens of teenage girls Mulligan— and Cootie—had planted in the house.

Still, their joy was offset by the specter of rock-n-roll being short-lived. *Enjoy it while you can* was the oft-repeated warning, and Lou strived to do just that.

CHAPTER EIGHTEEN

Sunday, November 20, 1955; 7:48 p.m.Washington.

For the sake of his health—mental and physical—Theo had trained himself to relax every bit as thoroughly on Sunday—all day Sunday—as he worked relentlessly on his five workdays, and many a Saturday. However, his respite was interrupted shortly after six that evening with troubling news from his home state.

A Negro, Cyrus Dailey, had been lynched the previous night in a small town sixty miles northwest of the capital. Thirty-five years old, a mechanic, the father of five, Dailey had lived a crime-free life. The local chapter of the Ku Klux Klan proudly claimed responsibility...but hours later learned it was a case of mistaken identity. Their real target was Dailey's cousin, with whom he bore a strong resemblance.

Now, in his den, Theo revised a speech he had made on three similar occasions, decrying such mob violence. For the fourth time, he would be filmed making this plea; it would be shown immediately across his home state and those that neighbored it. Theo would again emphasize that his anti-integration stance did not mean he harbored any personal ill will toward Negroes. He had made it clear at the start of his political life that he would never sanction the vigilante actions of the Klan. Legal segregation, yes; physical mistreatment, no.

After he finished his revision, he would contact the Reverend Jedediah Beales, his main liaison with the Negroes in his state. He would have Beales find out the cost of a first-class funeral for Dailey. Theo would make a check out for that amount, and another for five thousand dollars, to help tide the family through. Beales would be the go-between; Dailey's family was never to learn who sent the money. Moreover, Theo would give Beales orders to see to it that Dailey's family did not slide into poverty because of the loss of its breadwinner...

Mercy, Lord...there's always some shit...

He heard peals of feminine laughter from downstairs. He suddenly remembered that in a few days he and Virginia would have an anniversary of sorts—they were introduced formally, for the first time, twenty-one years ago, at a Thanksgiving dinner just blocks from where they now lived.

He could not help but notice her at the functions where the capital city's social upper-crust rubbed elbows. From afar, he judged her to have an understated attractiveness. He especially admired her patrician features—long, graceful form, and swanlike neck. He read the distance she kept from most people as equal parts shyness and a learned, tactful aloofness. Though he knew his queries about her would get back to her, he asked their mutual acquaintances to fill him in on her. From the furtive looks she gave him the first half-dozen times they crossed paths, he assumed—hoped—she was inquiring about him, too.

He learned she was from the vaunted, long-term Virginia planter class on both sides of her family. The branches of her mother's family tree included Dolly Madison. On her father's side, she was related to Richard Henry and Robert Edward Lee. He found out she was a graduate of Vassar, was seven years younger than he, and taught English, history, and social studies at an exclusive all-girls school in Georgetown. A healthy subsidy from her wealthy father, Artemis Culhane, supplemented her modest teacher's salary.

Several of her friends hinted, quite strongly, that at almost age thirty-three, the prospect of spinsterhood daunted Virginia Culhane more with each passing month.

After their formal introduction, they accompanied each other to parties, plays, arts-oriented events, and political fundraisers. When others asked, both were evasive as to the depth of their friendship. Yet, both realized they were not getting any younger, nor were either likely to have a better marriage option enter their lives. They decided they had more reasons for forming a union than for passing on each other, and they settled on a wedding date.

Because they married at relatively late ages, each realized the other might be set in his or her ways. Thus, before their wedding, they composed a list of by-laws for their union.

There was the class issue. Though as well-read and widely-traveled as anyone in Congress, Theo's origins were humble and hard. As for Virginia, her upbringing could not have been more privileged. Neither was to mention that difference, let alone disparage the other's background.

Moreover, though Theo's language skills—his talent for metaphors, painting vivid pictures in the clearest, simplest manner, and timely, clever wordplay—were widely admired on Capitol Hill, he was apt to get sloppy in informal settings. Among Dixiecrats, the grammar often went slack, the colloquialisms frequent and elaborate, the profanity unabashed, the voice loud, and the Deep South accent cloying or abrasive, depending upon the listener. In their home, and particularly around the children they would have, Theo was to speak the King's English, as if making a point before the Senate. Even in his den with his cronies, assumedly out of the earshot of others, he would keep his language clean and grammatical.

Then there was the matter of children. Both wanted them, but realized time was of the essence. Moreover, Virginia was adamant she would not become pregnant after age forty, and Theo abided by that choice. Given Virginia's age before the wedding and her self-imposed deadline, Theo figured they would have three children, at most.

Hopefully, at least one would be a son.

Because of Virginia's prim and proper carriage, Theo assumed, despite her age, she had never known a man physically. Indeed, when he delicately broached the matter of their conjugal life, she cut him short. "Don't worry: I'll do what I feel is within the bounds of decency to please *you*," she had said, in a clearly case-closed tone.

Yet, on their wedding night, Theo was surprised to learn he was not the first man to be with her—and rather miffed, though he did not let her know then, or at any time afterwards. He resolved not to dwell on it; after all, she was a sophisticated woman in her thirties. Then again, something would have been greatly wrong with her had she *not* acted upon certain natural yearnings, Theo decided.

Yet, the question nagged at him (like it would any other man, he told himself): who, when, and how many? Of course, he would not ask her. He waited for nearly a year, then began inquiring about her old beaux, but only to her casual acquaintances, never to a good friend. He deduced there were two definite bed partners in her past, and two middling possibilities.

Oh, well. It could have been worse.

Furthermore, though she did not address it directly before their marriage, Virginia was aware of his jaunts to the three top-shelf bordellos that catered exclusively to political high-hatters. She did, however, mention they would discuss *that* issue in the coming years.

At once causing Theo pleasure and surprise, but a degree of concern, Virginia was nothing like the distant, frigid bedmate he feared she would be. However, with the mid-life changes in her body coinciding with the growing duties of raising three girls, Virginia's ardor in the bedroom faded. A year after the birth of their last child, they made love once every two or three weeks, if that often.

She did not begrudge his excursions to bawdy houses—before they wed. But as the fires of their sexual life became banked by time, she turned a blind eye on his bi-monthly forays to the reputable houses of ill repute. As he grew older, Theo visited the houses not out of any great desire or need, but because he *could*. And though he had promised Virginia he would not favor any house over the others, let alone get stuck on any one girl, he broke his vow. Miggie Varner, a flame-haired woman of thirty was, over the last three years, the only one Theo patronized...

Now, with Thanksgiving Day nigh, Theo sat sprawled in his den, in a lounge chair given to him by some Alabama cotton lobbyists. He offered up a prayer to his Lord for this house, the two others he owned, three bright and attractive daughters, and an understanding wife. At times like this he had a special appreciation for how far he had come in life, with a minimum of interference run for him by others in his early years.

Yeah, I could've done a helluva lot worse than I have—and not much better, even if I do say so myself...

It was eight p.m., time for his favorite comedian, Allen Stevens. He turned on the television, and Stevens announced his guests. It mattered not to Theo who they were; Stevens and his regulars would be more than enough. He rose and went downstairs and into the kitchen, where he got a bottle of beer from the refrigerator and a glass from the cupboard. In the hallway, passing the living room, he overheard the program Virginia and the girls were watching:

"...and on tonight's rilly big shooo, making their second appearance, we have for the teeny-bopper set, Lou Cannon & the Blasters..."

Damn. Second appearance? Obviously I missed the first. I'm usually up on that sorta thing—and Hezekiah should of reminded me. Oh, well...

Unlike many of his friends who had children, Theo had never spoken to his about rock-n-roll, one way or the other, and neither had Virginia. It had not been necessary, so far. The music was not part of the girls' everyday lives; what they encountered was overheard rather than heard. Vicky Sue, at seventeen, had started to date—but only at well-chaperoned functions for the children of Washington's elite. Long-popular dances and classical music took precedent over the latest fads. At twelve, Janey Ann was already a grand snob about many things, music being at the top of her list. Anything not classical was garbage to her.

Fifteen-year-old Delia Mae, similar to Virginia and Theo, had a more eclectic appreciation of music. Delia listened to the stations that featured Virginia's beloved big-band jazz sounds of decades past,

Theo's favored country & western tunes, and those that played con-temporary pop songs. Included on the playlist of the latter were a few of the cleaner, tamer R & B songs—virtually all by artists aligned with Cootie Coutrere or Adam Freeman. That the girls were to avoid the stations that spewed gutbucket Negro music went without saying.

He returned upstairs and switched to Mulligan's show. He figured the blues band would not appear until the fifteen or twenty-minute mark. Suddenly, an idea struck him: *With so many li'l white gals goin ape over Cannon, I might wanna take a gander at mine, and how they react...*

On the heels of that came a second thought: *Careful. You might see something you wouldn't want to...*

A quarter hour later, Mulligan announced he would return after the commercial with the 'Cora Ann' men. Theo eased down the stairs, and stood outside the living room, where he could observe his daugh-ters, and yet not appear to be spying on them. Vicky sat on a couch, near Virginia. With her long, lustrous raven hair, ivory complexion, and large, aquamarine eyes, she had been a stunner almost since birth. She was still deciding which of the Northeastern "sister" colleges to the Ivy League institutes she would attend next year. She was by far the surest bet of the three girls to snare a rich lawyer, business mag-nate—or political kingpin.

Delia sat on the floor, a few feet from the television, her legs folded beneath her. She still had not lost all her baby fat, which was becoming a concern with her mother. In Theo's estimation, her tor-toise-shell rimmed glasses made her look owl-eyed and a bit combat-ive. She made many a joking remark about being the least attractive of the three girls. Her parents saw past the self-deprecating humor, but also felt that being pretty was a minor concern with Delia. Whether she were to find a husband or not, Theo would give the tow-headed Delia all encouragement to pursue a career in Law.

Janey Ann, paying no attention to the set, sat apart from the rest, also on the floor. She was drawing a charcoal sketch of the room itself. Ethereally blond, she was the only one of the three not tall for her age. A stare from her huge, smoke-gray eyes could puzzle, beguile, or intimidate. She was the thinker of the bunch, so much so that Theo and Virginia feared she would become the type of person who lives too much inside her own head. Her parents hoped she would never decide to essay the life of a professional artist...but would support that choice were she to make it...

After a raucous reception by the audience, Cannon and his band launched into a jump-blues version of "Don't Get Around Much Any More." Virginia, a big fan of Duke Ellington's music, tapped time with her toe and swayed her head to the muscular beat, but in a bare-ly noticeable manner. Janey Ann continued to disregard the television as she sketched on. Vicky Sue gazed blankly at the screen. By far the most animated, Delia Mae patted her thighs as she tried to sing along with the quirky interpretation of the jazz standard.

Then, something about Vicky registered on Theo in delayed reac-tion and pulled his eyes back to her. She was not staring at the screen, but at *Cannon*, her eyes glued to his as he warbled. Her back was rigid, her neck craned, shoulders taut, and eyes unblinking.

Mercy Jesus!

A flash of heat shot through him. The image of Peggy leaving arm-in-arm with her Negro from his cabin revisited him. The image departed as quickly as it arrived; yet, Vicky was still eye-locked on Cannon. If she was not staring at him with lust, then surely with admiration for his handsome features. *And she doesn't even realize she's staring like she's stuck on him! Lord!*

As though she had tuned into her father's wavelength, Vicky cut her eyes toward him, but did not acknowledge his presence at the cusp of the room. She flushed, her entire body slackened, she pre-tended to be no longer interested in what was on the screen.

He focused again on the set; the band had slithered into an instru-mental bridge. The camera shot, wide enough to include Cannon waist-high in the foreground and his bandmates behind him, switched to a tight shot on the lead singer's face. Cannon grinned sideways, coquet-tishly into the camera, then slipped America a big, slow wink. Before he finished it, he chuckled self-consciously at what he had just done, and appeared to be embarrassed about being seen in millions of homes.

As if letting Cannon off the hook, a new camera angle took over, this time panning on Cannon's three bandmates as they wailed away.

If Virginia noticed the wink, she did not react to it. Delia smiled grandly, having caught Cannon's parody of a sexy hipster.

Vicky resumed staring at the singer as he began the final verse.

Virginia spied Theo lurking in the doorway. "Have a seat, make yourself comfortable."

Delia Mae cocked her head at her father. "Shouldn't you be upstairs, watching *your* program?" she said with mock disapproval at his presence.

Theo grinned. "I heard the group that's causing so much commo-tion, so I thought I'd see what all the fuss is about."

Janey looked up from her sketch. "Rock and roll. *What* will they try to cram down our throats next?" she expelled, her face and voice belonging to someone five times older.

"Oh, don't be such a…" Delia said and drew an invisible square in the air with her forefingers. "It's the latest! The limit! All the kids dig it the most!"

"Delia Mae! On what planet did you learn *that* language?" Virginia was half-scolding, half-amused.

"If *all* the—kids—like it that much, then I *must* not be a—kid," Janey sniffed.

`As she often did, Delia pretended not to hear Janey. "The music is the living end! Kuh-raaaaay-zee, baby! It's got so much—energy!"

Janey kept her eyes on her sketch. "So does an atomic blast. Would you like to be in the middle of one of *those*?"

"Oh, get hep, girl! Jump to it and get, like, uh-ruh—with it, honey chile!"

"Delia!" Virginia's response was harsher; this time Delia had tried for a Negro inflection.

Delia rolled her eyes, then trained them on Vicky. "And what do you, Victoria, think of this new rock-n-roll?" She mimicked the self-consciously serious tone of some newscasters.

Vicky did not respond as she stared at the conclusion of the song. "Our eldest sister is otherwise engaged," Janey sniffed.

"Vicky!"

She snapped out of it. "Did you say something, Delia?" she asked, sneaking a look at her father, to see if he was still studying her.

Delia repeated the question. "It is—interesting," Vicky slowly replied. "Its mélange of styles is perhaps its most compelling feature."

"Well! And thank you, Professor Briscoe," Delia said, reprising her parody of an announcer's overly-precise delivery.

"Delia Mae. Sarcasm is the cheap tool of churlish individuals," Virginia chided mildly.

Delia stared at Theo with mock accusation. "Well, *Daddy* likes rock-n-roll!"

"Whoa, honey! Don't press that charge on *me*!" Theo said, chuckling.

"You *do*! And you know you do! Especially *that* song by that group!" Delia nodded toward the set, where the Blasters were huddled up with Mulligan, chatting.

"Alright. I admit I thought 'Cora Ann' was cute and catchy—"

"And it sounds a lot like some of those country-and-cowboy songs you like so much!"

"Delia, how many times must I tell you never to interrupt a grown-up?" Virginia scolded.

"Saaahhh-rrreee."

"As well you should be, miss! Pay more attention to your manners!"

"Yes, ma'am…"

Theo caught Virginia's eye. *Ease off the girl.* His gaze returned to Vicky, still focused on the set, where Ned Mulligan was handing a plaque to Cannon and his mates.

"…and this gold record represents a million sales of 'Cora Ann,' gentlemen," Mulligan said in his trademark stiff, nasal, but not unpleasant manner. The Blasters flashed broad smiles as the audience in the theatre applauded enthusiastically.

Cannon proudly fondled the gold record. "Thank you, America, for making the song the hit that it is," he said from behind a shy, boyish smile. More applause greeted this.

Mulligan clasped Cannon on the shoulder. "And on your next visit to our shoo, we'll present the same for 'Botheration,' which is well on that path."

Cannon swiveled to look at his mates. The piano player, a round, pleasant-faced man, cast his eyes downward, then stepped forward. He braved a look into the camera and recited, "Again, thanks America." He accepted the gilded disc from Cannon and held it aloft. "This is—nice," he said in a soft voice and with a smile even shyer than Cannon's. More applause.

"Lou Cannon & the Blasters will return later in our shoo, to sing their chart-topping 'Botheration,'" Mulligan announced. "And now a word from our sponsor…"

The image of Speedy Alka Seltzer commandeered the screen. With an eye on Vicky, but to the room at large, Theo said, "Fine-looking boy, that Cannon. *Right* fine-looking…"

"Yes…for one of—them," Virginia said, with no intentional condescension.

"I was not paying attention," Janey Ann yawned. "*I* would not look twice at any of those—rock-n-roll singers."

"One need not be a full-fledged member of the Caucasian race to be comely," Delia sniffed. This was more of a dig at her sister than a defense of dark people.

Theo's gaze prodded Vicky for her opinion. She flushed, and looked off as she answered. "Like Mother said, he *is* fairly handsome—for one of them. No, actually, he *must* be of mixed racial descent. Virtually all the better-looking Negroes are, you know."

"There's a picture in my geography book of a Cherokee Indian who looks just like him!" Delia chimed in.

"If anything, his face catches the eye for the same reason his music catches the ear," Vicky continued. "It is a mixture of so many elements."

"Oh, come off it! Stop making excuses for staring at him so hard!" Delia cried. "I saw you! Hypnotized! Mesmerized! You think he's adorable, so admit it!"

"Careful, Delia," Virginia said through clinched teeth. She slid her eyes to Theo, petitioning for him to cut in. He watched silently, weirdly amused. Virginia continued in a low, bristling voice: "Young ladies, this is neither the time nor place to discuss even the *ghost* of an attraction for members of any nonwhite races." Her two older daughters avoided her gaze. "Nor is there *any* proper time and place for a conversation of that sort," she added, her anger tempered by the evenness of her voice.

Vicky scowled. "I never said I had any such attraction—"

"You would do well, Victoria Sue Ellen, to address me in a less peevish tone!" Virginia snapped. "Now, you *may* apologize."

Vicky mumbled her regret. Delia stuck out her tongue at her; Vicky returned the favor.

In her corner, eyes still on her sketch, Janey said to nobody in particular: "Rock and roll will *really* become acceptable to those who matter when it finds its first white star."

The others batted around a ponderous look. "But it is *their* music," Virginia said. "Nobody can sing and play it with the same feeling as those people."

Janey finally looked up. "Jazz," she said and returned to her artwork.

Theo gazed at his youngest daughter, and let the others see his proud smile at her. *She's got something there.* He decided it was time to ask them something that had nagged him since Day One of rock-n-roll's explosion. He crossed to the television and clicked it off.

Vicky started to say something, but choked it back. Delia, however, was a detonating grenade. "Daah-deee! That was so—rude!"

"I want to ask my girls one simple, but important question—"

"But we were in the middle of watching—"

"Delia! Did I not just caution you about interrupting grown-ups, and talking back to them?" Virginia turned to Theo. "And, that *was* quite abrupt! For the sake of common cour—"

He stopped her with an upraised hand. "I'm *sorry*. The question, though: what do you girls *really* think of rock-n-roll, and all the terrible things some people will predict will happen because of it?" None volunteered a response. "Don't worry, there are no right or wrong answers here, only honest ones," he coaxed.

Janey first took the plunge. "Just the latest contrivance to siphon the allowances of childish children. Noise for lemmings. Anyone who appreciates *real* music would tune out that swill." Her duty done, she returned to her sketch, and missed Delia's scowl.

Vicky bit her bottom lip as she always did while in deep thought. "Those with a bent toward vulgar behavior have never, nor will ever require the soundtrack of Negro music for their base deeds. Just another excuse for the dregs of the Euro-American race to act like Neanderthals," she said, in a tone that dared dispute.

"Excuse me, but am I the only one who hears how much *fun* the music is?" Delia cried. "That's *all* it's meant to be—fun! And: 'jungle music?' Didn't people used to label jazz that? Dirty lyrics? Most kids don't really *listen* to the words. And those who do realize they're only rhymes to string a story together! I mean—some people need to get over themselves!"

"Present company included," Janey stage-whispered. *"Especially present company."*

Delia denied Janey even the faintest edge of her concern. "And those who say rock-n-roll is the highway to—the Devil—I'll bet they think everything close to fun is evil! Fiddlesticks to them! They're just pinning their hates and fears and insecurities onto some bright, bouncy, fun music!" She folded her arms, pooched out her lower lip, and stamped her foot. *So there!*

Theo allowed his daughters to catch his proud, sweeping look. *Smart girls. Articulate, each in her own way. Then again, they* better *be, much as we're paying for their education.*

Virginia broke the brief silence. "Why, thank you, Young Miss Freud!"

Her posture unchanged, Delia said haughtily, "The truth is nothing but the truth."

Theo flicked the television back on. "Thank you, Daddy." Delia's purring voice and sweet smile did not mask her sarcasm.

Theo started back upstairs. "And thank you, girls. Enjoy the rest of your program."

"You want us to call you when the Blasters come back on?"

"I'll pass on that, Delia, darling." He returned to his den, and added what he had just observed to the enigma that was rock-n-roll. Delia's reply strengthened his hunch that the fear of rock-n-roll corrupting American youth was mostly the brayings of extremists. It would not make a juvenile delinquent out of anyone not already on that track.

A plot by Communists to undermine America's youth? *Don't put too much stock in that one, bud. Ol' Joe McCarthy shot off his own dick chasing that ghost.* Still, Theo could not totally discount that. Yet, was there enough truth in it to merit some sort of action? He doubted it, but time would tell.

A kick-starter for the civil-rights movement picking up steam

The Man Who Invented Rock-n-Roll, Volume One

with Negroes? It *was* bringing white and colored kids together, at live shows and dances. The subtlest of cultural exchanges was gestating. And white girls *were* going bananas at the sight of some colored singers—or even the mere mention of their names. Especially Lou Cannon.

And Theo did not have to leave his own living room to observe Cannon's allure.

Still, he knew not to make too much of Vicky doing some long-distance mooning over Cannon. For his daughters to think of one of them as attractive was one thing, but to converse, alone, with a Negro male with whom there might be the faintest allure on either side was out of the question. Yet—if rock-n-roll increased *anything*, it would be the number of white women with black men, Theo reckoned.

Still, these were all the most immediate, obvious concerns. A line he had overheard at a recent gathering, from a politician from New Orleans, was looming larger and louder on his consciousness. The speaker mentioned that his brother, the owner of a Cadillac dealership on that city's Canal Street, had crowed: "Now that white kids're buyin them records by Little Robert and Luziyana Fats, I'm sellin a heap more Caddies. Everyone *faintly* connected with them boogie-woogie hits is makin out like a bandit, I'm here to tell you."

Big Picture, Theo reminded himself. Who was cashing in, big time, on this new fad? Negroes and Jews. Last week, with several colleagues, Theo discussed what would happen if rock-n-roll showed any staying power. Many predicted there would be a demi-monde with its own economy and by-laws. It would be similar to the Italians' mafia, though not as secretive or nefarious. And, already a handful of kingpins had risen in that corner of the music world.

The economic end of the whole shebang. That might turn out to be the nut that's gotta be cracked...

Think about that as your main area of concern. The money. Then again, it always goes back to the almighty dollar.

He grabbed a pen and paper, and began to jot out possible scenarios and strategies.

CHAPTER NINETEEN

Thanksgiving Day, 1955; 7:16 p.m.
The Brighter Day Baptist Church; Knoxville.

Oblivious to the din of dozens of guests on the floor below, Reverend Cannon half-dozed off his mammoth holiday dinner in his rectory. The serving had commenced at two; anyone, a member of the church or not, could get a plate. The feast, as always, would last until eight or thereabouts. He had put in two long hours ladling food, and his feet were on fire. He could not wait to get home and soak them in a tub of Mother Cannon's pickled beef brine.

Junior had called that morning from Denver. The company would scratch together its own dinner, using the facilities in a colored barbeque joint. Afterwards, they would perform two shows. He sounded exhausted, but happy. *Bless his heart*, the reverend thought after hanging up, *he's got the opportunity that most folks would sell their soul for: to do what they love most for a living—and get paid well, to boot.*

And paid well he was. Lou sent the brunt of all five of his twice-monthly paychecks to his parents. He kept a little walking-around money. Part of it went to Alba, who still lived with her parents while Lou toured. She set aside most of that for fixing up a house on Cruse Street she would share with Lou. However, the cozy little abode would be but temporary; depending on Lou's royalties and live-show income, they planned to build a home of their own.

However, most of Lou's money went to his father, as a loan of sorts. That money—along with that from the increased attendance at Brighter Day brought on by Lou's fame—was put into an account that would launch a plan Reverend Cannon had nourished for most of his adult life: a cooperative of first-rate, Negro-owned businesses in Knoxville's Black Belt. He had long discussed this with likely partners, but they could never raise enough start-up capital.

Now, thanks mostly to rock-n-roll, the seed money was, if not rolling in, filtering down at a reasonably fast pace.

Among his colleagues were three ministers with similarly large congregations, the town's three Negro undertakers, Knoxville's most influential colored doctor and attorney, and a few proprietors of modestly successful businesses. Their scheme included only establishments within the two Negro sectors of town, in East Knoxville, and Mechanicsville, on the north side, near Knoxville College. The enterprises would mostly render services that Negroes *had* to get from Negroes: funeral parlors; barber and beauty shops; restaurants—*real* ones, not greasy spoons, as Reverend Cannon was quick to point out; a clean, reputable hotel; dry cleaning shops; self-service laundries; shoe-repair shops; and automobile service stations.

Chadsdale Worthington had journeyed to Knoxville six weeks ago to help set up the cooperative. The basic plan was simple: the residents of the community would buy stock in the stores they would essentially own, operate, and patronize. Worthington's commanding presence—and his association with "Cootie" Coutrere—gave him instant credibility; many put aside their qualms and vowed to help finance the plan when matters became more concrete.

First on the agenda was the most accessible and necessary: a string of supermarkets. Reverend Cannon had already talked with Cal Walters, the local supermarket magnate, about the purchase of three of Walters' stores. They would be costly; Walters was still reaping big profits from them. Yet, because they were in Negro neighborhoods, Walters saw them as much of a headache as a financial balm, and Reverend Cannon used that to his advantage.

Yes, the cooperative would start slowly, with safer ventures like the supermarkets. The purchase and renovations should be well under way by the time warm weather arrived...then they could plot their next move...

God bless rock-n-roll, the reverend mused. *Still, we'll have to bake cakes while the oven is hot. No telling when that flame will die...*

He made a note to remind his congregation—yet again—how the so-called Devil's music would prove to be a blessing for so many of them.

CHAPTER TWENTY

Phil Samuels parked his car in a Union Street garage, a few blocks from his Moon Records studio on Second Avenue. The day after Thanksgiving was clear but nippy. Phil covered the distance across Union Street in purposeful strides. He smiled and nodded to people who recognized him. He turned right on Second and headed for the studio, near Church Street.

From nearly a block away he saw the handsome, tow-headed, guitar-packing lad. The youngster looked as if he had been waiting for some time. Phil knew what the boy wanted. As Phil strolled down Second, he purposely slowed. The boy never took his eyes from Phil, while Phil pretended not to notice him. When he reached the front of the Moon building, the lad cut off his path as politely as possible.

"Good afternoon, Mister Samuels, sir," the youngster said, his hazel eyes unmoving. "My name is Pervis Elmsley and I wanna be— am gonna be—a rock-n-roll star," he completed breathlessly.

Phil made a flash evaluation of the young man. He was a sliver under six feet tall, wiry, a few years from his full-man's girth. *Fine-lookin boy—though that mousy, sandy-blond hair ain't gonna cut it,* Phil surmised. He could not decide whether the boy's sideburns were flat-out old-fashioned, or so old-timey they were perversely cool. *The kid's tryin too hard to look like Marlon Brando,* Phil thought as he sized up the lad's denim jacket, blue jeans, cowboy boots, and leather motorcycle cap.

Beyond all, however, Phil sensed the boy could halfway sing— based on what little he had heard of his speaking voice.

Surely the lad realized that Phil was giving him a quick but thorough once-over. That was to be expected. The youngster spoke up, this time slower, less rehearsed, with more genuine confidence. "You're askin yourself: 'Is this cat any good?' Well, sir, there's only one way to find out." The kid named Pervis nodded to the studio.

Phil *wanted* to see and hear what the boy could do, but he had to make him sweat a little. "I 'preciate your drive, young man, but what makes you think you can waylay me, and have me just *give* you an audition out the clear blue?" Phil challenged.

Pervis smiled tightly. "Like I said, sir, I'm *gonna* be a big star, one way or t' other. If need be, I'll pack my grip and grab a Greyhound to Memphis, Noo Orleens, Nooyork, Chicago, Deetroit—anyplace I can get heard. But why should I go through all that when you, the great Mister Phil Samuels, has got as fine a record company as I could scrounge up in any-a them-there places?"

Phil angled a look at Pervis, but said nothing.

"Besides, sir, I figgered you'd see some of yourself in me. Suthrin boy, humble, workin-class folks, bristlin with the will and talent to buck the odds and make it big." Pervis's smile expanded greatly.

Phil had to laugh, if only to himself. The boy had hit it dead on the nose. Still, he had to make this kid named Pervis Elmsley sweat a little more. He looked at his watch; it was a quarter past noon. "Tell you what, Pervis. Go have yourself a Co-Cola or somethin. Come back at two. Sharp. I got business I gotta get at, but I *will* set aside a few minutes to give you a listen."

"I really appreciate this, sir!" Pervis cried.

"You got four songs ready, boy?"

"Of course, sir! Even more—"

"Four's all anyone would need to hear. Two sharp, son."

Pervis grinned uncontrollably. "Yes, sir! Two, sharp!"

"See you then." Without looking at Pervis again, Phil turned and entered the studio. He sauntered past the small reception area. He had given his secretary/receptionist the day off after the holiday. He was there only to re-listen to a half dozen recently-cut tapes.

Whatever this Pervis sounds like, he sure has the right look to be a star, once he eighty-six's that Brando bit, Phil mused. *If you could wad up that new rock-n-roll sound into a ball and have it come out a white boy, it'd look like that Elmsley kid.* In the past months he had signed three white boys about Pervis' age who sang chillingly well. One, Ron Iverson out of Wink, Texas, had a panty-creaming baritone, but a plain face. Another, Lee Jerry Lawrence, from Faraday, Louisiana, was a good-looking, piano-pounding blond lad with much of the Negro sound for which Phil was searching in a white singer. Yet, anyone could see that Lee Jerry was a series of mishaps waiting to unfold.

Phil opened a file cabinet, then shut it hard so the faulty latch would catch. "Who dat?" a scratchy voice called from a back room.

"Me, Gut," Phil called back. McKinley "Gutbucket" McDaniel, the legendary bluesman, oozed into the room. In 1950, during a lull in his career, Gutbucket signed on with Moon Records and became the label's first "name" artist. Until then, the two-year-old company had a few artists with true talent, but limited appeal in the blues or country markets. With a sizeable following in the South and Northern urban areas, Gutbucket's record sales pushed Moon Record's finances into the profit column. Moreover, Gutbucket cranked out at least one "jump" tune per year for the younger-geared R & B market, and they always landed in the race-music top ten.

"Whatcha up to, Gut?" Phil asked.

"Just fartin around, tinkerin with some tunes."

"Got a kid comin in for an audition at two. White boy. Just might be the goods." Gutbucket nodded and Phil continued. "Mind sittin in on the audition, give me your feedback?"

"If the boy hisself don't mind."

"He won't. You're *Gutbucket*—he oughtta be tickled shitless."

At two on the dot, Pervis was tapping on the front glass. Phil let him in and led him to one of the smaller studios in the back.

"Mister Gutbucket, sir!" Pervis shrieked, saucer-eyed, when he spied the veteran bluesman. He rushed to Gutbucket, grabbed the leathery right hand, and pumped it wildly. "It is indeed an honor, sir!"

Gutbucket meted out a smile. "Hope me bein here don't discombobulate you none."

"Oh, no, sir! No *true* artist lets any outside thangs mess with his performance. If anythang, you bein here's gonna fire me up that much more!"

"Let's hope so," Gutbucket replied.

Phil Samuels turned on a reel-to-reel tape machine and spoke into a tiny microphone. "Pervis Elmsley audition tape. November 25th, 1955; two-oh-seven p.m., Moon Records." He nodded to Pervis. "Whenever you're ready, son."

Pervis sucked in a deep breath, like someone about to dive from a high cliff. "This here's 'Cora Ann,' done originally by Lou Cannon & the Blasters." He launched into a guitar introduction that was almost a note-for-note replica of the one on the .30/.30 release.

Phil looked over to Gutbucket, who seemed to be thinking the same thing: *Not bad, but this kid is no Lou Cannon on that git-box.*

Then Pervis sang. If he were not but a few feet from him, Phil would have sworn he was listening to Cannon himself. Every note, every inflection. Phil traded smiles with Gutbucket. Phil—and surely Gutbucket, also—had long ago caught the irony of what Cannon had done on "Cora Ann." He was a Negro imitating the country pickers who copied the colored boogie-woogie shouters. In turn, Pervis was taking it—perhaps unwittingly, perhaps consciously— one step further: he was a white boy who imitated the Negro, who spoofed the...

The image of a man in a house of mirrors gazing at an endless series of self-reflections—however slightly warped—zipped across Phil's mind.

Pervis finished. Neither Phil nor Gutbucket spoke, but both nodded: *Not bad.*

Next Pervis performed the Hank Williams classic, "I'm So Lonesome I Could Cry." Again, neither Gut nor Phil commented verbally, but traded smiles. *This kid* can *sing.*

Next came what Phil regarded as a refreshingly oddball selection: a bluegrass-tinged rendition of "It Ain't Necessarily So." Phil flipped through his mental catalogue. *Gershwin Brothers. From* Porgy and Bess, *if memory serves. This cat's done his homework.*

By then Phil was sold. Convincing his board of directors could be another matter. Though Phil had the final say on who got signed, he still relied heavily on the judgment of the six people he had picked for their fine ears.

In the three songs, Phil listened hard for that Negro feel. Pervis' interpretations of "Cora Ann" and the Gershwins' tune had been *too* imitative. Ironically, Pervis sounded more like a Negro to Phil on "I'm So Lonesome I Could Cry," the song on which he did not even try to.

"Uh, Pervis...you got you one more 'Negro' song?" Phil asked casually.

Pervis swallowed hard and looked over at Gutbucket. He grinned sheepishly. "Yes, sir. Mister Gutbucket's 'Between Sundown and Daybreak,' sir."

Gutbucket offered something akin to a grin. "Hit it, whiteboy."

Three minutes later, Gutbucket was grinning without reserve. "Whiteboy, you ain't half bad. You sung that better'n most black-ass niggers could of."

"Gee, thank you, sir!"

Phil secured the tape. When he spoke, he struggled to conceal his enthusiasm. "Thank you, young man. I'll let my board of advisors give this a listen, and I'll get back to you. One way or the other."

That drained the blood from Pervis's face. "I understand, sir," he mumbled. "At your convenience." He paused, then added, "And thanks for the chance to audition."

"Thank *you*. Give us a week." Phil put out his hand.

Pervis pumped the hand, firmly. "Indeed, sir," he said as he squeezed out a smile.

After Phil heard the front door close behind Pervis, he turned to Gutbucket. "Well?"

"That 'whiteboy-with-the-Negro-sound-and-feel' you said could make you a million bucks?" Gutbucket nodded to the door out of which Pervis had just walked.

Phil smiled to himself. He had made that statement to perhaps a dozen people, but never to Gutbucket—or any Negro. "You think he's that good?"

"The *record-buyin public* will think he's that good. Better sign his ass, like yesterday."

"I cain't just go flyin up Second Avenue after him, Gut—"

"So be coy and wait 'til Monday. Tuesday at the latest. This company is Mecca for cats like him. They'd wait for you to say 'no' before they'll take a crack elsewhere. He'll keep."

Phil nodded. "You're right. First thing Monday morning, I'll have the board give his tape a listen. But that'll be just a matter of course. Even if they all turn thumbs down, I'll sign him irregardless." Phil patted the tape. "This boy is mine."

Gutbucket mimed flipping through wads of greenbacks.

* * * * *

On Monday, the board members agreed that Pervis was worthy of a contract. Half felt that, with some polish, he could be a star who straddled the country and rock-n-roll worlds. "And when that nigger-music craze goes ten toes up, he can always fall back on good ol' country & western," the oldest, most conservative member commented.

Yet, none shared Phil's belief that Pervis was a million-dollar baby.

At nine on Tuesday morning, Phil called Pervis to tell him the good news. At six that evening, after Vernon Elmsley got home from work, he and his wife Grace affixed their signatures to the contract Pervis was too young to sign.

On Wednesday, Pervis quit his truck-driving job with Humes Plumbing Supplies.

On Thursday, he was in his first Moon recording session, co-produced by Phil Samuels and McKinley "Gutbucket" McDaniel.

CHAPTER TWENTY-ONE

Monday, November 28, 1955; 6:17 p.m.
Washington, D.C.

After hours, in a bomb shelter beneath the chambers of the U.S. Senate, Theo Briscoe met with Chance Elam, Reece Stracker, and nine of the most right-wing members of Congress.

The topic of discussion was the stealthily spreading Negro rhythm-and-blues, which radio jockeys were palming off to young whites as rock-n-roll. Theo began with an update on the music, for those in the dark about its rising popularity. "As we speak, your sons and daughters could be listening to that—"

"Senator, *my* children have breeding and culture, so they wouldn't be caught dead listening to that hoodoo screaming," interrupted a senator from Indiana, with whom Theo had a long-term, chilly relationship. His words triggered murmurs of agreement.

"Okay, maybe not *your* kids, but not all white children have the advantages you-all's kids enjoy," Theo amended. "The point I'm making is that rock-n-roll is exposing our children—white children—to *Negro* culture."

"Not *culture*. Negro *customs*. Language. Morals—or lack thereof," Chance sniffed.

Theo thanked him and continued. "You'd have to of lived in a cave the last few months not to know that white and black kids are mingling like never before. Where?" he thundered, rhetorically. "I'll tell you where. At wherever rock-n-roll is played: record hops, rhythm revues, television studio shows." He paused to let than sink in, then continued:

"Why? Because somebody *finally* came up with the right blend that appeals to the *masses* of both Negro and white youths." He again paused to let them digest his words.

A senator from a Southeastern coastal state waggled his hand. "I've heard the hue-and-cry against rock-n-roll, but I must admit I've hardly paid any attention to the music itself." Several mumbled and nodded their agreement. The senator smiled. "You being Theo Briscoe, of course you've got some examples for us to hear."

Theo smiled back. "Of course." He plucked a portable turntable from its half-secluded spot in a corner, set it on a table, plugged it in, and placed on a 45 rpm record. "I'll play snatches of three records by Hal Dillard & the Moonlighters, one of the more popular groups. Yawl'll get the picture soon enough." He gave the first platter a spin.

"'Bunny's Got a Bun in the Oven?'" clucked a House representative from a lower Midwestern state. "They actually let *that* on the radio?"

"It was number one ten weeks in a row," Theo replied, neglecting to mention it hit the top spot on the R & B chart, but failed to make a splash with general audiences.

Theo played the next disc. "'If It Don't Fit, Don't Force It'?" wailed a senator from a state that bordered Theo's. "What the devil is this country coming to?"

"This here is Little Robert. White kids cain't get enough of him," Theo said, then played bits of "Hot Lana From Atlanta" and his new release, "You Drive Me Crazy, Miss Daisy."

"Shit-fire, that ain't *singing*," groused Thom Thurland, another senator from a Southeastern coastal state. "Sounds like somebody stuck that nigger's whanger in a light socket, then hit the switch."

"Somebody by-Gawd *needs* to," Reece Stracker squalled. "On *all* of 'em."

"And these are the better-made, best-selling examples," Theo said. "Need to hear more?"

"Thank you very much, Theo—you've more than made your point," Chance responded.

"Spare us, brother." A buzz of agreement punctuated Reece's words.

Theo filled the congressman in on the traveling shows of Coutrere and Freeman. He then pointed to a squarely-built man who had slipped in beneath notice. "I've had my Man Friday researching that scene, much of it first-hand." He introduced Hezekiah, who smiled and waved shyly. "Feel free to ask questions about what he saw," Theo continued.

The first issue the congressmen addressed was of crime generated by the music, directly or indirectly. Theo shook his head. "Nowhere's near as much as predicted. Yep, the usual tomfoolery when teenagers get together. But Coutrere and Freeman were prepared for the real crazy stuff." He nodded for Hezekiah to provide details.

"Soon as the slightest hint of trouble pops up at Coutrere's shows, his security boys are on it. Humongous apes, but all fast as lightning," Hezekiah relayed.

"Plus," Theo continued, "Freeman and Coutrere have enough of the Pied Piper in them that they can talk to an audience when things start gettin ugly, and shame 'em into behavin."

"If anything, that shows how much mind-control those jockeys have over the youngsters," Chance Elam noted. "Not good."

Theo's smile was that of a feather-mouthed cat near an empty canary's cage. "There's talk that some outside agitators have actually *paid* kids to throw their weight around at some of those shows, ignite a few sparks, if you know what I mean…"

"No!" Thom Thurland cried, his gray-green eyes glittering. "*You* wouldn't of had any hand in that sorta thing, would you?"

Theo blinked hard, twice. "You actually think *I* would stoop to such skullduggery? I'm insulted—insulted!"

"Too all-fired bad it didn't work," Reece said, pulling a shade on the light moment.

"Okay, so the wide-scale violence folks predicted for these shows hasn't happened—yet. Give it time. The music's still in the feel-good stage. That whole scene's gonna get darker," Theo declared.

"*If* it even survives," intoned a Northern conservative.

"I get the impression we're dealin with a Hydra's head here," Theo said. "That noise—in one form or another—is gonna be with us for a goodly spell."

Thom Thurland cleared his throat. "No offense," he began, "but doesn't Mister Hester stick out like a nekkid African in a snow field at those rock-n-roll shows?"

"Of course. That's why we've taken him off the case. Got some boys who look the right age servin as our eyes and ears," Theo replied.

"Still, even they'd be noticed from city to city," Chance played the Devil's Advocate.

"True. Every week or two we open a fresh can of spies," Theo said.

Thurland angled a look at Theo. "Who's paying for all this—espionage?"

Theo's face clouded over. "Don't worry. I'm not doin this on the taxpayer's dime."

Thurland shrugged his shoulders. "Well, then—more power to you and whoever's picking up that tab."

"I'll bet those traveling shows are never-ending orgies on wheels," the senator from Theo's neighboring state said in a change-the-subject maneuver.

"Shit, yeah, buddy. I bet those rockers get more wool in a month than a normal man does in a lifetime," Reece added.

Theo nodded. "That they do. Pussy like you would not believe."

"What about Coutrere his ownself?" Thurland asked. "He must of worn out about three or four peckers by now."

Theo shook his head. "Hate to disappoint you. Far as we know—and we been watchin him like a hawk—he hasn't stepped out on his near-white woman since the show began."

"That's because she watches him like a hawk, too," Hezekiah contributed.

"What about the 'Cora Ann' nigger? He gettin much?" Reece asked.

"I thought we were here to discuss a festering threat, and not the sex lives of traveling minstrels," the other Southeastern senator said, archly.

Theo saw a few nods of agreement. "Uh—we did get kind of off the track. Sorry if anyone took offense." The Southeastern senator accepted the apology with a wave of his hand.

Theo sensed restlessness in over half his audience. He summarized all he had said, and got a verbal commitment from the twelve to meet again in three months for an update. "If this mess is still alive by the end of the summer of '56, then we're gonna have to take some *very* direct action," he said, then released them.

Once they were gone, Theo had one more bit of business. He raced upstairs to his office and placed a long-distance call to Clifton Clowers, one of the surviving participants from that summer night, thirty-eight years ago.

"Theo? Is this Theo Briscoe, or is some joker shittin me?" croaked a voice Theo had not heard in thirty years. The voice was scratchy with age, but still clear and strong, still Clifton's.

"It's me, ol' buddy. Callin to see how the old marbles champeen of Irish Alley Flats was makin it," Theo answered.

Clifton guffawed loudly in Saginaw, Michigan. "Yup, you're Theo, all righty. *Only* Theo and a handful-a others'd remember that." Theo heard a pause on the other end, then, "Thought the ol' senator'd forgot his boyhood chums."

Theo apologized for the years—decades—of no communication. He deftly got the catch-up questions about Clifton's work, career and family out the way. That done, Theo asked, "You ever get that *Jet*-book I sent you in the mails?"

"Yup. Thought that was some sorta prank, too. What would an ol' boy I ain't seen since Methuselah was a tyke be sendin *me* a colored folks picture-book for?"

"Got it handy?"

"Nellie! Fetch me that-there colored pocket magazine! Over by the tee-vee!" Theo heard Clifton shout. "Hold on, Theo. Here 'tis. What's up?"

"Look at Cannon in the middle."

"Unh-hunh, I'm lookin…"

"Think hard, Clifton. He look like anyone you—we—know?"

Silence. "No," Clifton finally answered. "Should he?"

"Look hard, Clifton. Think hard, remember hard," Theo said, patiently.

Another silence, then: "Sorry, but I cain't rightly recollect *anyone* this Cannon is suppose to resemble."

Theo breathed hard through his nose. Through clenched teeth he whispered, "That summer night. Lake Como. Peggy's—friend—"

"Steady there, Theo," Clifton cautioned softly from a thousand miles away. "You got *enemies*, bub—no tellin who might be listenin—"

"I realize that, Cliff. But you *do* know who I mean, now, right?"

"Yup." Clifton was silent, then spoke again. "Since *you* mentioned it, he does—but I wouldn't of made the connection on my own."

"So they *do* look similar to you?" Theo's voice was unnaturally high.

"Deep brown skin, Injun features—they *share* a certain look more'n they look alike, at least to me. And don't forgit, Theo: I ain't seed him but once. And real fleetin like. I didn't exactly commit his map to memory." Clifton paused, then added, "Why don't you call Polk Caterfield and get his—"

"He's a tough man to get aholt to," Theo lied.

"Yeah—went Christian on us. Big time," Clifton said with a chuckle.

Theo thanked Clifton for his time and promised to call more often. "And don't take this the wrong way, but if you're ever in a bind for some ready cash-money, Clif—"

"Ol' General Motors is doin okay by me. Gonna retire in a few years, nifty pension lined up. But thanks, Theo. And don't wait another thirty years to call me, dadgum it."

"Be good, Cliff. Talk to you soon enough." They hanged up.

Theo leaned back in his leather easy chair. Was it mere coincidence that the Negro who had stolen his girl—his first love—resembled the man who was bringing white and colored kids together? White girls and black boys. *I can spot the resemblance, if nobody else can.*

Then there was the near collision with Cannon—if that was Cannon—outside Knoxville that night. *Could of been. I take that route often; he probably drives that highway a lot, too—that multi plies the chance of somethin like that happenin. I'll check to see if he has or had a pattern of drivin that way...*

He needed something to slow the thoughts that careened in his head. He reached inside his drawer, pulled out his emergency bottle, and took a long pull straight from it. The fiery liquid soothed his nerves and reined in his thoughts to normal speed.

No, none of it was coincidence, he decided, finally. The resemblance, the near wreck, Cannon giving the music the push it needed to take it over the top—it all tied together. *If nobody else sees what's goin on—yet—then I do. That's the Good Lord's way of tellin me to be the first to take up the sword against rock-n-roll.*

He took another long swig and plotted his next move.

CHAPTER TWENTY-TWO

Despite the growing opposition to the new music, Cootie's Rhythm Revue forged westward across America.

November dissolved into December. The Upper Midwest cities, with sizeable Negro populations, were behind them. The company faced two weeks of unknown territory before it reached large, friendly audiences in the San Francisco Bay area and Southern California.

Their goal in such towns as Topeka, Wichita, Denver, Portland, Seattle, and others was to tread water at the box office—and leave without any major trouble. For, as the success of the Revue grew—the Negro press tracked and trumpeted the show weekly—the picketing at the venues increased. Especially in the towns with few—or no—Negroes, protestors routinely picketed and dared ticket buyers to cross.

At first, the pickets amused the cast and crew. The protestors, with their bad skin, ugly teeth, eyes glazed and unfocused, veins bulging in their flushed necks, looked like the first cousins of the zealots who screamed that the end of the world was nigh. Their signs and chants depicted rock-n-roll as the Devil's Music, jungle sounds, and audio voodoo designed to steer white children to the beds of oversexed Negroes. According to the picketers, the jukeboxes in Hell blasted only rock-n-roll. The Communists were using it as part of a mind-control scheme that would reduce the United States to a nation of coffee-colored, curly-haired mongrels.

Some even claimed the music was foisted by the advance guard of invading Martians.

From Day One, Cootie had instructed his charges to ignore the taunts hurled against rock-n-roll and the Negro race. Miraculously, there were only a half-dozen physical altercations. Most were simply overblown shoving matches. In Peoria, a fat, fiftyish man singled out Hal Dillard as the anti-Christ. Hal, a former Golden Gloves bantamweight champ, cold-cocked him with an eye-blinking seven-punch combination. Cootie and Willa walked the police commissioner behind the hockey arena where that night's show was to take place. After some haggling, all agreed that three hundred dollars would keep Hal's record clean in the state of Illinois.

In the beginning, the pickets cost the Revue little, if any business. Now, venturing deeper into the Bible Belt heartland, Willa and Cootie wondered if the half-filled houses were because of a backlash—or because there was little demand for the music. Comparing notes with Freeman, Cootie learned that his friend's integrated roster was meeting similar animosity.

But not as much as my all-Negro revue, Cootie assumed.

Still, Cootie and Willa were braced for such a box-office slump. From New York to Kansas City, the show was profitable beyond their grandest visions. The two weeks in California, and the return to the Apollo for the Christmas-to-New Year's week would surely be a windfall. Moreover, the investors were overjoyed, though not surprised, by the Revue's success. Willa employed a team of bookkeepers to ensure that each investor's first dividend check—to be paid after the start of the new year—was accurate to the penny. She and Cootie paid their troupers handsomely; the last thing they needed was a mutiny over short money.

As for their personal finances, they would soon be able to pay off the loans from friends and relatives. Willa calculated the Christmas Week Apollo engagement would put them over that hump. For the time being, they relied on their original sources of income. Cootie, from the road, taped shows and sent them to New York for WPLC to play. He brokered a deal with the WPLC management to lease the tapes to stations across the country. Thus, Cootie became syndicated—and compensated smartly.

Since Willa managed all the artists in the show, ten percent of their pay boomeranged back to her. As for her clients who were *not* in the show, it was difficult for her to juggle their bookings from the road. An assistant she hired before she left New York was largely inept; five of her clients had jumped ship in the three months since the tour began. However, her most valuable artists were with her every night.

They had to fire two company members. One, the alto sax player in the orchestra, violated the rule about underage girls. He spent most of his free time during a three-day run in Detroit with a fifteen-year-old girl—who did not even look thirteen. Willa paid the girl's mother a grand in hush money, warned the mother and child that that would be the first and last payment, then sent the horn player packing.

Much to Hal Dillard's sadness, Willa and Cootie had to give one of his Moonlighters a pink slip. Tony Jones, Hal's best friend since the first grade, violated *both* of Cootie's most serious rules. Willa caught Tony in the act, backstage at Chicago's Regal Theatre, with a fourteen-year-old blond, her back propped against a brick wall. Willa waited until Tony and the girl finished, then calmly asked to speak with him. Tony, knowing what was next, offered no argument and accepted his bus ticket back to Buffalo.

They saved their biggest worries for Little Lydell Franklin. His mother had chaperoned the Lexingtons for the first three weeks, then returned to Lydell's four younger brothers. Willa monitored the Lexingtons as best she could, which was not much, given her sundry other duties. Wynona Williams had *her* hands full keeping the hounds at bay from the Belles.

As expected, Lydell and his fellow Lexingtons went hog-wild after Gloria Franklin returned to Manhattan. The boys could easily talk their revue mates—or fans—into obtaining alcohol. They learned that the affection of many female fans did not end with screams from the audience. In every hotel they stayed, Cootie and Willa made sure the Lexingtons' room was next to theirs. *Still* the lads were able to sneak girls in.

That is, the other four Lexingtons sneaked in girls. Lydell fooled around mostly with women twice his age. He strutted arm-in-arm with them, his tiny frame and baby face making the age and size difference all the more pronounced. Yet, when Willa and Cootie cornered him about his reverse jailbait scenarios, he pleaded innocence. "She was my *cousin*. I come from a large family—we have relatives all over the country," Lydell explained more than once.

"So how come all your cousins are pretty, curvy women between twenty-five and thirty-five?" Willa challenged.

"It only *seems* that way, Miss McAshan," Lydell would reply with indignation, his hands on his hips and lip pooched out. Willa never knew whether to scold him or give him a kiss.

Yet, as the weeks toddled by, the sneaking of booze and against-the-wall-backstage quickies with their fans was becoming old news for the Lexingtons—except Lydell. Just days after Willa lectured them on the hazards of venereal diseases and jealous boyfriends, Sherman Garner, the bass singer, caught a dose of gonorrhea in Leavenworth, Kansas. In Wichita, the ex-husband of a thirty-year-old woman whom Lydell was putting the moves on threatened to pistol whip him. "I don't give a fuck how many hit records you done made, midget-assed nigguh," the man, just released from a ten-year manslaughter conviction roared as he waved a .44. However, one of Cootie's troubleshooters intervened, and, ex-con to ex-con, talked the man out of doing any damage.

"Good thing Big Ben stepped in," Lydell later crowed, "or I'd of *kilt* that motherfucker."

Though the episode hardly slowed Lydell with the women, that—and Sherman's case of the clap—cast a damper on the other Lexingtons.

To nobody's surprise, Moanin' Lisa became a huge headache. Off stage, she sought men—and women—with reckless abandon. Any man connected with the show who wanted her had her. And, despite Cootie's warnings, Lisa tried to put the make on two of the Philadelphia Belles—though she had the good sense to leave Shirley Williams alone.

On top of that, Lisa was drinking heavily, though each time she performed she was sober enough. With the Lexingtons' rising popularity, Cootie had them and Lisa shift places in the show. Now Lisa's three-song set served as a bridge between the teen groups. After the revue crossed the Mississippi—and started playing before mostly white audiences—Lisa got but paltry applause when compared to the crossover groups that sandwiched her. This only made her more surly, and she withheld energy from her performance. By the time the show reached Denver, Lisa was merely walking through her songs.

The more Cootie and Willa called attention to her attitude, the surlier she became. The surlier she became, the more she drank. The more she drank, the more Cootie and Willa called attention to her attitude...

For reasons neither could explain, they could not muster the heart — or lack thereof—to fire Lisa in mid-tour. That they would cut her loose when the Revue returned to New York was a foregone conclusion.

Yet, they wished such disciplinary problems were the worst of their concerns. Until others mentioned it, Willa thought she was the only one to notice the same faces showing up in several cities. She remembered a squat, muscular, bespectacled white man from Syracuse, Rochester, Buffalo, Erie, and Pittsburgh. That he was at the doorstep of middle age, and looked the personification of a "square" made him stick out like a seven-foot redhead in a pygmy village. She made it a point to stare him down in Pittsburgh; she had not seen him since.

In his stead came younger men. Willa never forgot a face, no matter how nondescript. Youngstown, Akron, Zanesville, Cleveland, Sandusky, Toledo: three young men sharing a Freddie Frat-boy look were always in the house. She noticed other young men, solo or in groups of two or three, who would be present in five or six consecutive cities, then fade away.

Willa told Cootie about this, and learned he saw the same pattern, the same faces.

Who were they? Who sent them? What did they want? What do we do? How do we approach them, if at all? They asked themselves these questions, but could come up with no viable answers. They were loath to inform Goldfarb and Worthington—and Lumpy Jackson, the gangster sultan—about the situation until something more concrete developed.

And they hoped whatever action they took would not be too late.

Yet, the pattern continued, becoming more obvious with time. In both Kansas City's, Lawrence, Topeka and Wichita—four lads, blond, bland, crew-cut, around twenty—were at every show. By now Cootie, Willa, and the security men were on the strictest lookout for uninvited camp followers. Finally, certain these were the same four, Cootie, flanked by his three largest, hardest-looking peacekeepers approached them in the parking lot after a show in Dodge City.

The ex-jocks towered behind Cootie, arms folded, legs spread, their faces tight, but noncommittal. Cootie smiled brilliantly. "I need to cut you cats a rebate," he drawled pleasantly.

The lads traded sheepish looks. The largest one spoke up. "Why's that?" he asked in a Southern accent Cootie could not place as to region.

"Because you've caught our show for the last five, six nights," Cootie replied calmly.

The young men passed around another look. Two flushed pinkly. The leader, however, remained composed. "You must of mistaken us for others, Mister Coutrere, sir," he said politely.

"I don't forget faces." Cootie's smile was caustic.

"Sir, I assure you we have better things to do than trail a bunch of—rock-n-roll singers," the leader said firmly.

From the corner of his eye Cootie saw Willa give him several light head shakes. He grinned coldly. "Maybe you cats are right. I *could* be mistaken. And why anyone would shadow a rhythm revue is beyond me," he said, his gaze sliding, landing, holding, then moving on from each one. "Sorry if I compromised your time."

"No problem—sir," the spokesman uttered. He dipped the last word with just enough sarcasm *not* to cause the three skulking Negroes to react in any fashion.

Without turning his back on the men, Cootie walked over to Willa. "I'm sure they got the message," she said. "Whoever sent them will take care not to be so obvious from now on."

"Which only means they'll get slicker about it," Cootie replied. "Whoever *they* are."

"They're not amateurs, that's for damn sure," Willa said. "Still, we can't worry ourselves ragged about some phantom force, always looking over our shoulders."

Before the first of three shows in Denver, Cootie repeated his pre-Apollo pep talk, and reminded his charges of who was fired, and why. "You-all have been mostly cool," Cootie told them. "We've had a few scraps among ourselves, but we've kissed and made up. We know how to circle the wagons when we have to. But now we're under even closer scrutiny than before…" His voice trailed off.

Lou raised his hand. "Can you be more specific?"

"Yeah—like name us some names," Little Robert said.

"We wish we could," Willa replied, "All we can say is: be good."

"We'll try," Lydell trilled.

"Don't try. Do." With that, Cootie had Lou lead them in a brief prayer.

* * * * *

Tuesday, November 29, 1955; 8:26 p.m. Knoxville.

Alba was in the living room watching *The Red Skelton Show* with her mother when her phone upstairs rang. "Gotta be Lou!" she gushed as she dashed to answer it. She picked up the receiver. "Heh-loooow," she crooned.

"Hello?" a soft, tentative female voice echoed.

Alba could not place the voice. A strange, cold wave washed through her. Yet, she replied calmly, "Evans' residence. With whom do you wish to speak?"

"I'm sorry, dawhrling," the voice purred, Southern, white. "I *must* have the wrong number. Lou Cannon, the famous singer, gave me this and—"

"This is Lou Cannon's *wife*! Who are *you*, and how did you get this number?" Alba surprised herself with the heat and volume of her voice.

"I tole you, hunny: Lou gave it to me." This time defiance filtered into the voice.

A bucketful of reason doused Alba's racing thoughts. "This is not even his number; it's mine—his wife's—so why would he give you *my* number?" she whispered fiercely.

"Lou ain't never tole me nuthin 'bout no wife," the caller groused indignantly.

Alba felt ropes tugging on her from opposite directions. She soaked her tone with confidence. "I don't know who you are, or what your game is, but my husband does *not* fool around—and least of all with low-class cracker trash like you!"

A haughty laugh answered her. "Guuurl, wake up and smell the per-fume! All them niggers in that show is screwin around like monkeys—and mostly with white gals—"

"You lying hoojie bitch—!"

"They's on the *road*, hunny. Gittin what they cain't git at home. All of 'em, and 'speshly *your* man, the finest one of all—"

A sudden surge of confidence—in herself and in Lou—shot through Alba. "Aren't you a bit too old to be making prank calls?" she said with finality.

"Okay, Miss Goody Two Shoes. Keep thinkin this is just a prank. Keep thinkin your man ain't stickin ever'thang in a skirt, whilst you sit at home pinin for his return, sittin by the phone, waitin for him to call. Keep livin in your dream world, sweetie."

"BITCH!" Alba slammed the receiver down as hard as she could.

Footsteps padded rapidly and Hurlene was at the bedroom door. Her face was maroon with worry. "Alba! What's wrong?"

Don't cry. Don't cry, Alba told herself. "Just some crazy woman, calling for Lou."

"Who? Why? How'd she get your unlisted number?"

"I don't know, Mama—"

"Well, she got it from *somebody*!"

Alba angled a look at her mother, then spoke. "You're not suggesting that Lou—?"

"I suggested no such thing," Hurlene retreated.

The phone pealed again. Alba let it ring three times, picked it up, but said nothing. She then recoiled, nearly dropping the phone.

"DON'T YOU DARE CALL *ME* A BITCH—NIGGER BITCH!" the voice brayed, then sent the phone crashing to its cradle.

"Her again?" Hurlene asked. Alba nodded. "I don't know what's going on, but—"

The phone rang again. Alba pounced on it. "BITCH, IF I EEEVER FIND OUT WHO YOU ARE—"

"Whoa! Hold your horses, Alba!" Lou's voice, surprised yet soothing, commanded gently. "This *is* Alba Cannon, isn't it?"

Alba swallowed hard before she spoke. "Yes, Lou, honey. Sorry, but—"

"Baby, what's wrong?" She heard deep concern, even fear, in Lou's voice.

She told him about the call. "Just a prank," he said calmly, confidently.

"But why would anyone want to pull a prank like *that*, Lou?"

"Who knows why crazy weirdoes do what they do? That's *why* they're crazy weirdoes."

"But she got my *unlisted* number, Lou."

On the other end, Lou laughed. "Yeah. Alba Cannon's unlisted number. Not Dwight Eisenhower's. Not Winston Churchill's. Not Nikita Khrushchev's. Alba Cannon's."

"That's not funny, Lou. And she harped on all the wicked things— the performers in the revue—are doing, everywhere they go."

Silence, then: "And you *believed* her? You think I might be part of that scene—?"

"That's *not* what I was thinking, Lou—"

"Yes you were. In the least, deep in the back of your mind. Or you wouldn't have said it."

She knew he was deeply hurt. "I'm sorry, honey. That call just got me so undone—"

"It was just some fool who—God knows why—wants to shovel some mess between us," Lou said, his voice heavy. "And she's off to a doggone good start."

Alba sighed. "I'm *sorry*. I just wasn't thinking clearly. But you're right." She paused, and sensed his unspoken words: *Of course I am.* She continued, "Can you forgive me?"

Now it was Lou's turn to sigh. "Of course."

"Can you really, Lou?"

"Yes. Yes." His irritation read through.

She decided to quit while she was behind. "G'night, baby. Love you madly," she cooed.

"That goes ten times double for me." They hung up simultaneously.

* * * * *

The next morning, Lou rode with Cootie and Willa to Pocatello, Idaho. Cootie's coffee-colored Cadillac convertible was always the lead vehicle in the four-car, two-bus caravan. Despite the brisk Rocky Mountain air, Cootie—and Jimmy Jameson, Hal Dillard, and Louisiana Fats behind him in *their* brand-new Cadillacs—had the tops down.

Lou told them about the call. "Most likely the same jokers who've been spying on our shows," Cootie speculated.

"That's a safe bet," Willa said. "*Somebody's* sharpening their knives, for sure."

"Some of the trouble at the shows—I'd wager it was the same yahoos," Lou said.

"And the vandalism afterwards, in a few towns—which folks tried to blame on us," Cootie added. "Lightweight stuff that got nipped in the bud—but the press tried to make it sound like World War Three."

Silence. "Who? Why?" Lou grumbled.

"Why? Because we're Negroes making money, doing something positive. Who? People who think all Negroes should be dirt-poor, illiterate, one remove from slavery!" Willa spat.

Another silence. Cootie scanned the mountainous terrain and its endless evergreen trees. "I feel like a bear that's being stalked by some invisible hunter. If I could just *see* who it is…"

"Like I said before: eventually they've got to shit or get off the pot," Willa said.

From the back seat Lou softly remarked, "You told us on Day One this tour would be no picnic in the park…"

"That I did…that I did," Cootie softly replied.

CHAPTER TWENTY-THREE

Sunday, December 4, 1955; 7:03 p.m. Knoxville.

Alba, Hurlene, Florence, and Sarah Cannon sat, planted in front of the brand-new Philco television in the Cannon's living room. Upstairs, in Reverend Cannon's den, he met with Sam Evans and several men. They plotted the purchase of three Cal Walters' supermarkets, and converting them into cooperative businesses. In the kitchen, Ruth prepared a pitcher of Kool-Aid. On the television, stiff-necked Ned Mulligan promised America a "rilly big shoo," as he did every Sunday evening at that time. Mother Cannon entered at the precise moment Mulligan cut to a commercial. "Alright! Who colored is on tonight?" she asked the room at large.

"The Five Fevers. They sing 'On My Front Porch,'" Sarah replied.

"Oh, yeah! That's a cute, jumping li'l tune!" Hurlene gushed.

"Girl—don't get too heavy-handed with the sugar in that Kool-Aid!" Florence shouted to Ruth in the kitchen.

"Okay, Mama," she called back. The phone rang. "I got it," Ruth said. She picked up the wall phone and spoke. "Good evening. Cannon's residence."

In the living room, Alba felt her heartbeat quicken. The others smiled as she rose.

"Good evening. Is Lou there?" Ruth heard from the other end of the line.

"Who may I ask is calling?" Ruth replied, with an edge to her voice.

"A friend of Lou's." The voice, pleasant and clear, sounded white.

"I repeat, who is this calling?" Ruth fought to remain civil. She glanced up to see Alba standing before her, puzzled. Ruth motioned for Alba to put her ear to the phone.

The caller paused, as if to muster patience. "My name is immaterial. Lou said I could reach him at this number."

A flash of heat tingled throughout Alba.

"Is that Junior on the line?" Florence called from the living room.

"No, Mama! It's—a friend," Ruth called back. Into the phone she snapped, "Listen, Miss! My brother is in Portland, Oregon, so there's no way *he* could have told you to call here!"

"He said he had to fly home for a few days. Family emergency," the caller replied.

Alba, her anger—and curiosity—mounting, mouthed: *Lou? Fly?*

Ruth snorted. "You *must* be talking about someone else. You couldn't *melt* my brother down and pour him into an airplane. Listen: whoever you are, whatever you're trying to pull—"

Alba yanked the phone from Ruth. "Who?" she hissed into the mouthpiece.

"Who is *this*?" the caller asked, with serene arrogance.

"Lou Cannon's wife. And don't tell me you didn't know he was married." Alba remembered to keep her voice low enough not to be heard in the next room.

"Oh, I know," the caller replied casually. "So what? He's famous, he's handsome, he fools around. You should've seen that coming when you married him, sweetie."

Alba sifted for the slightest glimmer of truth in the woman's words. She noticed this caller sounded better-educated than the previous. Alba snickered. "I don't know who's putting you white-trash sluts up to this, but—"

"Honey, keep denying the truth. That only makes it easier for him to run around on you."

Alba had a notion to slam down the receiver, but a morbid curiosity overruled that. She halted herself in mid-slam, then returned the phone to her ear.

"Still there, sugar?" The caller sounded strangely polite.

"Still here."

"Who *is* that yawl're talking to?" Hurlene called from the living room.

"Girls, you're about to miss the Five Fevers!" Florence sang.

"Yeah—they're all cute! And can *dance*!" Mother Cannon shouted.

"In a minute!" Ruth shouted back.

"You want details, sweetie?" the caller cooed. "I'll give you details. Last week in Denver, the biggest stars in the show and me and my girlfriends had us a party—if you get my drift. Lou's got a half-moon scar near the base of his spine, just atop the crack of his—"

"Stop it! Stop it, you filthy whore!" Alba screamed in a whisper.

"And his ding-a-ling—his big, black, beautiful cock—curves to the right—"

"You lousy slut," Alba shrieked, but remembered to keep her voice down.

"I probably know that body as well as you," the caller crowed. "Need more details?"

Alba said nothing as she pushed back tears of impotent rage. Ruth tried to snatch the phone away, but Alba held it in a death grip.

"Let *me* talk to that slut!" Ruth pleaded. Alba fiercely shook her head. At that instant Reverend Cannon entered, an empty metal water pitcher in each hand. His eyes quickly absorbed their troubled looks.

"What's going on here?" he demanded.

Ruth covered the mouthpiece and whispered, "Some white woman calling about Lou."

Reverend Cannon stabbed out his hand. She relinquished the phone.

"Who is this?" he roared quietly.

"Who is this?" a female voice replied, tentatively.

"Louis. Cannon. Senior."

A sharp click followed. The tears, dammed up in Alba's eyes, now overflowed. Ruth and the reverend tried to console her. Soon Florence, Hurlene, and Sarah joined them.

"What's wrong, baby?" Hurlene asked. "Another one of those calls?" Alba nodded. "Same caller?" Hurlene inquired. Alba shook her head. "Lordha'mercy!" Hurlene clucked.

The four Cannons eyed Hurlene; all caught the hint of mistrust in her tone. She did not see their looks, though Alba noticed.

"It's time to end that meeting," Reverend Cannon sighed as he nodded toward his den. "The rest of you, into the living room, please."

They complied. He returned to his den and addressed his guests. "Gentlemen, I hate to end this so abruptly—especially since things were going so well. However, a situation has arisen that demands my immediate attention." Five of the six nodded understandingly.

Sam Evans tossed him a puzzled look. With a tiny nod of his head, Reverend Cannon told his in-law to stay. He saw the others to the door. Within ten minutes, everyone was up-to-date on the two calls. Reverend Cannon stood over Alba and gently squeezed her shoulder. "Junior would not want to see you this upset, would he?"

"No, sir."

"Especially since you have absolutely no reason to believe such hogwash, correct?"

Alba hesitated. "No, sir. I would not," she said in a watery voice.

"Don't sound so convinced," Sarah said, as sneeringly as she dared.

"Sarah!" Florence scolded, unconvincingly.

"I'm sorry if I sound like I—but she had—details!" Alba said, mildly defiantly.

Florence arched an eyebrow. "Such as?"

Alba looked down. "I can't repeat them. About...secret parts..."

The reverend clamped his gaze on his daughters. He pointed to the upstairs bedrooms. "Ruth. Sarah. And don't make me have to tell you twice."

The girls pouted, but said nothing as they dragged themselves from the room. When they were on the stairs, Sarah mumbled, just loud enough, "Treats us like we're ten years old."

"Girls! What'd I just—?"

"We're going, Daddy!" Ruth shouted from the stairs.

Alba kept her eyes on her shoes. "I'm embarrassed to say this before *any* of you—but especially Mother Cannon!"

"Girl, if you want me to pull a Houdini, then keep on wantin," Mother Cannon huffed. "I can hear *anything* that concerns my Sonny-boy!"

The reverend stood before Alba. "These—details—were they accurate?"

"In a general sort of way," Alba waffled.

"Either yes or no," Florence said.

"You need not talk to my daughter in that tone!" Hurlene snapped.

"Exactly!" Sam agreed, and thumped twice on a table.

"Everybody calm down!" Reverend Cannon commanded. Quiet returned. He faced Alba again. "Was this person *dead-on* accurate?"

Alba thought about the half-moon scar. *I never noticed it, one way or the other.* She recalled the remark about Lou's curving...and whispered it into her father-in-law's ear.

When he pulled his head away, he could not contain a smile. "So do most right-handed men in this world." His grin broadened to mirror Alba's sheepish embarrassment. He then addressed everyone. "Rather than wait for Junior to call us..." He rose, went to his den, and returned with a copy of the revue's itinerary. He picked up the living room phone and had an operator put him through to the company's hotel in Portland.

"Good evening," he greeted the switchboard operator. "Lou Cannon's room, please." He glanced up to see Alba staring, wide-eyed.

Seconds crept by. "Sorry, sir, but Lou Cannon is not in at the moment. Would you care to leave a message?" the operator replied.

"Yes. Tell him," he looked at Alba, her eyes dull with disappointment, "that his father called, and to call me back. Thank you." As he hung up, Reverend Cannon caught the suspicious looks of Sam and Hurlene.

Their expressions were not lost on Florence. "It's his day off. You know Lou—hates to be cooped up," she said, trying not to sound defensive. Alba and her parents were silent. The Cannons offered no further comment.

Finally, Alba spoke. "Look. I'm tired. When Lou calls, tell him I've gone home."

"We'll do that," Florence said with a glued-on smile. "I'll get your coats." When she returned with them, the families exchanged perfunctory good-night's.

As Hurlene started out the door, she wheeled around. "I hope you don't think *we* think Lou would—"

"There's no telling what *we'd* be thinking if we were in your shoes," Florence diplomatically interrupted.

"Frankly, this is a big worry-fest over nothing," the reverend declared.

Alba crossed to him and hugged him. "You're absolutely right," she said. "Tell Lou to call me when he's finished talking to you all."

A half-minute later, as Sam turned on his car's ignition, Hurlene railed: "Imagine them getting snarky because Alba hinted there might be something to those calls!"

"Where there's smoke…" Sam hummed.

"Oh, stop it!" Alba snapped from the back seat. "You know as well as I that Lou would never do what those women claimed he did."

Her parents turned and flung her twin looks. "Alba," Sam began, fumbling for the correct words, "you're not going to want to hear this…but if Lou *is* running around on you—"

"Sam!" Hurlene hissed. *Be careful…*

"You went into this knowing what I felt about a musician's life—"

"Lou is not just any 'musician,'" Alba muttered hotly.

"Not saying he would—or wouldn't," Sam shifted gears, "but with his sudden fame, women pursuing him—"

"This isn't helping matters—not right now, anyway," Hurlene cut him off.

"Yes it is, if only because it'll help prepare Alba for any blow that might be coming. The worst thing you can do is bury your head in the sand," Sam said.

"I've got a *brain*, Daddy. I can decide for myself what's going on," Alba said as she sat upright, then leaned forward in her seat.

Within five minutes, Sam wheeled the Plymouth into the drive-way. "Home, sweet, home," Hurlene said. "Thank God for nearby in-laws."

Alba went straight to her room, shut the door, picked up her Bible, and tried to read it. Her thoughts—and eyes—kept drifting to the phone.

* * * * *

When Lou got the message, he rushed to a bank of pay phones just off the lobby and called, collect. "Dad! Heard you called! How's everything?" Lou blurted. *What's wrong?*

"Fine. Everything and everybody is fine," came the reply. You *tell* me *what's wrong!*

"Since I call every Sunday night, I thought it odd that you'd call *me*," Lou tiptoed.

"No. It was getting late and we hadn't heard from you yet..."

Lou glanced at his watch. "Dad. I've called later than this several times before. What's doing?" He heard a long sigh from three-quarters of a continent away and braced himself.

"It's Alba. Some woman called here, looking for you, and Alba got all—"

"Where is she?"

"She went home. Soon as we finish, call her; she's awaiting it."

"Of course I will." Lou sucked in a breath, then released it. "So...what happened—this time?" Reverend Cannon filled him in. "I *hope* she realizes what utter nonsense that is," Lou said. He heard no response. "I hope *you* don't believe any of that," he added, carefully.

"Of course not." His father sounded wounded by the comment. Silence, then: "Don't take this the wrong way, Sonny-boy—but I've *got* to ask—"

"No—I know absolutely nothing about the callers. And I'm disappointed that *you'd* even consider I might—"

"It's my duty to ask, son. I've got an obligation to Alba, too, you know."

"Every rumor contains an ounce of fact...is that it?"

"I'm just trying to get to the truth. Don't take that tone with me!"

"Sorry, Dad," Lou mumbled.

Another silence. "What're you thinking?" Reverend Cannon asked.

"I thought I'd straightened this out with Alba after the first time. If she *really* trusted me, she wouldn't've let this caller get her goat."

"That's the same thing I told her." The reverend paused, then, "Give her a call and try to put her worries to rest..."

"Yeah...*if* she chooses to believe me. Let me speak to everyone."

Lou talked briefly with them. All avoided mention of the calls. Before he ended the conversation, Lou told all to listen in. "I wouldn't do *anything* to disgrace this family. Especially something as low and—typical—as those callers claimed," he swore.

"We know that, Junior," Ruth said.

"Love you," Sarah chimed in.

"Be well, Junior," Florence cooed.

"Good night, Sonny-boy. Call your wife," Mother Cannon commanded sweetly.

"Will do." Lou hung up the phone. He started to call to Alba then and there, but decided to do it from his room.

Excitedly, Alba answered. "Hey! Whatcha up to?" Lou said with forced nonchalance.

"I'm *so* glad you called, honey!"

"Don't be so surprised. Sunday night, remember?" He added, in a pre-emptive strike: "Called my folks, you weren't there..."

"Had a slight headache." She paused, then continued: "How was your day?"

"Fine. Just fine." Lou said vaguely, to draw her out.

"What all did you do today, honey?" she asked.

Lou picked up the forced nonchalance in *her* voice. He tried not to sound quarrelsome. "Are you *really* asking where I was and what I was doing when my dad called?" He heard a loud exhale of irritation.

"No, Louis. I merely asked about your day."

"Okay. Met a bunch of folks after last night's show, including a nice young couple, Bill and Rosie Hempstead. Reminded me of you and me. His dad's a preacher, too, so they invited the entire company to Sunday morning services..."

"Bet they didn't have too many takers on *that*," Alba chuckled.

Her lightened tone relieved him somewhat. "Nope. Just Fats, the Belles, Robert, a few others. We spent the whole day together, even watched *The Ned Mulligan Show* at Bill's parents' house. Guess what *that* made me homesick for," Lou said.

"That sounds sweet," Alba trilled.

Something overruled Lou's better judgment and compelled him to say: "If you want to call the Hempsteads and—"

"Confirm your—alibi?

Her hurt tone was like a punch to his stomach. "Sorry, honey," he muttered. She did not reply. Carefully, he forged onward. "Heard you got another crank call..."

"Yes...and it *did* shake me for a second—but I'm never going to let that nonsense faze me again, no matter how many times those sluts call!"

"That's my girl!"

"I apologize for doubting you for even a tenth of a second, baby…"

"I understand," Lou replied. "You get a call like that, instinct says there *could* be something to it. Human nature."

"I'm *so* glad you understand!" Her voice was breathy, sunny, girlish. She paused, then purred, "Looouuu…I *really* miss you, baby…"

A warning light flashed in Lou's head. "I miss you, too," he said, cautiously.

"Just can't *wait* to see you, honey…"

Lou saw what might be coming, and knew he had to deflect it, somehow. "It'll be soon enough. After L.A., and before the return gig at the Apollo, we'll have a few days—"

"Sweetie, can't I see you *before* then…?"

"Aaaaalbaaaaa…" Lou moaned.

"If I could just fly out to L.A.—it'd be so exciting! My first time on an airplane—and that far from home!"

"Baby, *I'd* love to have you with me," Lou began slowly, "but it wouldn't be—practical. We'll be busier than heck, you'd have to make last-minute reservations—and are you *sure* you want to be five miles high, for ten hours?"

"In other words, you don't want me to—"

"It's not that," Lou argued. "It's just—remember the mild upset in Cinci when—"

"Other people had a problem with that, Louis. Most of whom you hadn't met a year ago, and will have forgotten a year from now," Alba huffed.

"That may be true, but for now I've got to work with them." Alba did not respond. Through the wires he could sense her disappointment.

"Okay, Louis…if you say so…"

He tried not to hear how deeply dejected she was. "We'll see each other a week later, anyway," he said, soothingly.

"Yes, in—Knoxville."

Silence padded the mounting long-distance bill. Lou spoke. "Don't be like this…"

"Like what?" she replied, and he knew her innocent inflection was fake.

"Trying to make me feel guilty over *your* disappointment…"

Alba exhaled grandly. "I'm not going to lie. I *am* disappointed."

"Honey, look at the Big Picture," Lou began as he borrowed a phrase Cootie often used. "If you think your presence in *Cincinnati* made some folks itchy, imagine how they'll feel with an outsider—a wife—among them in L.A., Hollywood..."

"Oh, Louis! How can I make them see I could care less about what *they're* doing?"

"That's the number-one rule of the road. Nobody is above that rule."

"Looouuu...I promise to stay *way* in the background. Nobody'll know I'm in town."

Lou tried to laugh. "Not likely, babe." Yet, her last plea sparked a flash-memory of every warm moment they had shared. *This'll be one of the highlights of her life.* His stomach tightened into an iron, icy fist. He felt poised to dive, naked, from a high cliff into freezing, shallow waters.

"Okay, Alba. We'll try to work something out..."

"You mean I *can* come out?" she screeched.

"We'll *try* to work something out, I said—"

"You don't know how much this means to me!"

She doesn't hear me, or doesn't want to, Lou thought. Aloud: "Yes I do, babe." *More than you realize what it could mean to me.* He thought of how Jimmy and Deuce, emboldened by the distance from home, were now catting around like many of the guys in the show...

"I'll make plane reservations first thing tomorrow!" he heard her say. "The tickets'll be as expensive as all outdoors—but they'll be worth it."

"Nothing's too good for my baby..."

"Uh, Lou...I know how you hate to fly...but maybe I should get a ticket for you on the return flight—?"

"Not so fast. Me and the band are gonna drive back to K-town."

"But that'll mean two fewer days of seeing you, honey!"

Lou gave it a moment's thought. "You're right." He paused again. "Tell you what. Reserve me a ticket back—just in case. Not saying I'll fly or not."

"Will do! Love ya, love ya, love ya, Lou!" Alba squealed.

"Love you, too. G'night, doll. And see you soon." He heard an extended smooch and giggle, then a dial tone. When he fell asleep ten minutes later, he had a broad smile on his face.

He snapped awake when Blondie entered. He looked at his watch: midnight. "You're in early tonight," Lou chuckled.

"The chick I was with decided at the last minute she was a *good* girl, after all," Blondie said, at once amused and disappointed. "Call K-town?" Lou nodded affirmatively. "What's shakin on the home front?"

Lou told him about Alba's planned trip.

"Are you crazy, or what?" Blondie cried. "Call her back, convince her to cancel!"

"I can't, man! This'll be one of the high points of her life. I mean, L.A.'s going to seem like some faraway, exotic planet to her."

Blondie slumped into a chair and buried his head in his hands. "Man oh man oh man oh man oh man! Dumb move, Cannon. Dumb. Stupid. Retarded."

"Will you stop making it sound like she's on a *mission* to be a wet blanket?"

"This is gonna go over like a sack full of rattlesnakes at a church picnic."

"You're footloose and fancy free, Blondie. What've you got to worry about?"

Blondie sat at the foot of Lou's bed. "That no-wives-or-girlfriends rule is not just some random thing. They *always* find a way to muck something up on a tour."

"Man, you need to quit. How much damage can *Alba* do?"

"Hope we don't have to find out."

Lou sat up and clapped Blondie on the shoulder. "Let's get some sleep, buddy. Got a nine a.m. train to catch."

"Yeah—and that's about the only reason I'd get up that early."

"Good night. Sleep tight. Don't let the bedbugs bite." Within ten minutes, Lou was asleep again. Blondie, always wide-awake at this hour, joined the poker game in Hal Dillard's room.

* * * * *

As the Seattle-to-Los Angeles Union Pacific train sailed southward, Willa stood at the front of a car and beamed proudly at her charges.

Against her protests, Cootie—and the Fantabulous Fontaine— had splurged and rented two coach cars on the Portland-to-Oakland leg. Business in the Pacific Northwest was better than expected. Paranoid Floyd, the show's co-promoter in that area, was largely responsible. He saturated the airwaves in Idaho, Oregon, and Washington State—where he owned a half-dozen stations—with plugs for the show. Cootie regarded the rented coaches as an early Christmas present for his soldiers.

Now, an hour from Oakland, the coach was jumping. Once word spread that the R & B stars were aboard, many passengers beat a path to the cars, for autographs, chit-chat...and other possibilities. The inevitable happened. Guitars and horns were unsheathed; hands became drumsticks. The performers took requests and jammed.

Cootie was in a far corner, holding court with three reporters who just happened to be making the trip. As they soaked up every word, he pontificated on the universe of R & B, and its role in the Big Picture. The Blasters were bunkered in another corner, working on a new song. Nearby, Louisiana Fats did likewise with his longtime producer and co-composer, Dan Bartolomeo. Willa crossed into the other rented car for a headcheck; all but Lydell Franklin, Hal Dillard, and two members of the Rhythm Revue Orchestra were present.

Willa smiled acidly. As the company boarded in Portland, Lydell breezed on arm-in-arm with a statuesque, olive-complexioned woman who looked enough like Willa to be her sister. She was at once perversely flattered and peeved over the lad's brazenness. She and Cootie would have to talk to him—again—about his ways. They were too wild for a grown man, let alone someone barely fourteen.

Yet, in no way could they fault him as an artist. To everyone's pleasant surprise, the group's second release, "The Alphabet of Love," was taking off nearly as fast as their first, which had peaked at number-one on the R & B, and fifth on the pop chart. Moreover, she and Cootie were relieved at the lack of friction from the other four Lexingtons over the new release's billing. "Lost Love, Last Love" had been credited to "The Lexingtons," while "Alphabet" was labeled as "The Lexingtons, Featuring Little Lydell Franklin."

They had just received good news for some of the performers. Adam Freeman was producing and starring in a rock-n-roll movie that would begin shooting in late January. Of course, the staples of his Rock-n-Roll Road Party had featured roles. Of the Rhythm Revue artists, Freeman chose the Blasters, Little Robert, Louisiana Fats, and the Lexingtons. Willa knew the reaction from those not chosen would range from middling disappointment: The Belles and Moanin' Lisa— to downright crushed: Hal Dillard & the Moonlighters.

She returned to where the Blasters worked on new material. She watched as Deuce, with an imaginary stand-up bass, made sounds with his mouth as he responded to the notes Lou played on his guitar. Blondie tapped out the beat on an armrest. Jimmy scrawled it down, roughly, on sheet music. They stopped when they noticed her observing them.

"Sounds good, boys." They thanked her. As she strolled away to check up on the latest Louisiana Fats-Dan Bartolomeo compositions, Lou fell in step behind her.

"Miss Willa?"

I simply can't get these guys to kill that "Miss" jazz...

"Yes, Lou?"

He frowned and started to say something, but pulled the words back. "Nothing important. It can wait."

She studied him quickly. "You sure?"

"Yes, ma'am," he said, uncertainly.

"If you say so, Lou." She smiled to herself as he walked away. *Bless his heart. He must have the worst case of blue balls in history. He's turned down more cooz in the last three months than most men fantasize about in a lifetime. He must miss his little cutie-pie until it's about to drive him mad.*

The train passed through a tunnel, which threw her window reflection into bold relief. She looked around to make sure nobody noticed as she studied herself. *Not bad for thirty-three.* Three barely visible lines crossed her broad, high forehead; the twice-daily applications of Vaseline and Noxzema were so far holding the crow's feet at bay.

She glanced at the dozen or so young women who had gravitated into the coach. She noticed several who, while conversing with others, slipped longing looks at Lou and Cootie. *The only thing these little mommy-o's have on me is a fresher date on their birth certificates,* she told herself, not immodestly.

She looked to the far end of the car, where Cootie was ending his monologue at the reporters. As far as she knew, he had been faithful to her, while on the tour. Often she traveled a city or two ahead, to shore up any last-minute loose ends. The opportunities for him to fool around were ample. Yet, had he done so, she would have known immediately. He would have radiated guilt like fallout from an atomic bomb. Yes, he was a cool customer, a consummate actor, but she was an even sharper judge of human nature.

Moreover, in such a tightly-knit company, word would have filtered to her. Practically all the performers would have kept mum, but Moanin' Lisa—and maybe Wynona Williams—would have jumped at the chance to rat him out.

In their fifteen months together, he stopped eyeballing pretty women while he was with her. He had continued to sneak glances at first, as most men would. Now, however, his attention—and eyes—stayed on her when they were together. She realized he had either learned to study an object without openly looking at it...

Or maybe—just maybe—he doesn't see them any more, she dared to consider. *That Creole kid and I just might make it, after all.*

As if he had read her mind, he gave her a big, corny wink from the far end of the coach.

"Oakland, California. Next station stop, Oakland in ten minutes," the conductor called as he threaded through the musicians, their instruments, and their fans. Minutes later, the train slowed into the terminal. The platform was crowded with teens and young people of all races. Many jogged along the platform as the train eased in, jumping, trying to see into the cars. Suddenly, one spring-legged kid's face exploded with joy. A tall, thin Asian lad, he pointed to the first car with the R & B stars. "There they are!" he cried. The coach became a flesh magnet; instantly, dozens of shrieking people gathered outside the car.

"Rhythm Revue!" they chanted wildly. Inside the car, the troupers were profoundly surprised and flattered. "Rhythm Revue! Rhythm Revue!" The chant spread like a forest fire.

Willa sidled up to Cootie, who stared at the mob outside, his face frozen in a grin. "Friends of yours?" she said, dropping her voice in mock deepness.

Cootie looked at her and laughed. "Not this time, baby. I had nothing to do with *that!*" he said as he pointed to the clamoring crowd. "Maybe Fontaine—but not me, not this time!"

Willa hugged him and nibbled his ear. "They might have come on their own. Ever think about that?"

Cootie continued to stare at the mob. "They love us, baby. They really, truly, flat-out love us," he said softly. "We've gotten some wild receptions before—but always *after* the show. But—this..." He waggled a hand toward the fans, who obediently moved back as a squadron of policemen ordered them to do so.

Willa addressed the company. "You see what they think about us. We can not disappoint..."

"No worry about that, Miss Boss Lady!" Little Robert wailed. "These folks is gonna see the *best* of this show, hunny-chile, baby-doll, let me tell it like it I-T, is!"

"Amen on that, brother!" Lou shouted, and all roared agreement.

CHAPTER TWENTY-FOUR

At roughly the same moment the Union Pacific train cruised into the Oakland terminal, Theo Briscoe met with Chance Elam, Reece Stracker, and Hezekiah Hester on the opposite side of the continent. They convened in the same underground bomb shelter where Theo had met previously with his dozen cohorts. He sat at the head of a rectangular table. In the corner was a cafeteria-style coffee urn, cups, and fixings. He knew from the last session that the room's chill and gloom would shorten attention spans, if not tempers.

"Let's get this over with before the icicles start to form," Theo began. The others chuckled dutifully. "I truly appreciate you boys granting me this extra time, all things considered..." He gestured in an arc at the room.

"And with Christmas nigh," Chance said in a faintly impatient tone.

"Yeah, but Theo wouldn't of called us in here just to shoot some empty shit," Reece defended his mentor.

"Of course not," Chance agreed in a warmer tone.

Theo propped his half-moon reading glasses at the midpoint of his nose and scanned several typewritten sheets. "Here goes. The latest on rock-n-roll: as yawl surely know, it's *still* spreadin like a house a-fire." His audience gave him a get-on-with-it head nod. "Lotsa folks who'd normally be pushin a broom or a clothes rack are rakin in money hand over fist."

"Yeah—mainly niggers and Jews," Reece inserted. "That music's the best thing to happen to jigs since the Emancipation, and for Jews since Moses parted the Red Sea."

"A writer or performer can make more off one hit record—which probably took all of fifteen minutes to write and an hour to cut—than an honest, working-class stiff can bring home after a year of busting his hump," Chance groused.

"Life's unfair. That's turrible," Hezekiah muttered.

"As the dust settles on 1955, the people benefittin the most are five boys we discussed the last time out: Claxton, Freeman, Coutrere,

Paranoid Floyd, and Fontaine," Theo declared. "Ol' Hez here's done a shitstorm of research on them…and they all got the same mode of operation…" He dangled the last sentence before them.

Chance grabbed at the bait. "Which is…?"

"They got their hands in every possible pie, bleedin each of their artists drier'n hell."

"Details, Theo, details," Reece said.

"Case in point: Coutrere and Cannon. Coutrere 'discovers' Cannon, plays his first record to death 'til it cain't *help* but reach number one. Meanwhile, Coutrere's common-law wife signs on Cannon to manage him. Coutrere 'steers' Cannon to such-and-such a record company—and if that Creole *don't* have big stock in that company, I'll kiss his yellow ass in front of Robert E. Lee's tomb."

"Mercy!" Reece hissed. "Do all the jockeys have similar control over their artists?"

"Just about, if they can yoke the performer in—and if he's worth the investment," Theo replied. "Each of the five fat-cat jockeys has at least a half-dozen artists—*best-selling* artists—who they practically own, lock, stock, and barrel." He explained how Coutrere and Freeman had built shows around their artists, how Claxton was forming a rock-n-roll empire on television, and how Fontaine and Paranoid Floyd ran interference for all three in their West Coast ventures.

"Lord love a duck," Chance sighed. "Before long, those guys are gonna be richer than an Arabian sheik—because rock-n-roll's not gonna die a natural death anytime soon."

Reece gave his head three hard shakes. "Great googly-moogly! Who'd-a thunk there'd be so much moolah in them jacked-up blues? Mercy, Lawrd!"

"So what've you got in mind, Theo?" Chance asked. "Do we take a shot at rock-n-roll while it's still such a fast-moving target?"

"That wouldn't be smart. The ground keeps shiftin. Nobody's established any rules yet," Reece said. "Plus, no matter how much adults hate the music, the kids think it's the greatest thing since paved roads."

"I gotta differ about 'the rules,' Reece. The jockeys *do* have their rules, though they'd seem corrupt to an honest person. Compoundin that, their pay-for-play set-up, and all the cross-dippin they do is *not* illegal," Theo replied.

"At worst, in some places, plugola constitutes a bribery misdemeanor," Chance, the legal wizard, corrected. "But—in most jurisdictions, if the station owners accept gifts, *that's* a felony."

"Yeah, like they don't skim from their jockeys' takes," Theo spat.

"The question remains: what're *we* gonna do about rock-n-roll?" Reece asked. "If we try to stop it now, it'd be like throwin ourselves in front of a tank."

"Then you wait until that tank slows down enough." Theo's grin was vulpine.

"That could be *years*. By then the damage could be irreparable," Chance grumbled.

Theo said nothing as Reece and Chance were poised for his next words. He looked over to Hezekiah and smiled. "Reece, what's your favorite meat dish?" Theo lobbed. Reece scowled as if this were a trick question. Theo waved for the ex-footballer to answer.

"Uh-ruh...roast beef ..."

"Reece. Chance. Someone gives you an immature cow, a calf. Not for a pet, but for future food. You gonna kill it, butcher it, eat it right away?"

"Of course not. I'd feed it, fatten it, wait 'til it's just right for slaughter—"

"Exactly. And that's what we do with the niggers and Jew-boys of rock-n-roll."

Chance laughed dryly. "You mean we let them build up their empires, then when it's to *our* advantage, yank the rug from under them?"

"Now you're gettin the picture. The Big Picture. We couldn't stop 'em at the start; things happened too fast, too unexpectedly. Why wait 'til they're on their way down and out? Who wants to fuck a dried-up woman? Set our trap just right, they'll walk into it on *our* time."

Reece poured a cup of coffee and added cream and sugar. "We fatten 'em, Theo. But how do we lead 'em to slaughter?"

"Oversight committee."

"Beg your pardon?" Reece responded.

Chance, with an idea of Theo's plan, smiled. "Since there are no laws that make cross-dipping illegal, we *create* some," he said.

"Yeah—but wouldn't that be lockin the barn after the horse busted loose?" Reece said.

Theo snorted. "Reece, my friend. Have some faith in our—wiliness."

Chance's round, pinkish face brightened as the picture became even clearer to him. "We'll hook a lot of those fish after the fact. Less than legal on our part, yes, but the greedy grubbers that they are, a bunch of them'll mosey into any trap we set."

Theo pounded his attorney on the back. "Chance, boy, I don't keep you on that fat retainer for nothin. And boys—I admit, this *is* gonna take us a goodly while—"

"Hell, Rome wasn't built—or destroyed—in a day," Reece drawled.

"Timing is everything—especially in somethin like this," Theo continued. He stared hard at Reece and Chance. "Well, boys—you in, or what?"

Reece smiled thinly. "Theo, you're a tough man to say 'no' to. Besides, there ain't many roads I wouldn't walk with you. Count me in like Flynn, bub."

"Ditto," Chance chimed. "When do we start?"

"We have already." Theo turned to Hezekiah. "How'd the calls go?"

"The girls did what they were told," Hezekiah replied in his usual toneless voice.

Chance leaned forward in his chair. "Calls? Girls? What're you talking about?" Theo briefed Chance and Reece on the calls made to Lou Cannon's wife.

Chance pursed his lips. "I'm missing something. You're biding your time with rock-n-roll's fat cats, yet you're diddling with some flash-in-the-pan singer and his wife?"

"Hell, I could care less about Lou Cannon, *whoever* he is. It's what he *symbolizes*. Whilst we wait to get the big cheeses right where we want 'em, we can warm up on smaller fish like Cannon, keep the killer instinct sharp."

"I see what you mean," Reece cut in, "but Cannon ain't never done you nothin."

"From all accounts, he's a decent colored kid," Chance added.

Theo grimaced and shook his head. "Yawl *still* don't hear me. It's not about *Cannon*. It's about knockin the most popular colored singer—with white gals—out the box. And he opened up a Pandora's Box with 'Cora Ann.'"

"If it hadn't been Cannon, it would've been another good-looking colored boy with a monster hit a few months further down the road," Chance contended.

"Exactly," Theo agreed. "And it would of been *his* black ass we'd be after. But it was Cannon." Theo paused. "C'mon, boys. It's not as if I've—we've—never put my enemies through similar hounding."

Chance grinned despite himself. "You're right about that. Nobody plants a burr under his opponent's saddle and drives him to the brink like *you* do."

"Amen, Brother Ben," Reece piped in. "I'm glad I'm on your side."

"Besides, Cannon's had it easier in life than any of us in *this* room. Middle class, both his parents college graduates. Despite where we're at now, none of us can make that claim," Theo said. "Nigger-rich before his twenty-fourth birthday, monster hit first time out the chutes—that boy ain't paid no dues."

Chance grimaced. "I still don't think you should waste a hard-on over Cannon. If you're gonna mess with anyone's personal life, it should be Coutrere, or one of the other fat cats."

Theo shook his head. "That could throw off our long-range plans. Like removing one card from a house of cards, the whole thing comes tumblin down. Save the best for last, and as plush as we want 'em to be," he repeated his basic battle plan. He studied Chance and Reece, and could tell they did not fully support his harassment of Cannon.

"Believe me...I have my reasons for targeting Cannon," he said softly. A dark brown face that merged the features of Dion Eason and Cannon flashed across his mind's eye.

Chance gave him a hard look. "I'm sure you do. We're with you on your long-term, Big Picture bushwhack, but whatever's between you and Cannon is between you and him."

"Yup. Between me and him. And when the day comes where I can't bring down some Johnny-come-lately..."

"I hear Coutrere's show is packin 'em in out on the Wrong Coast," Reece said in a change-the-subject maneuver.

"You betcha," Theo replied. "You *know* they're gonna cut the fool out in Hollyweird, give us plenty of ammo we can use later. Ol' Hez is gonna fly out there, supervise the boys I got trailin Coutrere's crew." He eyed Reece's barely-touched coffee cup, then the urn in the corner. "Noticed you boys didn't put much of a dent in the java. Since business is concluded here, might as well break out somethin that should tickle your fancies more." He pulled two pints of bourbon from his inside suit jacket.

"I was *hopin* that's what them bulges represented," Reece crooned, reaching for a cup.

"You know what to do. Kill 'em both," Theo smilingly commanded.

And they did, in little time.

CHAPTER TWENTY-FIVE

Sunday, December 11, 1955; 4:43 p.m.
South of Los Angeles.

"Good Lord! Who would ever believe this was the middle of December?"

Lou looked to his right at Alba in the passenger's seat. To their right, two hundred yards away, was the Pacific Ocean. The reddish-orange sun descended gracefully into the water. *So far, so good*, he mused. Aloud he said: "This is the life, hunh, baby?"

"*Viva la* rock-n-roll!"

Lou swerved to his right as a northbound eighteen-wheeler took up more than its share of the two-lane Pacific Coast Highway. Lou honked as the truck faded in the opposite direction.

"California Road Hog!" Alba twisted in her seat and shouted vainly. Lou stared at her for a long second, then guffawed. "What?" she demanded pertly.

"Your hair. It's so—mussed up," Lou replied. "Want me to put the top back—?"

"No! What's the fun of flying down an oceanside highway in a drop-top Cadillac—if you're gonna keep the roof *up*?" Alba asked, then adjusted her oversized black sunglasses.

"Yeah—you're only young, in California for your first time—"

"With your baby by your side and a hit record on the charts—" Alba sing-song-ed.

"—Just once," Lou finished.

Alba raised her arms above her head, clasped her hands, and did the closest thing she could to a cat stretch from where she sat. "Wow!" she cried in summary of her feelings.

"Something else, hunh?"

"You betcha, babe!"

The day before Alba's arrival, he told Blondie she was on the way. "Thanks for letting me know," Blondie responded, with a glance toward Jimmy and Deuce's room next door. "Now I can start warning cats who need to be warned."

"Yeah. Just jump on your horse and pull a Paul Revere," Lou snipped.

Thursday morning, just before he drove in a rental car to meet Alba's flight, Lou knocked on Cootie and Willa's door. Cootie's delayed, vexed "Who dat?" and the chasm of time he took to crack open the door told Lou what he was interrupting. Cootie's face remained frozen as Lou told of Alba's visit.

"Indeed," was all Cootie said. He turned and traded looks with Willa, buried in a thick, extra-large bathrobe, hiding in the middle of the room. Cootie then returned to Lou, nodded curtly, and gave the door the twelve-inch push it needed to be closed.

Whatever it was that Alba was saying jarred him back to the present. "Sorry, babe. Say again, please," he requested.

"Sure was sweet of Mister Fantabulous Fontaine to let you use his car," she repeated.

"*One* of them. He's got enough to start his own dealership."

"Still, he didn't *have* to tell Mister Cootie and Miss Willa you could borrow it."

Fontaine would loan his wheels to anyone who helped fill the houses all over Southern California, Lou thought, but knew it would sound cynical if he put it into words.

"Why does he live so far outside the city, honey?" Alba asked. "Why couldn't he just buy a mansion in Hollywood or Beverly Hills or one of those movie-star places?"

"He tried to. Never mind that he had the cashola—several times over. Folks just wouldn't sell, not to him. So he built his own. In about the only place he could buy enough decent real estate. Way out here, near the ocean, miles from L.A. proper."

"Why couldn't he have just built a mansion in one of L.A.'s nice colored neighborhoods?"

"Sometimes distance has its advantages, babe. Like the old-time kings used to build moats around their castles…"

"I see." Alba paused, then: "That mansion had *better* look like it does in the *Jet*-book…"

Lou laughed and pinched her leg. "There's some things you can't fake for a camera."

"No…I guess not," she said, "how silly that must've sounded…"

Lou pinched her leg again. *So far, so good.* He had caught no resentment the few times his revue mates spied Alba in her three days there. And though they knew beforehand of her arrival, Willa and

Cootie reacted with arch surprise when they saw her with Lou Thursday afternoon in the motel parking lot. Lou's mentors' greetings were cool and curt. Conversely, shortly thereafter, Willa and Cootie overdid the politeness bit, in Lou's judgment. He figured their suggestion that Fontaine loan him the '54 baby-blue Caddy was their way of apologizing.

Deuce and Jimmy, as always, displayed their big-brother graciousness to Alba, but were chilly toward Lou when she was not around. Lou sensed Willa and Cootie had warned the troupers that a wife was on board; the few Alba chanced upon were neutral toward her.

She did, however, stay out of the way, as promised. On Friday she caught a city bus downtown, shopped, and took the shoe-leather tour. She returned to the motel to rest and freshen up, then jumped in a cab as showtime approached. She watched the two Friday night performances from the recesses of Wrigley Field, the home ballpark of the Los Angeles Angels of the Pacific Coast League.

Her Saturday was much the same: early sightseeing and shopping, then to the stadium.

Yeah, so far, so good, Lou repeated to himself. That the company enjoyed a two-week box-office bonanza in California did not hurt, either.

"Lou! Aren't those the three boulders we're supposed to look out for?" Alba asked as she pointed to the huge rocks on the beach, halfway between the water and highway.

"That's them. We're just a mile away now. Keep your eyes peeled on the left—thought I doubt we could miss the place."

A minute later they found it. The compound sat a quarter mile from the highway atop a small hill; an iron gate surrounded it. Lou wheeled up the freshly-blacktopped road to the gate. As they drew closer, Lou noted that the cast-iron vertical spokes, spaced inches apart, reached twice the height of a tall man. The ends tapered to spear-like points. The front gate was about two hundred yards across. They stopped at the security hut at the mouth of the gate. A swarthy, thickset man in a dark suit greeted them with a professional, military smile. "Mister Cannon..." his voice trailed as his gaze slid from Lou to Alba.

"And The Missus," Alba said with a big smile.

"Indeed. Just go to the top; a valet will take the car from there."

Lou tried to slip the guard a five-dollar bill, but he politely refused. "M'sieur Fontaine takes *exquisite* care of us, to be sure," he said.

"Sounds like he's done some Shakespeare," Alba said as Lou drove to a circular driveway at the hill's crest. A slender Latino lad bounded over as Lou brought the car to a halt. The young man opened Alba's door, then Lou's, took the keys, and drove off.

"Mercy!" Alba said. "That Mister Fantabulous has got an entire army on his payroll!"

Lou laughed. "I'm afraid our friend's not *that* plush. Most of these folks jumping at our beck-and-call tonight were hired through an agency."

"Still." They began the trek up the forty-eight steps to the front door—one for each state, as Fontaine was fond of pointing out.

"Oh. My. God!" Alba exhaled when she *saw* the nineteenth-century Spanish-style abode for the first time.

"Beautiful, isn't it. Just like in the *Jet*-book, right?" Lou responded. They stopped in mid-climb to admire the house. Three stories high, the back part built into the hill, the doors of the second story led to a level that had been sculpted out, then flattened by landscapers. The stucco exterior was painted in a greenish-gold blend. The roof was pinkish-burnt orange, corrugated sheeted iron.

"Lord! I'm waiting for the Cisco Kid to come charging up any minute," Alba chuckled.

"A few more hit records and we can build us something like this, right, baby?"

"No thanks, Lou. How much luxury does a person need? Or can stand?"

They reached the front door. It eased open and a stately ebon-skinned woman in her late forties filled the passageway. She wore a leaf-green evening gown woven from pure silk. Her hair was tied in a green, gold, and brown African headwrap. Her broad smile revealed teeth that resembled ivory piano keys.

"Welcome, Mister and Missus Cannon," she trilled in a pleasantly husky voice. Given her regal bearing, headwrap, and exquisite African features, Lou was surprised when he detected an unmistakable, albeit cultured, Southern accent. She extended her hand. "I'm Yvonne Fontaine."

"Oh! *Missus* Fontaine!" Alba gasped.

Lou choked back a smile as he recalled what Cootie had told him days ago. Yvonne was Fontaine's first, *legal* wife; he had married her in his native Beaumont, Texas, when he was twenty and she sixteen.

"Yes. Gretchen will show you around," Yvonne said and gestured toward an equally tall blond woman, about forty years old. Lou studied her quickly. *Gretchen. Fontaine's second "wife," been with him since 1938.* By then, Fontaine's array of businesses, legal or otherwise, had made him the wealthiest young Negro in Los Angeles. According to Cootie, Gretchen had fled Nazi Germany and nested in California to be in the movies. Her accent was too indelible for casting directors, and she settled into Fontaine's household, who "sponsored" her attempt at an acting career, as he had done—and was still doing—with a select few. Gretchen had borne Fontaine a boy and a girl, both teenagers, to go along with his two sons and daughter, all young adults now, by Yvonne.

"Follow me," Gretchen said softly.

Lou and Alba complied. "Who's she?" Alba whispered. "The maid?"

"Nope," Lou replied as softly as he could, "I'll explain later."

Gretchen showed them the dining and living rooms on the first floor, which were three times larger than in an average-sized home. She led them to the kitchen. "Good Lord! I'll bet even the ritziest restaurants don't have such swell equipment!" Alba whispered as they surveyed the gleaming stoves and utensils. "Who do they cook for here? A pro football team?"

Next was the recreation area at the back of the ground floor. One half was reserved for the youngsters. The Lexingtons—minus Lydell—played pinball games and shot pool. With them were a dozen teenaged boys and girls; Lou figured the boy and girl with curly, sandy hair and gray eyes had to be Fontaine's by Gretchen. Then she led them to the "adult" side of the cavernous rec room. It featured a roulette wheel, several gaming tables, a specially-made table for shooting dice, and three tables with painted-on chessboard tops. Along the back wall ran a lavishly-stocked bar. Though unfamiliar with the brand names, Lou assumed the bottles on the shelves represented liquor and wine from every corner of the planet.

"Would you care for a drink?" Gretchen asked, politely.

"No, we will have something at the party, thank you," Alba replied in a voice more proper than normal.

"Let us go outside," Gretchen said. She led them to the second floor and along a short hallway. From there a door opened to the carved-out-of-the-hill pool area. Gretchen nodded to the rooms they had passed. "Bedrooms. Six in all. Three full bathrooms, three half," she recited in a half-proud, half-complaining tone. "I'd show you the bedrooms, but—" she grappled for the correct words "—some of them are a mess right now."

Lou felt Alba's pinch on his forearm, but he dared not look at her.

They stepped outside to the pool area. A dozen circular, white-painted metal tables dotted the concrete rim of the pool. The pool itself was in the shape of a jukebox, with the bottom painted to resemble a classic nickelodeon. Countless lounge chairs were set up, along with a temporary bar. A jazz sextet played sedately on a permanent bandstand at the far end of the pool area. A lad about twenty, who Gretchen said was Fontaine's nephew Carlyle, was recording the party on film—as he did with all the soirees at the mansion.

Lou soaked in the scene. Around fifty people were already there, many of them from the Revue. He winced when he saw Jimmy and Deuce; they were sprawled at a table, each with an arm around a pretty girl. The young women had the same lustrous, medium-brown skin and shoulder-length black hair; Lou assumed they were related in some way.

"Oh, look: there's your friends," Alba said, too airily, as she nodded toward them. She wrapped her right pinky around Lou's left, and off she sailed toward them. When they saw her approach with Lou in tow, neither blinked. Lou smiled to himself; his buddies had prepared themselves for this moment.

"Alba. Lou. What a surprise," Jimmy said, not the least bit surprised.

"A pleasant one, I would hope." Alba's drawl was as sweet as her smile. She shifted her gaze to the young women.

"These are—uh—Lorraine and Marva," Deuce said. "Cousins. Actresses."

"Yes!" Alba's eyes brightened in recognition. "I saw you in—" She braked her tongue and put her memory in gear.

"Actually, we haven't *been* in anything—yet," Lorraine said reluctantly. "But I *was* Dorothy Dandridge's stand-in when we filmed *Carmen Jones* last year."

"Yes…you do resemble Miss Dandridge…slightly…both of you…" Alba said from behind a two-hundred watt smile. "Oh—by the way—this is Lou Cannon, and I'm his wife," she said as she offered her hand.

"Yes…we knew the first part and assumed the second," Marva said, her warm smile at odds with her mildly testy tone.

"Well, we must—circulate," Alba cooed, as she steered Lou from the table.

People began to trickle in, Negro and white. All were well-dressed, and reserved in manner. "Lou!" Alba whispered. "Everyone here is so—successful-looking!"

"Yep. They've either already made their mark, are well on their way, or can fake being important. Only *le crème de le crème* get invited to a Fontaine blow-out."

"All these pretty women—actresses, I'll bet. All the colored ones are trying to look like Miss Lena Horne or Dorothy Dandridge—"

"Or a combination thereof," Lou interjected.

"And the white gals must've stopped off on their way to a Marilyn Monroe or Jayne Mansfield look-alike contest."

"Hoo-ray for Hollywood, babe."

Taking a closer look at the guests, Lou recognized many of them. Some he had seen in films and on television; he saw four boxers he knew from *The Gillette Friday Night Fights.* Any West Coast-based jazz or R & B hotshot who was not already present was on the way. Anyone approaching or past middle age whom Lou did not recognize as an athlete or entertainer was surely a big wheel in the business world, he assumed.

Lou and Alba continued to mingle, glad-handing as if candidates for office. "Ya never know," Cootie recently told him, "but the hand you shake at a party on Saturday could open the door on a brand-new opportunity for you on Monday." Not for nothing had Lou studied Cootie and Willa for the past three months. They took the time to speak with everyone—even for the tiniest moment—at social gatherings, regardless if that person were great or small, seemingly important or insignificant.

They mingled on. Lou modestly deflected all compliments about his hit records. Alba smiled graciously through the "you're so *cute!*" declarations often punctuated by a pinch of her cheeks. The gathering swelled and the pool area became more crowded. Alba clung tightly to Lou and squeezed his arm—sometimes consciously, sometimes unconsciously—every time an aspiring starlet buzzed closely and fixed an overlong glance on Lou.

"Hey, Lou! Alba!" They pivoted to see Blondie at a table, with his left arm on the bare shoulder of a green-eyed redhead, and his right hand dangling dangerously closely to the well-filled cleavage of an amber-eyed blond. Alba and Lou crossed to them. "Cindy. Melinda," Blondie introduced. "UCLA co-eds. Dancers. Actresses. Models. Cheerleaders. Yawl *know* who the cat is; the kitty is his wife."

"Oh, my!" Alba said, pleasantly. "So many—titles."

Lou noticed how Blondie's friends winced at the wispy sarcasm. "Nice meeting you-all," he mumbled as he steered Alba away.

"Well," Alba said, "I doubt he'll be bringing *them* back to Knoxville to meet the folks anytime soon—"

"Don't start, Alba. Folks go out with who they want to out here—"

"*That's* not what I was getting at, Lou—"

"Like I said: don't start. C'mon, we're supposed to be enjoying ourselves."

"Lou! And Missus Lou!" They looked up to see Lydell Franklin grinning wildly. His arm was interlocked with that of a handsome brown woman more than twice his age and nearly a foot taller. "Just *had* to come out to L.A.?" Lydell directed to Alba.

"Uh—yes," she replied, looking sideways at him.

"Where are my manners?" Lydell said, with a tiny slap to his own head. "This is my mother." He tugged on the woman's arm. "Missus—uh-ruh—Annie Franklin."

The woman tried not to scowl. Lou battled to keep a straight face. Alba looked away from Lydell and his friend and bit her lower lip to keep from shrieking in laughter.

"You have a *most* talented son—Mrs. Franklin," Alba drawled sweetly. "I'm sure you're too proud of him for words."

"Yes...I sure am," the woman mumbled, then turned to Lydell. "Honey, I'm hungry; let's get something to eat."

"Yeah, let's—Mama," Lydell said in a liquid voice.

"Nice meeting you...Mrs. Franklin," Alba said, her jaws tight to dam back the laughter.

"Likewise," the woman said as she walked away, arm-in-arm with Lydell. The pint-sized singer could not resist looking behind the woman to admire her full, rounded buttocks as they shimmied beneath her tight woolen skirt.

When Lydell and friend were out of earshot, Alba and Lou howled with laughter. "Gracious! How many mothers *does* that child have? And not counting his real one I've already met in New York," Alba croaked.

"At least one in *every* town we've played—two and three in some," Lou replied. "A young girl doesn't stand a chance with Lydell. The only thing a chick his age can do for him is go fetch her mother—*if* her mama is a killer-diller."

"My feet are starting to complain," Alba said. "Let's find an out-of-the-way table." They seated themselves in the far corner of the pool area, near the shallow end, and watched the parade of people. Time whisked by as smoothly as the cool sounds from the jazz ensemble. Lou checked his watch: nine o'clock. Fontaine had yet to arrive at his own party.

Louisiana Fats floated by their table. "Man, I'm ready to head on out," Fats said.

"But you barely got here," Lou said. "And you haven't met Fontaine yet."

"I'll meet him later. All these phonies and people strivin to be somethin they ain't is workin my last nerve."

"Suit yourself. Later, Fats." As Fats left, Lou looked around for his other revue-mates. He spied Moanin' Lisa strolling in, sandwiched between a hulking heavyweight boxing contender and a tiny, dark-skinned Negro girl in a platinum-blond wig. Deuce, Jimmy, and Blondie were still with their original dates. In the corner diagonally across from them, Little Robert soaked up the admiration from a score of his fans. Hal Dillard sauntered by to tell Lou that Fontaine had been holed up in the house the entire time. "He's havin a major pow-wow with Cootie and Willa," Hal explained, then scooted off after a pair of tawny twins.

"What are they plotting?" Alba asked. "The Second Coming?"

"You know how it is with those high-drama types," Lou said. "Always got to wait 'til the time's just right for their big entrance."

"Hiii, Lou," a honeyed voice purred from behind them. They looked up and into the smiling topaz eyes of a copper-skinned woman in her early twenties. Her well-endowed cleavage threatened to spill out of one of the tightest dresses Lou had ever seen a woman stuffed into. Even in a setting stocked with stunning women, this one stood out—and was acutely aware of it. "Mind if I sit for a moment?" she asked innocently.

Lou glanced over to Alba, who bounced looks between him and the woman. Alba's jaws tightened, but her eyes betrayed no emotion. He squeezed Alba's hand. *Be nice.*

"Uh," Lou mumbled as he tried to kick-start his memory.

"Have a seat, deary," Alba said in a flat tone as she gestured with her right hand. She rubbed Lou's forearm with her left.

The realization of who the woman was struck Lou like a snake bite. "Oakland. *Hal Dillard's friend*," he said, then cut his eyes toward Alba.

"No...you just *happened* to see me with him a time or two," the woman coolly corrected. "Ginger Catlett...remember?" She offered her hand.

Out of sheer politeness, Lou took the hand and answered, "Yes."

She slowly wiggled her pear-shaped rump downward and into a chair. "I'm in the same Adam Freeman movie *you're* going to be in—"

Lou stopped her as Alba cleared her throat, grandly and at length. "Ginger, this is my *wife*, Alba..."

"Charmed, I'm sure," Ginger replied in a barely audible voice. She did not look at Alba when she offered a limp hand, and withdrew it after the slightest contact.

Alba leaned back and shot Ginger an indigo glare, which went unseen by its target.

Ginger forged on. "Lou, I hate to bother you with something like this, but..."

"Go on," Lou coaxed. He pulled back a wince as the heel of Alba's shoe twisted downward on his instep.

"You see...I've already gotten the scene I'm in—and I've only got one line...so far..." she said, with a pout, but hopefully.

"That's—awful," Alba clucked. "But it's one more line than most people on this planet have, isn't it?" Now it was Lou's turn to grind his heel into her foot.

To Ginger, Alba was no more than a fly on a discarded morsel of food.

"So...why are you telling *me* this?" Lou asked, carefully.

Ginger leaned forward to give Lou a better view of her charms. "Perhaps you could, you know, use your—influence—with Mister Freeman and Mister Coutrere, and, you know, try to persuade them to upgrade my role."

Lou glanced at Alba before he addressed Ginger. He smiled kindly. "Friends though I am with them, I have absolutely zero say-so about the film. I haven't gotten *my* script yet."

Ginger acted as if she had not heard this. "I've talked to people," she plowed on, "on the inside of the project. I'm *only* playing one of the high school kids"—she missed Alba's amused, arching eyebrow—"but I thought maybe...you...we...could talk to Mister Freeman and convince him that your character should have a 'love interest.'" She finger-curled strands of her shoulder-length auburn hair as she awaited Lou's response. "You know...maybe a little girlfriend..."

Lou smiled, cut his eyes toward Alba, and silently told her to take the wheel.

Alba propped her elbows on the table and leaned forward until her face was a half foot from Ginger's. "Excuse me, but from what we've heard about the movie, all the performers will be playing *themselves*. That being the case, Lou Cannon *already* has a 'love interest.'" She waggled her wedding band beneath Ginger's nose; the movement resembled a backhanded slap in slow motion.

Ginger did not blink. "Oh, no. I was talking about in the context of the story itself. Lou's *character*," she said, slowly, as if explaining something to a six-year-old.

"I read you, sister," Alba snapped. "In more ways than one." She locked Ginger's gaze with her own. "Nice try, girlie..."

Ginger's head and shoulders rolled back as if tugged by ropes. "You actually think I'd try to come on to your husband—with you sitting right here?" she said in a steaming whisper.

"You just did. *Tried*, that is," Alba said evenly.

Now it was Ginger's turn to prop her elbows on the table and lean forward. Her nose was three inches from Alba's. Her smile was that of a beautiful reptile. "Honey," she said, sounding bored, "if you're *that* insecure about where you stand in your man's—"

"Girl, if you don't get your face out of mine," Alba purred gruffly, "I'll smack it clean into that swimming pool." Alba flinched slightly, quickly, as if drawing back to do just that. Ginger shot upward, like a high jumper bounding to clear the bar.

"Small-time, country-ass bitch," Ginger said from beneath a lethal grin, cutting her eyes in all directions to make sure she was not giving Fontaine's partygoers a free show.

Lou clamped his hands on his chair's armrests and sank lower. Using his peripheral vision, he made a quick scan to see if anyone was watching the brewing brouhaha. Miraculously, nobody seemed to pay them any attention.

Alba rose, her eyes sweeping the grounds, to make sure they were not creating a spectacle. "You want to 'upgrade' your part? Just do what you did to get your sorry little walk-on in the first place—but do it with more guys, and more often."

Ginger's eyes paintbrushed Alba from top to toes, and up again. "How would *you* know anything about that, Miss Goody Two Shoes?" she sniffed.

"Read a book the other day," Alba replied in a sweet voice. "*Confessions of a Hollywood Whore Masquerading as an Actress—*"

Lou stepped in. "Ladies, why don't we just end things before they get out of hand?"

"You're right, doll," Alba trilled. "In a cat fight, the biggest pussy always wins." She snapped her fingers less than an inch from Ginger's nose, pivoted on her heels, and tossed a triumphant glare over her left shoulder.

Ginger looked around before she spoke in a low, gear-grinding voice. "Honey, if we weren't where we are, I'd be in your big hillbilly ass like an enema."

"We won't always be at this party, slut! We can arrange a time and—"

"Alba! This has gone far enough!" Lou barked, though he was amused and amazed at this side of Alba. He then realized a tent was rising beneath his zipper.

Ginger looked past Alba and at Lou. "Despite your—wife—trying to make something out of nothing, my offer is legitimate, purely business, and still stands. Just give me a—"

"Sister—you *still* haven't gotten the message yet?"

"Alba!" Lou snapped, then smiled wanly, neutrally at Ginger. *You'd better go.* She pursed her lips and walked away, rolling her hips wickedly. Lou took yet another look to make sure they had not created a scene. "Thank you for *not* drawing a crowd—"

"She started it!" Alba squalled. "And you could have nipped it in the bud by—"

"She had a genuine reason to approach me like she did, this being Hollywood—"

"Which means she can just walk up to you, show all thirty-two and push her boobies in your face, while she treats me like a piece of furniture?"

"Okay, so she was a bit forward, and—insensitive—to your presence—"

"'Forward?'" Alba whispered shrilly. "'Insensitive?' If I hadn't been here, she'd've tried to give you some in front of all these folks!" Lou's thunderclap of a laugh stopped her. "What's so doggone funny?"

"I wish I had a camera to record this! Then I could show you later how *silly* you're acting. Over a trifling piece of eyeball candy like *her*!" He grabbed her upper arm and pulled her closer.

"No, what galls me is *how* she just totally disregarded me and—"

Lou drew her even tighter. "Forget about her—and the entire incident. Consider it water under the bridge. Now give me a kiss to let me know everything's all right."

Alba took a self-conscious glance around. "Looouuu…people are watching us…"

Lou laughed. "That wasn't much of a concern when you were ready to put your foot up Miss Aspiring Starlet's behind."

Alba thumped her fists into his chest. "That was different! I was angry!" Yet, she smiled broadly, which put Lou at ease.

"Gimmee smoochee," he hummed.

"Looouuu…" Alba protested, without conviction.

"Kiss! Kiss!" Lou demanded. No sooner did their lips brush that an explosion of applause jerked them apart. The jazz ensemble swung into a playful slice of "Hail to the Chief."

"Dollars to donuts that the Fantabulous Fontaine just made the scene," Lou said as he searched for the host.

"There he is!" Alba cried as she pointed to the opposite end of the pool area. Fontaine was the hub in the wheel of his fans, business colleagues, and sycophants. He wore a deep purple tuxedo with matching cape, a top hat perched on his shaved head, white spats on his shoes, a monocle over his left eye, and brandished an African walking stick. On Fontaine's right arm was Yvonne; Gretchen entwined her right arm with his left. Flanking Gretchen were Cootie and Willa, who seemed self-conscious about being part of this parade. Fontaine moved among the horde, grandly, fluidly, a sponge for the admiration and affection, be it genuine or feigned.

Fontaine returned the love, with smiles, nods, handshakes, words of encouragement. The uncelebrated received as much of his notice as did the well-known athletes, entertainers, and business sultans. He drew the hired help into his orbit, praising them for keeping the party a well-oiled machine and inquiring about their families. As he made his way across the area, a wave of humanity washed beside him, behind him.

"Lou!" Alba rose, grabbed his arm, and shook it vigorously. "Let's go meet him!"

"Have a seat. Relax. We'll get to kiss his ring when he's good and ready to meet *us*!"

Alba sat back down. "Okay, Lou. I'm relaxed." Yet, five seconds later she kicked off her shoes, stood in a chair, and placed a hand on Lou's shoulder to balance herself.

He stared up at her. "Girl, if you don't get down from there—!"

"Oh, my!" she gasped, not having heard. "He doesn't look too awful much like he *sounds*," she said, clearly disappointed.

"How so?"

"He's only about average height, and medium-complected—not bad-looking, mind you, but nothing to write home about, either," she said as she climbed down from the chair.

Lou chuckled. "What did you *imagine* he'd look like?"

"You know—six-and-a-half feet tall, broad, handsome as all getout—maybe like Woodie Strode, only with a beautiful jet-black complexion."

"Can't have everything."

"Oh my God, Lou—he's looking at us and heading straight this way!" she squealed. Sure enough, Fontaine was making a dramatically slow beeline toward them. He had seemingly tuned out everyone and everything else, his eyes fixed on Alba and Lou, a nebulous smile on his thinnish lips. When Fontaine was certain he had eye contact with them, he lifted his arms akimbo, at mid-angle between outward and straight up, his palms pointing inward.

He breezed closer. "Gracious," Alba whispered fiercely, "what do we say to—him?"

"For starters, 'hello.' Tell him what a fine time we're having. Relax, he's only a man."

Seconds later Fontaine and his retinue loomed before their table. Lou stood and Alba followed his lead. The host's arm unfurled to full extension toward Lou. "Mister Loueee Cannon." The words parachuted in Fontaine's much-imitated affectation of an upper-class British accent: a furry, clipped, basso profundo. He gave "Loueee" the French pronunciation.

Lou took the hand and returned the hard squeeze. "At long last, the pleasure is all mine."

"No, young man—the pleasure is all *mine*. You, esteemed sir, are the alchemist who transformed rhythm-and-blues silver into rock-n-roll gold."

Lou smiled modestly. "I had tons of help from Fats and Robert and Hal and countless others—"

"Indeed. A team effort for sure. You did, however, make the play that broke the game wide open, so to speak." Fontaine aimed an admiring, paternal gaze upon Alba. He beckoned for her to extend her hand. She did, after looking at Lou and pushing back a wild grin. Fontaine took her tiny hand in his and brushed it lightly with his lips.

"My soul!" Alba could not help but gasp, and everyone chuckled.

"This sepia vision of pulchritude *must* be Missus Lou Cannon," Fontaine declaimed.

"Yes I am," Alba trilled in her most honey-drenched drawl.

"How are you splendiferous lovebirds enjoying my humble little soiree?" Fontaine asked rhetorically, with a sweeping wave of his hand.

"Greatest party I've ever been to," Lou said in total honesty. "By far." Beside him, Alba bobbed her head in wide-eyed, animated agreement.

"Indeed. If there is anything—anything—you desire, then by all means inform me, or one of my charges. I assure you that no energy nor expense will be spared in accommodating you."

"Thank you, sir…"

"But we're fine for now," Alba completed.

"Indeed, if you say so." Fontaine panned his dukedom with a gaze. "As much as I would love to stay and discuss the world and the way things are, I *must* play the dutiful father and show equal attention to all my children. A longer, more profound discourse is in our mutual futures." He then released Cootie and Willa from his parade with an avuncular smile and nod. "Tut tut and cheerio. Page me if you need me." Fontaine genuflected and breezed off with his entourage.

"Wow!" was all Alba could get out as she slid slowly back into her seat.

"My sentiments exactly," Willa concurred as she sat.

"If his self-esteem could be melted into fuel, there'd be enough to fly rockets to the ends of the universe and back," Cootie laughed. "But I love him—and he helped me more than anyone when I got started in radio. All praises due to the Fantabulous One."

Lou gave Cootie and Willa his most charming smile. "You-all and Mister Fontaine were huddled for quite a while," he fished. "Big doings in the works, no doubt...?"

Cootie traded a look with Willa before he answered. "Let's just say that...Fontaine and we are traveling up the same road, so we've been deciding who has what right of way, which vehicles we'll share, who our drivers will be, and whatnot..."

"Oah-kaaay," Lou replied, to let them know he got their message: *And that's all you or anyone needs to know for now...*

"Uh-oh...it's closing in on somebody's bedtime," Willa said as she caught Alba stifling a yawn. "Somebody who's got to ride back into town with us."

"No, I'm fine—"

"Don't worry; we're ready to vamoose, too," Cootie interrupted. "We'll stay for another hour or so. Protocol. That okay with you-all?" Lou and Alba nodded affirmatively.

A commotion about thirty yards away snared their attention. Lydell, now wedged between a tall, thin Asian woman and a zaftig Latina, yammered at the host: "Fantabulous, you know what you got here, Daddy-O?" The teenager made an arching motion with his left arm and nearly lost his balance. "You got you a motherfuckin *Taj Majal*, man! Xanadu! Bucking-fucking-ham Palace!"

Fontaine's grin was sheepish with embarrassment and dark with warning.

"Oh, Lord," Willa moaned. "That child is lit up like a Christmas tree. Clai, go over there and pull him aside before he—"

Cootie threw up his hands. "I can't do anything with that boy! When we get back to New York, we're gonna have a looong talk with his parents—"

"A friggin *Gone With the Wind* mansion!" Lydell cried, "swim-min pool and all!"

By now everyone was tuned into the scene. Fontaine did a quick search for the plainclothes security officers peppered throughout the crowd. Many people chuckled.

"They think it's cute," Willa hissed. "They're just egging that kid on."

"Young man. Obviously, you have imbibed more than your system can tolerate," Fontaine bit the words off politely, but with subtle menace.

Lydell heard not one word. In four eye-blinks he had stripped to his boxer shorts, and began to kick off his shoes. "I don't know 'bout the rest of yawl—but I'm game for a li'l moon-light swim!"

"Oh. My. God!" Alba exhaled over a cascade of titters and encouraging catcalls.

"Ev'rybody into the pool!" Lydell ordered. The guests laughed; Fontaine backed away, called off his security men, and assumed a let's-see-where-this-goes stance. Lydell yanked down and stepped out of his shorts, waved them above his head and howled, "Yawl ain't heard me! I said: EV'RYONE INTO THE GODDAMN POOL—LIKE RIGHT MOTHERFUCKIN NOW!" He punctuated that with a violent twist of his hips, which caused his penis to ping-pong from thigh to thigh. He posed long enough for everyone to get a good look.

"Ooooo, baby! We can't call you *Little* Lydell any more!" cracked a starlet-in-waiting.

"So *that's* why chicks twice his age can't get enough of him," Cootie whispered to Willa.

"Follow me!" Lydell cried, cupped his privates with his hands, and belly-flopped into the water. Four women, already clad in swim-suits, eased into the shallow end. A dozen other party-goers stripped to either their underwear or birthday suits and hit the tank. Once in the pool, they splashed water on those at poolside and dared them to join in. Fontaine repaired to a corner of the pool area and stood between his wives, arms folded as he watched, amused but not sur-prised at the development. Carlyle filmed away, dodging people that rushed past him and into the water.

Lou took it all in silently and wondered if this were some sort of erotic dream.

"This is too, too, too much!" Willa cried in utter glee.

Alba could only stare ahead. "I can't believe these people would be so—disrespectful!"

Cootie grabbed Willa's arm. "Honey, how 'bout it?"

Willa gave it a flash of consideration. "Oh—why the hell not?" She rose and unbuttoned the top of her dress. Cootie yanked off his alligator shoes.

"Miss Willa! Mister Cootie!" Alba howled, sounding like a child who had stumbled upon her parents as they prepared to make love.

Willa went as far as her pastel-green cotton bra and panties; Cootie stopped at his leopard-spotted silk briefs. Hand-in-hand, they skittered to the rim of the pool and hopped in, feet first. Willa scooped up a handful of water and tossed it at Lou and Alba. "C'mon in! The water's perfect, it's heated. Don't be chickens!" she hollered, then shrieked as Cootie grabbed her head and ducked her under.

Lou had to laugh at Alba's look of outrage. "What's so funny?" she snapped.

"You." Lou cut his eyes toward the pool, then back to Alba.

"Lou! Don't even *think* about us—"

"What? You think I'd want to join—that? No thanks, I'll stay on the scenic route."

"You love this sort of confusion, don't you?"

Her acid tone jolted Lou. He waited before he replied. "It's just a bunch of folks—show-biz folks—having what they consider fun. They're not hurting you in any way."

"It's just so—indecent. Naked and half-naked in front of folks they don't even know."

Willa bounded out of the water and over to the table. The way the water clung to her panties, she may as well have been naked below the waist. She grabbed Alba's wrists. "Girl, we're gonna *baptize* you—show-biz style."

Alba pulled back with all her strength. "No, thank you. And pardon me if I do not find *any* of this amusing."

Willa dropped Alba's wrists. "Suit yourself," she sniffed, then returned to the pool.

"Lou!" Alba punctuated this with a jab to Lou's shoulder. "I *saw* you! Staring at her thick old hairy—business—down there!"

"Mercy!" Lou hissed, trying to inject outrage into his tone. Alba was right, though; Willa's nether foliage had arrested his gaze for an overlong moment.

Soon the pool's shallow end was so packed that people could barely flail about. "I want to go home," Alba pouted.

"How are we going to get there?" Lou snapped back. "Our ride is frolicking in that pool."

"Not back to the hotel—well, that too. But *home* home."

Lou emitted a mammoth sigh and looked skyward.

"When we're back in Knoxville, Lou, we've got some things to discuss."

"There's nothing we can't discuss when we get back to the motel that has to keep 'til K-town," Lou said, biting off the words.

"Just so—wicked! Un-Christian! Heathenistic!" Alba said as she pointed toward the pool.

"Yeah. Show-biz is one big Sodom and Gomorrah," Lou snarled softly, then dared to add: "Just like your dad always says it is."

"Well—obviously he is perfectly correct."

Lou gave his patience one last stand. "It's just folks having *their* type of fun! What's with this Miss Self-Righteous caper all of a sudden? It's not like you to be so judgmental!"

"I've never been—exposed—to anything like this before," she sniffed. "Literally."

That was it for Lou's patience. "If it offends you *that* badly, then go in the house where you won't have to look at it."

Alba rose. "I'll do just that." With her head high and back straight, off she marched.

As Lou watched her exit, he squelched an impulse to follow her. *What the heck? Let her stew. Soon enough she'll realize how silly she was.* He relaxed in his seat. *In the meantime, it's not gonna kill anybody if I eyeball some butts and boobs and bushes...*

Soon he felt someone by his side. He looked up and was not surprised that it was Ginger Catlett. Lou did not motion for her to sit, nor did she do so on her own.

"Got a bit too risqué for the little wife?" she said, detachedly.

Lou nodded. *Obviously.*

"I still want you to lobby for me, however you can," she said, her voice now syrupy. "And I can—will—make it worth your while..."

Lou braved a look at her, then had to avert his eyes from her smoldering gaze.

Ginger cut her eyes toward the house. "Don't look now...but we're being observed..."

Lou chuckled glumly. "I don't need to look. I can *feel* her staring at us."

Ginger gave her long auburn hair a toss. "You can kill ants with the look she's giving us," she said in a mildly triumphant tone.

Lou battled an urge to turn and watch Alba as she watched them. He sucked in a breath, then freed it. "Ginger...this only complicates things, gives me more I'll have to explain..."

"I understand, Lou." She placed her hand on his; Lou liked the feel of her skin; at the same time, he wanted to jerk his hand away. She took three tiny steps away from him. "My offer is...permanent..."

To Lou, Ginger appeared to sleepwalk to the pool's edge. She stood there, her back to him, for an extended moment, then slowly unpeeled her tight dress. Beneath was not one stitch of underwear. She squeezed the cheeks of her well-toned, honey-colored buttocks several times, as if performing an exercise, then slid into the shallow end.

Lou surrendered to an impulse to look toward the house. Alba was in a second-floor window, mostly obscured by a curtain. She granted Lou three seconds of eye contact, then faded from his view.

Lou was now ready for the party to end.

* * * * *

"Lou. Wake up, honey. Nine o'clock."

The words trickled into Lou's mind from another realm. He climbed toward wakefulness. Above him, Alba smiled. He frowned, puzzled. *Is this the same person who didn't say one word on the ride from the party last night?* He realized something beside her mood was off kilter. She was already fully dressed and neatly coifed.

"Up and at 'em, Lou, if you want to meet those movie people at eleven," she chirped. Even though he was still half asleep, Lou caught the feigned pleasantness.

He sat up in the bed. Alba's quartet of matching luggage was stacked, in stairstep fashion, neatly by the door. "I got a break from the airline," she said when she saw Lou eye the bags. "Got a flight out today at half-past noon, instead of the one I had for Tuesday night."

Lou continued to stare at the bags. "Unh-hunh..."

She touched him on the shoulder. "It's not what you think, Lou—"

"It isn't?"

"I remembered your original plan to drive back with the guys, and it now makes all the sense in the world. You-all have business and whatnot to iron out."

Lou said nothing.

"I'm *not* angry at you—or whomever—about last night. Not any more," Alba stated. "I didn't want to be in the way, so I took advantage of the earlier flight. Last night had nothing to do with that decision, I assure you."

Lou said nothing.

"Lou—say *something*!"

"You sure this is what you want, baby?" he asked in a soft voice.

"What do *you* want? Tell the truth, Lou. You *have* been looking forward to driving back with them, and I can't blame you. That was obvious when you told me about it."

"Yeah, you're right about that," Lou conceded. "But that doesn't mean I didn't *want* to fly back with you—"

"What's a plane flight? I'll see you when you get home. After all, we'll have the rest of our lives together." She paused. "I'll catch a taxi to the airport. I know you'll be in your meeting. I'll call you when I get home."

"Okay. Let me shower and shave, and we'll have time to catch a bite of breakfast."

"Sure," she replied airily.

He bolted out of the bed and into the bathroom. As he showered, ropes from opposite poles pulled on his emotions. He wanted—needed—the time with the Blasters. Though he did not want to fly, he did want to be in Alba's company for that time. And he felt that had she stayed until Tuesday night, regardless of how he chose to return to Knoxville, he could have patched things up with her.

Maybe. Now *we know why wives, girlfriends—outsiders—are bad news on a tour.*

Their breakfast featured blueberry pancakes, fresh fruit, and self-conscious politeness. Neither mentioned the previous night. After the meal, Lou got her bags from the room, hailed a cab, gave her a quick kiss, and held his hand aloft, a smile etched on his face, until her taxi was out of sight. Seconds after Alba was gone, Cootie wheeled up beside him.

"Hop in, Daddy-O! This baby's bound for Holly-woooood!" Cootie crooned. Lou climbed into the back seat; Willa, riding shotgun, was the only passenger.

"Not to be meddling," Cootie said, "but have you lovebirds kissed and made up yet? On the way back last night, I thought I'd have to turn on the heater, she was so cool to you."

"I *guess* she's okay," Lou replied.

"I pulled her aside before you woke up and had a woman-to-woman talk with her," Willa said. "Let her know how childishly *I* thought she reacted. And, that between this and what I told her in Cinci, this was *absolutely* the last time we would have this conversation."

"Good for you," Lou responded. "It's better she heard it from you—she thinks you're the sharpest, knowingest, doingest colored woman there is." *And so do I.*

"Got to keep my artists happy, babe."

Lou waited a while before he spoke again. "Thanks. For not giving me the 'I-told-you-so' about spouses on the tour."

Willa turned to face him. "Well. *Now* you know why, am I right?"

"Yes, ma'am, you are. As always."

"Not always. As *usual*, maybe, but not always," Willa corrected, then laughed heartily.

* * * * *

For Lou, the meeting was surprisingly brief. In a screening room on a Hollywood studio lot, Cootie's—and Freeman's—artists met the film's creative team: Carson Sinclair, a co-producer; Mason

McGuiness, an overall advisor to Adam Freeman; and Eastwick Sanders, the twenty-seven-year-old writer and director of the film. Freeman and McGuiness filled everyone in on minor details; a secretary handed the performers their sixty-five-page scripts.

Sanders, dark-haired, tall, reed-thin, addressed the "talent," as he called the rock-n-rollers-turned-actors. Nervously, chain-smoking, he told them: "Basically, we have a kid, Packy Parker, who brags that he knows Lou Cannon, Louisiana Fats, et. al., and can get them to perform at the high-school prom. *Of course* he's never met them. Yet, he has the prom committee put out the word they'll be appearing. *Of course* everybody and his brother wants to go to the prom now. So Packy's in big trouble. He's got to put up or shut up."

"Let me guess," Blondie said. "Packy somehow *meets* Lou, Fats, et. al., and convinces them to play at the prom. Ta-da!"

"Yes!" Sanders said, his eyes wide in disbelief. "How on earth did you know? Have you read the script already?"

Blondie's smile was smarmy. "Not *this* one." A few feigned coughing so as not to laugh.

Lydell raised his hand and stood. "That's all fine and dandy—but what's the *plot*?"

Nearly everyone choked back a laugh.

Eastwick Sanders stared at Lydell. "That was *it*."

"Oh," Lydell said with a sheepish grin, then sat down.

"Nobody's gonna mistake this flick for Shakespeare," Lou whispered sideways to Fats.

"Beyond payin the performers, I betcha this movie's got a budget of about ten bucks," Fats whispered back.

When they got back to the motel, Cootie gathered his charges. "Technically, you're on your own. See you on Friday the twenty-third, brush-up rehearsal, noon sharp, Apollo. Get safely to where you're going." The troupers began to filter out. "I love you all," Cootie added. He held his gaze on Moanin' Lisa. *Even the ones who I've got to cut loose.*

An hour later, he and Willa were snuggled in Fontaine's guest house, where they would relax for two days before they caught a train to New York, with a stopover in New Orleans.

* * * * *

The first days of 1956 found Lou in Knoxville. He listened closely for any squeaking wheels in his marriage. Alba had vowed all was forgiven after the incident at Fontaine's, and she seemed to be her usual chipper self. Yet, Lou was not fully convinced. Maybe it was just his imagination that had him hearing a tinge of sarcasm in otherwise harmless remarks, or maybe her tone at times *did* betray some lingering resentment.

Still, he tried to look at the issue from her viewpoint. Things *had* gotten out of hand that evening—but as he had attempted to explain, the incident was an aberration. *Yeah. Try telling that to someone convinced that life on the road is an endless circus featuring all the things that'll get you a first-class ticket to hell.*

However, Alba's speculations on what he and others might be doing loomed small in, as Cootie called it, The Big Picture.

Despite rock-n-roll's strong start in 1955, hardly anyone would wager that the music, or at least its initial "sound" and first wave of artists would endure. The make-it-all-while-you-can mentality remained the consensus. Like most, Lou's earliest goal had been to ride the tide, squirrel away as much as possible, and face any fade the music made with few, if any regrets. Now, after his three-month stint on the road, he reveled in the adoration at the live shows, the attention he got in public, and seeing his name and picture in the papers. Then there was the money, which was several times over what he would ever need to keep a roof over his head and food on his table. He knew he had only entered the front vestibule to the Lush Life—and now yearned to see the rest of the mansion.

Whatever career that lay ahead for him if rock-n-roll were to capsize anytime soon would never compare to his short ride atop the R & B world. And though he did not want to be one of those people whose life was all downhill before he even got out of his twenties, he realized that was a distinct possibility.

Moreover, his father's plans for the business cooperative hinged on loans from the hefty royalties and live-show salaries of Lou and his bandmates. All involved could only pray that the music stayed robust enough long enough for that plot to unfold.

He tried not to fret about the show's phantom stalkers. Those behind that mess *had* to be fairly powerful. Lou could only imagine what they could do to Cootie, the company, and him if they *really* wanted to lower the boom. And yes, though the crank calls to Alba had stopped, Lou's heart leapt every time the phone rang. It had become a case where, as Mother Cannon would say, "the worryation is worse than the confrontation." Still, being the only person in the company who had received any such personal harassment only made him wonder if someone were, beyond all, out to get *him*.

Though he struggled to toss that thought from his mind when it imposed, the fear kept finding ways to slither back in…

* * * * *

"NINETEEN-FIFTY-FIVE!" Willa exhaled when they returned to Hamilton Heights. "We lived a decade in that one year, babe."

Cootie eyed a calendar of 1956, but his vision saw beyond it. To his relief—and partial amazement—the revue had survived its maiden tour with a minimum of internal damage…and had earned a nifty profit, to boot. They popped open a bottle of champagne and drank a toast to the trouble they had been able to sidestep, or at least minimize.

"Hopefully, we didn't use up too much of our luck these past few months," Willa said. Cootie nodded grimly to her unstated reference to the revue's upcoming swing through the Deep South.

They had wagered that the potentially fat revenues behind the Cotton Curtain would offset any problems sure to unravel. Yes, Willa, Cootie and the others would take all precautions against the menu of trouble inherent in the trip. Still, the worst imaginable was not out of the question: race riots, maimings, maybe even murder. They would school their charges on the ethics of surviving in Jim Crow land. They would point out ways the troops could deal with whatever the race-baiters flung at them, in a manner that could save lives in the long run, if not momentarily injured feelings. Their toughest task would be to temper that take-no-shit-from-nobody attitude many in the show had, especially those who had come up in hard Northern burgs.

Given the opposition they had faced in the Midwest, the company's penetration of Dixie would surely subject it to much worse. Many had expressed appreciation they would not be going South in the maiden tour. Now, Willa and Cootie faced the daunting task of telling them about the spring-and-summer excursion through the South.

And, if Cootie suspected, their phantom stalkers were Southern right-wingers with reasonable clout, they could be marching into the mouth of the beast…

Like everyone connected to rock-n-roll, Cootie and Willa had no true idea of how long it would last, or how to enjoy fully its strong out-of-the-gates popularity. Their Rhythm Revue, as thorny as it had been to bankroll, organize, and launch, was just the springboard to a series of plans. They realized that the degree of difficulty with each succeeding step would increase geometrically. If all their plans worked out, the hardships endured in the Rhythm Revue '55 tour would seem like a church picnic.

That thought was nearly as frightening to them as the fear that rock-n-roll would not strive long enough for them to begin these endeavors in the first place...

Another area of concern came from whispers Alan Payton Howell had heard on Capitol Hill. That rising kingpins like Cootie, Fontaine, Freeman and others were cleaning up *in so many different corners* of the broadcasting/music industry had not gone unnoticed. "Never mind that it's always happened in business," Howell warned, "but when spades and Jews can make hay without getting clearance from the Big Cheeses..."

That Willa and Cootie's bookkeeping was immaculate was not a consolation to them. They had long known that if Uncle Sam wanted to trip anyone up, he would command the I.R.S. to stick out its foot. Still, they would never give anyone a pistol to shoot them with.

Willa, his mother Felicia, and several others often told Cootie, in so many words, that he was addicted to combat and confrontation. Sometimes it was said as a compliment, sometimes a complaint. Regardless, Cootie saw that part of his nature as his greatest strength in the odyssey that loomed ahead in the next years.

* * * * *

In Washington, Theo Briscoe tried to forget about his impending war with rock-n-roll, and enjoy the holidays with his family. Still, his resolve was challenged every time he heard the music overspilling from a television or radio.

Let the fruit get just ripe enough...then pluck it, he kept reminding himself...

Theo was now convinced that rock-n-roll—or something from it and close enough to it—would be around for more than a short while. The strong, post-war American economy had trickled down to the teenagers. They had jobs and allowances that allowed them to create their own culture, and they enjoyed a sense of freedom youngsters from previous times never knew. If Johnny and Janey wanted to spend some of the money *they* earned from their after-school jobs on phonograph records, how could a reasonable parent tell them no? That sense of freedom led to a rebellious spirit shared by many in their generation. The music had opened a Pandora's box on that spirit, and Theo sensed that the lid would never be shut back in place, fully.

Yes, rock-n-roll, or whatever it evolved into, was here to stay, Theo reckoned.

Theo's list of future targets was short, but stocked with high-rollers. He was not so arrogant to think any would be easy marks. Though each had his own Achilles heel, every hotshot jockey-mogul had a history of landing on his feet. Most of them, anyway, more or less.

Above all, Theo looked forward to the upcoming war. He was one of those persons who relished the combat more than the enjoyment of the spoils.

* * * * *

Though Phil Samuels loved and respected the men on his Moon Records board of directors, he could not fathom their blindness to Pervis Elmsley's potential. In the weeks between Thanksgiving and Christmas, he and Gutbucket worked with the boy. They smoothed the rough edges in his voice, widened his range, and found suitable material. Though the lad was not a great natural dancer, he did have the wiggliest of hips, so they exploited that. They agreed upon his stage wardrobe—eye-catching, but "nothin so pimp-nigger flashy it'll have yahoos rushin the stage to stomp yo' ass," was how Gutbucket phrased it.

They would test Pervis at a teen-age sock hop, New Year's Eve, at Cumberland High School. He would go on, unbilled. His only payment would be the exposure and experience before a live audience.

Still, even if Pervis flopped like a fish at Cumberland, Phil had all the confidence in the world in the boy...even if nobody else did. The lad seemed to have the resilience to rebound from any setbacks he might suffer—and the level-headedness to take a smashing triumph in stride. All in a day's work. Some cats are born to succeed.

That Pervis was *not* the million-dollar baby he had dreamt of seldom crossed his mind. Every time Phil gazed upon Pervis, he saw a bountiful check waiting to be cashed at a bank that had yet to open.

Phil Samuels counted down the days to when Pervis Elmsley's music-world boot camp would be completed.

* * * * *

End of Volume One